Stories of Heaven
and Earth

Stories of Heaven and Earth

BIBLE HEROES IN CONTEMPORARY CHILDREN'S LITERATURE

Hara E. Person
and
Diane G. Person

continuum

NEW YORK • LONDON

2005

The Continuum International Publishing Group Inc
15 East 26 Street, New York, NY 10010

The Continuum International Publishing Group Ltd
The Tower Building, 11 York Road, London SE1 7NX

www.continuumbooks.com

Printed in the United States of America

Library of Congress Cataloging-in-Publication Data

Person, Hara.
    Stories of heaven and earth : Bible heroes in contemporary children's literature / Hara E. Person and Diane G. Person.
        p. cm.
    Includes bibliographical references and index.
    ISBN 0-8264-1468-0 (hardcover : alk. paper)
    1. Bible stories, English.   2. Bible. O.T.—Biography.   3. Picture books for children.   I. Person, Diane Goetz.   II. Title.
BS546.P47   2005
221.9'505—dc22   2005000763

In memory of

Stanley Person, a teller of stories,
and hero in his lifetime—

and to our next generation
of storytellers and heroes,

Liya Naomi, Yonatan David,
and Golda Shalom

Contents

Acknowledgments
9

Introduction
11

1
CREATION
24

2
NOAH
56

3
JOSEPH
90

4
MOSES
116

5
DAVID
154

6
JONAH
188

7
ESTHER
216

Conclusion
261

Bibliography
265

Index of Biblical Books
273

Index
277

Illustrations are found between pages 128 and 129.

Acknowledgments

WRITING A BOOK, under the best of circumstances, is a challenging proposition. When we told people that we were writing a book together, it was generally assumed that a mother-and-daughter writing team would encounter more than the usual book-writing challenges. It is true that we have, not because we are a mother-and-daughter team, but because we belong to the same family and are affected by the same ups and downs. And what a tumultuous time it has been, with both the best and worst of what life can bring. The period of time in which this book was written truly has turned out to be a story of heaven and earth, and a story of life and death. There have been the not-so-tragic curveballs of life, like a home renovation, child-rearing, and professional responsibilities. But these challenges have also included both the joyous arrival of Goldi, the newest member of the family, and the hospitalizations and untimely death of Stanley, spouse, father, and grandfather. Whole drafts of chapters were passed back and forth at hospital bedsides and the family waiting rooms of Long Island College Hospital, Beth Israel Hospital, and Columbia Presbyterian Hospital in New York. And yet despite all the delays and attendant frustrations, we are grateful to have had this book to work on, a positive focus in dark times.

One of our greatest blessings in writing this book has been the chance to combine our professional interests and personal passions. We have also been blessed with the help and support of many others, without whom this book could never have come to be. Our respective spouses, Yigal Rechtman and, until his death, Stanley Person, were unbelievably encouraging of this project, despite the time it took away from them. Jenni Person and Chaim Lieberman have been enthusiastic supporters. Dr. Janine Pollack of the Lamm Institute of LICH, the Executive Director's office of the Brooklyn Public Library, the libraries of Brooklyn Heights Synagogue, and St. Ann's Lower School Library were all generous in providing us with important source material. Thank you also to Dr. Alexandra Juhasz, for giving helpful feedback on a difficult chapter, to Stephen Mark Dobbs for helping us track down Dr. Josh Sherman, and to Dr. Sherman for allowing us to use Ori Sherman's beautiful art on the cover.

Hara is thankful for the support of her children, Liya and Yoni, whose love of stories inspired this project, and who indulged her passion for King Arthur tales. She is particularly grateful to Yoni, for generously sharing his vast knowledge of fairy tales and mythology, and to Liya, for being a challenging, insightful student of Torah. Hara would also like to thank her colleagues at the Union for Reform Judaism and the URJ Press, Ken Gesser, Rabbi Jan Katzew, and Rabbi Danny Freelander, for their initial encouragement of this project. Thanks also go to the members of the Chavurah at the Brooklyn Heights Synagogue, for being wonderful Torah–study partners, for not being satisfied with easy interpretations, and for letting her experiment with new ways of reading familiar text.

Diane thanks all those who encouraged the completion of her work on this book when she was most despairing. She thanks her family for their faith in this project, and for ignoring the piles of books and manuscripts. And, always, thanks to her Special Angel.

We are truly blessed to have Evander Lomke as an editor. We are grateful for his faith in us, for his wise guidance, and for his infinite patience. Last but not least, we would like to thank our copy editor, Bruce Cassiday, for his careful work.

Introduction

THROUGHOUT HISTORY, the Bible has served as a rich source of themes, motifs, and ideas for adult literature. In the last one hundred thirty-five years, since the rise of a body of literature created specifically for children, stories from the Bible have become a mainstay of children's literature as well. Books based directly on stories from the Bible, and with themes related to such stories, characters and events, have appeared frequently among award-winning titles for children.

While at once one of the oldest and most canonical of the texts of Western Literature, by modern standards the Hebrew Bible does not immediately present itself as a collection of stories suitable for children. There are the well-known narratives of Genesis and Exodus, and a multitude of stories wedged into the later books between accounts of wars, lists of genealogies, discussions of skin diseases and bodily emissions, and the chronicles of kingdoms, priests and prophets. Yet there is so much that is potentially problematic for children, including stories of family conflict, incest, rape, seduction, violence, and murder, not to mention divine retribution. The questions of how much of the story to tell to children, and how much to leave out, what to add and what to subtract, who to hold up as a hero and who to present as an anti-hero, are questions that parents, teachers, and clergy have been grappling with for hundreds of years.

There is of course a difference between the Bible itself, and Bible stories. Collections of Bible stories originally developed in response to the difficult question of how to present readers with an appropriate version of the biblical text. Early children's Bibles were in fact not actual Bibles at all, but collections of stories in which biblical material was edited, reshaped, and reframed to make it more palatable, more educational, more morally beneficial, or more in keeping with the values of the time. As philosopher, novelist, and publisher William Godwin wrote to his friend Charles Lamb in 1808:

> You, or some other wise man, I have heard to say,
> It is children that read children's books, when they read,
> but it is parents who choose them. (Kegan, unpag)[1]

The stories were now intended for children, but they were being shaped by adult sensibilities, based on what adults thought children should and could read. Using the framework of the biblical story, some of the aspects highlighted in children's Bible stories, such as the importance of obedience and parental authority, reveal adult concerns vis-à-vis children that span generations. In others, these familiar stories become mediums for such contemporary issues as the environment, human conflict, multicultural understandings, sibling rivalry, homelessness, racism, and saving endangered species.

The earliest versions of Bible stories that were read either to or by children were not originally intended to be specifically for children. Peter Comestor's *Historia Scholastica,* which appeared in Europe in the 12th century, was a widely distributed and much copied collection of Bible stories. This volume, which included only narrative sections, became a model for many of the collections of Bible stories which were to be published in Europe in the next three hundred years (Bottigheimer, p. 15). In 1529, Martin Luther's *Passional* was published. Written in the vernacular, it used some of the actual biblical text and relied heavily on illustrations as a story-telling technique. *Passional* was to provide a new model for Bible stories, one that remained a standard for several hundred years (ibid, p. 23-28).

Passional, and similarly modeled books like it, were read by adults and children alike. However, as publishing for children began to in-

---

[1] *William Godwin: His Friends and Contemporaries* (London: Henry S. King & Co., 1876), Vol. II. The book is out-of-print, but text can be found online at dwardmac.pitzer.edu/anarchist_archives/godwin/friends/tocv2.html

crease and take on a life of its own in the eighteenth century, Bibles and Bible stories specifically for children began to appear throughout Europe and North America. Long before there were dedicated children's departments in publishing houses, retellings of Bible stories were written for children, to instruct them and teach them morals as adults saw fit.

Special editions of the Bible intended specifically for children were published in the American colonies as early as 1763 by Andrew Steuart of Philadelphia and were soon followed by abridged, easy-to-read editions illustrated with woodcuts referred to as Thumb Bibles. The market for children's books began to increase in the eighteenth century at both ends of the economic spectrum, resulting in high quality books for the children of the educated moneyed classes, as well as inexpensive, mass-produced books for the children of the lower classes (Hunt, p. 26). In Europe, the rapid growth of the Sunday school movement, through which even children who worked in factories during the week were able to obtain some education, contributed to the rise in demand for these books, as did the simple fact of the decreased death rate for children brought about by advancements in medicine (p. 29–33). Though the first books published by John Newbery for children were not Bible stories, he did publish several, including *Holy Bible abridged . . . for the use of children* [sic] (1757), *Bible in Miniuture* [sic]; *or, A Concise History of the Old and New Testaments* (1789), and *Pocket Bible for Little Masters and Misses* (1772) (Carpenter and Pritchard, p. 60). However, in the United States, mainstream commercial and educational publishers, influenced by the dictates of separation of church and state, did not begin to publish children's Bibles until the middle of the nineteenth century. Instead, these books were mainly published by religious publishers (Bottigheimer, p. 47–48).

The goal of children's Bibles in the eighteenth and into the nineteenth century was mainly to inculcate into children values acceptable to the community, in other words, social indoctrination. There was a short-term objective of using the material to teach children to behave with parents and teachers, and the long-term objective of educating children to grow up to be fine, upstanding citizens who would contribute to society in positive ways (Bottigheimer, p. 4). As Ruth Bottigheimer writes:

> The pages of children's Bibles communicated more than a simple redaction of Bible stories; they also incorporated class-specific social values in a godly context that rendered them virtually unassailable. Children's Bibles are powerfully persuasive handbooks for inculcating social responses. Unlike the explicit directions of worldly manuals of courtesy, the social directives of children's Bibles are, and have long been, embedded in holy language from, as their editors assure the child reader, the Holy Penman himself. (p. 51)

Through careful editing, children's Bibles have typically reflected the values, concerns, and sensibilities of the eras in which they appeared.

In children's Bibles and Bible stories, the illustrations are a critically important element. Considered one of the first illustrated children's Bibles, "The Youths Visible Bible," was published by Elisha Coles in 1675 as part of *Nolens Volens: or, You shall make Latin whether you Will or No* [sic]. This section of the book was called "The Youths Visible Bible" and featured brief passages from the Bible arranged in alphabetical order according to a key word system accompanied by copperplate prints (Carpenter and Prichard, p. 60). Later, children's Bibles often used woodcut illustrations. As art became a central feature of Bible stories for children, illustrations took on the role of commentary. This was sometimes a way to deal with controversial text, by simply illustrating it instead of including it in the narrative. At other times illustrations are used to resolve problematic issues in the text, such as the binding of Isaac, in which Abraham is allowed to express a range of emotions, such as doubt, fear, and love of his son, not readily apparent in the text itself (Bottigheimer, p. 76). As Bottigheimer puts it, "Because illustrations in children's Bibles function in close partnership with text, they provide internal exegesis and play a central role in resolving puzzles thrown up by the stories themselves" (Bottigheimer, p. 57).

One type of illustrated Bibles popular in the eighteenth and early nineteenth centuries were referred to as Hieroglyphic Bibles. Similar to modern-day rebus puzzles, key nouns that were considered difficult or controversial for children were presented as pictures. Readers were meant to cover the answer key at the bottom of each page with one hand and only use the key as needed or to verify their answers. The most popular of these hieroglyphic Bibles was T. Hodgson's 1783 title, *Curious Hieroglyphick Bible . . . for the Amusement of Children* [sic]. Isaiah Thomas of Worchester, Massachusetts was the first to publish an American edition of an illustrated hieroglyphic Bible in 1788. With its nearly five hundred woodcuts, it contained passages from both the Old and New Testaments. According to Thomas, a popular figure in early American publishing, his *Curious Hieroglyphick Bible* was intended "for the Amusement of Youth: designed chiefly to familiarize tender Age, in a pleasing and diverting Manner, with early Ideas of the Holy Scriptures." Thomas noted in his preface that "by Experience" the use of illustrated Bibles was an easy way to teach children to read (Rosenbach, p. 57).

The representations of God also reveal a changing sense of how to introduce children to God. In *Icones Biblicae* of 1625, God is first illustrated as the four Hebrew letters that make up God's name (though incorrectly rendered) shining through a Trinitarian triangle. In *Andächtiger Catholischer Schriften Gott-heiligter Bibel-Lust* of 1684, God is a voice speaking the name Adam, and in *Erbauliche Erzählungen* of 1761, God is simply a triangular shape radiating light in the sky. These illustrations, though designed for adults, made their way into children's books. From those images, God evolved in later eighteenth century children's Bible stories into primarily a father figure, and by the nineteenth century, God had become almost human-looking, with a beard and robes (Bottigheimer, p. 65–69). This evolution of God coincided with the ongoing re-editing of the Bible stories themselves, in which God becomes an increasingly benevolent figure as the tales of violence, divine retribution, and divine anger are omitted from children's texts (p. 63).

Despite the many retellings of biblical text published for children, and the critical success of some retellings, today Bible stories are not generally considered an important source of stories for children outside of a religious context. While children learn about Native American and Greek mythology, multicultural folktales, and fairy tales from around the world, Bible stories are often no longer seen as an essential part of the canon of recommended literature for children. Professional anthologies of children's stories, such as the acknowledged standard among librarians and teachers, *The Arbuthnot Anthology of Children's Literature* (1976), do not include any selections of stories based on biblical text. Late twentieth century editions of textbooks most widely used in teacher preparation courses did not include any reference to the Bible as literature. However, the 2002 fifth edition of Cullinan and Galda's *Literature for the Child* has a brief discussion of the Bible as literature, and suggestions for how to use Bible stories in a public-school setting. A suggested list of stories and songs is included at the end of the chapter. The 2004 eighth edition of noted educator Charlotte Huck's *Children's Literature in the Elementary School* now includes a section on the Bible as literature as well. Huck and her co-editors look at both collections and single editions of Bible stories from major well-known commercial publishers; they avoid children's books that present a particular religious belief or point of view. There are of course many reasons why teachers and parents shy away from Bible stories, not the least of which are issues of politics, church versus state, and a discomfort in dealing with the role of God in the stories. Yet not introducing children to the biblical stories is to do a disservice. For beyond the issues of morality, faith, and belief, the Bible text is a source of deep, important, stories of human development.

The similarities among myths, legends, folklore, fairy tales, and Bible stories are not coincidental. As Elizabeth Cook writes in *The Ordinary and the Fabulous,* Bible stories "are as poetic and dramatic as anything in Greek or Northern mythology" and have greatly influenced imaginations for generations.

> They [Bible stories] were the only highly developed, literary mythological stories that were heard by uneducated people in the Christian period, and they meant as much as the Greek stories to poets and men of letters. (p. 38)

These stories, like the mythology of other cultures, have survived because of the power of their narrative structure, and the way in which they present people responding heroically in dramatic situations. Wrapped in the cloak of legitimacy granted to them by religious institutions, Bible stories filled a need in people's lives for narratives that were entertaining, inspiring, and helped give meaning and structure to the chaos of human existence.

Though these various genres of what were once oral tales, handed down from generation to generation, are a reflection of the specific historic and geographic contexts in which they arose, they share common motifs and themes. Bettelheim asserts that fairy tales originated and were most popular and influential at an earlier time when religion exerted a strong influence on people's beliefs and behaviors, finding what would be considered religious themes underlying many Grimm brothers' stories such as "The Seven Ravens," "The Old Man Made Young Again," and "Hansel and Gretel," as well as in many of the stories from the Arabian *Thousand and One Nights*. Many of the stories in all these genres emphasize obedience to an authority figure, questions of good and evil, and the attempt on the part of the hero to make the right decision when faced with a choice. All of these types of stories are attempts to fulfill the basic need to try to make sense of the world and the role of humans within it.

Northrop Frye noted the connection between mythology and the biblical stories, writing:

> Every developed mythology tends to . . . show in perspective man's origin, his destiny, the limits of his power, and the extension of his hopes and desires. A mythology may develop by accretion, as in Greece, or by rigorous codifying and the excluding of unwanted material, as in Israel; but the drive toward a verbal circumference of human experience is clear in both cultures. (p. 32)

Many of the stories in all these genres are tales of growth, featuring a central character moving from the simple world of childhood to the complex world of adulthood. They tell of recognizable characters making difficult decisions in circumstances generally beyond their control, sometimes failing but learning an important life lesson, and at other times even managing to triumph heroically. These stories also often feature a protective figure who helps and guides the hero along his or her journey. In Bible stories this figure is God, in fairy tales it is what Joseph Campbell calls "the helpful crone and fairy godmother" (p. 71), and in the legends of King Arthur it is Merlin.

Stories of Heaven and Earth is meant to be a helpful resource for parents, educators, librarians, and clergy. It is intended to be, in part, a critical examination of children's picture books based on stories from the Old Testament, and an exploration of the role of Bible stories in the world of children's literature. Beyond the obvious use of these stories as a way to pass on religious values, faith, and traditions, there are a significant number of these retellings that are recognized as outstanding children's literature by librarians and educators in the field of children's literature. Such stories are usually framed as hero journeys or epic myths. This book will focus on a select group of well-known biblical characters, about whom a critical mass of literary retellings for children have been written. Many of them have been recognized as award-winning books.

The stories that are focused on in *Stories of Heaven and Earth* are tales in which a significant transition takes place on the part of the hero, a transition from innocence, naiveté, and youth, whether metaphoric or actual, to adulthood. This book offers an analysis of these stories as powerful tales of emotional development. Emphasis is placed on the power of these stories not as a way to provide a quick morality fix, but rather as a source of literature, rich in universal archetypes, ethical dilemmas, decision-making, and emotional growth. Biblical narrative itself is full of ambiguities and morality is not always clear cut. The characters and situations are complex, neither purely "good" nor "bad." Joseph, for example, is portrayed as both an arrogant young man resented by his brothers, and as a heroic dreamer revered as a leader. Moses is a wise leader who is not always able to handle his anger appropriately or reign in his impulsivity. These stories can teach children the value of learning from one's own and other's mistakes, having courage, taking risks, and believing in one's own abilities. It is this complexity that makes these stories so well suited as a basis for teaching children about real life, with all its attendant shades of gray.

In examining the body of children's stories based on these narratives, *Stories of Heaven and Earth* will evaluate how these stories deal with the ambiguity and very real humanity of the biblical characters, while encouraging those adults who are involved with children to view Bible stories critically themselves. Any adult reading a story to a child, helping a child choose a suitable book, or developing a curriculum needs to ask important questions rather than just accept a book at face value. A story about Adam and Eve is not just a story about the creation of the world or about the first man and woman. A story about Noah is not just a story about a flood and animals. What parts of the stories get told, and what get left out of these versions? How do varying editions of the same stories reflect the different priorities or worldviews of the reteller, or the changing values in each generation? What do these publications tell us about ourselves as a society? How do these books reflect societal attitudes about children and childhood? What do adults think children need to learn and be told? What universal themes of human development can be seen in the emotional journeys of the biblical characters?

The biblical stories are an important source of stories about human psycho-social development. Esther, for example, is not only an individual with her own personality and history, but she is also a universal character whose story shares many elements with other similar hero stories from folklore and mythology. Many of the stories being examined here are mythological journeys into the self, journeys of maturity and development from a naive, self-centered state of childhood into a more altruistic, empathetic state of adulthood. The research of experts in child development, such as Jean Piaget and Erik Erikson, will be referenced, as well as the work of Bruno Bettelheim, in whose groundbreaking work, *The Uses of Enchantment,* the connection between fairy tales and human psychology was so persuasively made.

Likewise, the paradigm of Joseph Campbell's hero's journey will be used as another way to examine the lives and adventures of the biblical characters in the context of similar stories and myths from other cultures. Many of the familiar stories of biblical characters revolve around what Campbell calls "rites of passage" (p. 10). They are stories of transformation, as when David fights Goliath, or when Theseus fights the Minotaur and in the process is transformed from a boy craving his father's approval into a man in charge of his own destiny. For Campbell, the hero figure is one who goes through an ordeal of some sort, and is reborn, able now to help others with the knowledge learned in the process of transformation. He writes:

> A hero ventures forth from the world of common day into a region of supernatural wonder; fabulous forces are there encountered and a decisive victory is won: the hero comes back from this mysterious adventure with the power to bestow boons on his fellow man. (p. 30)

Adam, Eve, and Noah, the first stories examined in *Stories of Heaven and Earth,* are like pre-heroes; their tales share some qualities with the hero-journey model, but are not as fully developed. The other biblical characters focused on in *Stories of Heaven and Earth* more neatly fit Campbell's paradigm. After having been thrown in the pit by his brothers and then sold into slavery, Joseph is able to ultimately help save the entire nation of Egypt as well as his own family from starvation. After slaying the Egyptian taskmaster, running away, and encountering the mysterious burning bush, Moses is able to go back to Egypt and lead his people out to freedom. After having slain Goliath, David is able to become a great King and leader of his people. After his sojourn in the belly of the fish and the recognition that he cannot escape from God and God's bidding, Jonah is able to save the city of Nineveh. And Esther, after having faced up to King Ahasuerus and Haman and revealing her true identity, is able to save her people.

Our focus is on Old Testament stories. Both individual stories and collections will be considered. Stories similar to these appear universally in other cultures that are not part of the Judeo–Christian tradition. The significant body of children's literature based on Bible stories is concerned with Old Testament narratives and character development. The majority of trade books based on the New Testament revolve around holiday celebrations or are primarily intended for the purposes of religious education. They do not follow the prescribed literary conventions of the hero's journey and mythical epics but rather are non-narrative in nature and meant to be used as teaching tools, and are thus outside the scope of this endeavor.

In choosing the publications to be covered in *Stories of Heaven and Earth*, we limited ourselves to books published by commercial, mainstream publishers to the general book trade. Because our goal is to show why Bible stories are an important body of Western literature for children, we purposely excluded books and publishers whose publishing mission is primarily religious and didactic in nature. However, there are several notable exceptions to this rule. We included *Tomie dePaola's Book of Bible Stories* by the celebrated author Tomie dePaola, issued in 1990 by Zondervan, whose mission is to publish Christian books, as well as Dandi Daley Mackall's *Joseph, King of Dreams* (2000), published by Tommy Nelson, a publisher of faith-based books for children. Two books from Wm. B. Eerdmans, a publisher specializing in general religiously oriented books, were used, *Exodus* (1998) and *Joseph* (1997) by Brian Wildsmith. In addition, we have also included *A Prayer for the Earth: The Story of Naamah, Noah's Wife* (1996) by Sandy Eisenberg Sasso, published by Jewish Lights Publishing, whose goal is to publish books drawing on Judaism for people of all faiths and backgrounds. These books all added perspectives not found elsewhere, were of literary merit beyond the religious aims of their publishers, and were meant to appeal to a broad readership rather than a specific religious group.

Bible stories are part of children's literary legacy. Parents, teachers, librarians, and clergy have a responsibility to make sure that children are introduced to this important body of literature. These stories come from the Bible, and as such have an important place in Judeo–Christian religious and ethical traditions. Yet reading the stories as texts related to religious identity should coexist with reading the stories as literature. Part of the very richness of biblical text is that it can be read on many levels simultaneously, as ethical teachings, as part of a faith tradition, and as literature, history, and anthropology, to name a few. If adults limit the meaning and layers of the stories, or give pat answers about the contradictions and complexities, children are discouraged from returning again and again to these stories with a critical eye. They will outgrow the Bible both emotionally and intellectually. Adults must let children know they can ask questions, disagree, and read between the lines of the biblical stories. When children are given multiple ways of reading stories, they are able to become critical thinkers as readers of biblical stories. In doing so, they take greater ownership of them and can enter into a dialogue with the stories (Huck, p. 238). The stories will thus grow as children grow and become lifelong companions.

The Bible has long been the inspiration for a stirring source of stories for children, a way to pass on heritage, values, themes, archetypes, and role models within the context of a story. It has inspired modern children's authors to create memorable characters, heroes, and narratives. In their universality, these characters have the power to become important guides themselves as children embark on their own hero-journeys. Just as in numerous fairy tales and myths, in many of the popular biblical stories for children the hero begins his journey as a child. As in the beloved stories of Arthur coming to understand his true identity and role as leader of England, it is no accident that in these stories it is generally the least powerful, whether because they are the most innocent (Noah), the youngest (Joseph or David), the one with a defect (Moses), the orphan (Esther or Moses), or the least outstanding character (Jonah), who triumphs. These stories impart a crucial message for children, that despite all the road blocks they may see before them, they have the internal tools necessary to be the heroes of their own journeys and thus their own lives. As Campbell writes, "The godly powers sought and dangerously won are revealed to have been within the heart of the hero all the time" (p. 39).

The making of independent choices, and going out into the world are central themes in many fairy tales. Bettelheim suggests that "it is important to provide the modern child with images of heroes who have to go out into the world all by themselves and who, although originally ignorant of the ultimate things, find secure places in the world by following their right way with deep inner confidence" (p.11). The child needs this reassurance in order to confront the world and find his or her own place of significance within the universe. It is through doing so that the child is able to eventually emerge as a mature adult with a fully developed and integrated personality.

Like fairy tales, folktales, legends, and mythology, Bible stories are powerful pieces of literature that allow children to dream of themselves as heroes. Bible stories provide children with all-too-human role models with recognizable flaws who struggle to make ethical decisions and answer the challenges that confront them as they try to make sense of the purpose of their lives. These stories suggest to children a range of possible behavioral models for making the developmental journey from childhood into adulthood while reassuring them that though emotional growth is painful, it is also both necessary and rewarding. Bible stories matter deeply, because they allow children to envision becoming the heroes of their own lives as they make the difficult but essential transition from childhood to adolescence and into adulthood.

A Note about Translations of Biblical Text

There are a multitude of different translations of biblical text. Various authors of retellings chose different translations, or created their own. For the excerpts of biblical text used within this book, we have chosen to use as our standard the New Jewish Publication Society translation (JPS, 1999). This translation is a well-respected, scholarly, but modern translation of the *Biblia Hebraica Stuttgartensia,* for which the foundation is the Ben-Asher/Leningrad Codex, the oldest extant version of the Hebrew text. Because translation is an art and not an exact science, sometimes the text excerpts provided within are different from the quotes excerpted from retellings. The result is variations like "favor in God's eye" vs. "grace in God's eye" or "outrage" vs. "anger."

1

CREATION

In the beginning, God created the Heaven and the Earth. The biblical story of creation is both a story about beginnings, of the earth and of people, and a story about separation. Order is created out of chaos as God separates the heavens and the earth. Night and day are divided. Dry land and water are separated. Light is separated into the big light of day and the small light of night. The separations go on and on. On the sixth day, after God had created light and the sun and the moon and the waters and vegetation, God created humanity. Out of the swirling, primordial waters of creation emerge two human creatures (Genesis 1). The creation of this humanity, distinct from God's self, an "other" than God, is a further separation.

After God has rested on the seventh day from all the work of creating, God forms man out of the clay of the earth, breathes life into him, and sets him in the Garden of Eden, full of beautiful and bountiful food-bearing trees and water (Genesis 2:1–10). Also in the Garden is the tree of the knowledge of good and bad, which man is told not to eat from lest he die (Genesis 2:17). The man, now called Adam, is seen to need a suitable human companion, and so God creates woman out of Adam's rib (Genesis 2:22). These first people, who come to be called Adam and Eve, have been bequeathed a perfect world. All they have to do is obey the rules explained to them by God. Yet before long they begin to struggle internally, to push the limits of God's authority and demand their right to make their own choices. The woman, not yet called Eve, is then tempted by a serpent to eat from the tree of knowledge, who tells her that she will not die but gain knowledge, and she succumbs (Genesis 3:1–5). She in turn convinces Adam to also eat from the tree, after which both of them come to see the world in a new way (Genesis 3:6–7). It does not take long for them to lose their paradise and be thrust out into a harsh world, a world in which they will have to suffer and learn to take care of themselves. Ashamed at their newly perceived nakedness and afraid of God's reaction, they try unsuccessfully to hide. God then punishes Adam, the woman, and the serpent, and banishes them from the garden forever (Genesis 3).

For all its primal simplicity, the biblical story of creation is actually quite a complicated story. A close reading reveals that it is composed of two different stories of creation. First people are created in God's image, "male and female God created them." (Genesis 1:27). It is not until the second chapter of Genesis that the more familiar story is introduced, in which God first creates a man, Adam, and then out of his rib creates a woman, who comes to be called Eve.[2] There has been much written about the inconsistencies of the two accounts, and the significance of the two different versions of human creation. It might even seem as though God initially created either both genders together, or a bi-gendered person, and only later made two separate people. And in fact an early rabbinic Midrash reads this text as evidence that the first person God created was a hermaphrodite.[3]

However the details of these two versions are read, the second account represents a further stage of separation that occurs as God takes that undifferentiated person and separates out a distinct male and then a female. Campbell writes,

> The removal of the feminine into another form symbolizes the beginning of the fall from perfection into duality; and it was naturally followed by the discovery of the duality of good and evil, exile from the garden where God walks on earth, and thereupon the building of the wall of Paradise . . . (p. 153)

As soon as there is duality, the self and other, the me and not-me, the male and the female, there is also good and evil. God will not be able to protect Adam and Eve from encountering this duality forever. Eventually they are going to have to separate from God entirely and leave the garden.

The response of Adam and Eve to the situation into which they were brought by God remains a theological touchstone until today. The very concepts of original sin and the Fall of Man, so central to Christian theology and practice, comes from this story. Yet that is only

---

[2] The woman is not actually called Eve until just as they are about to being expelled from the garden, in Genesis 3:20. However, for ease of reference, she will be referred to as Eve throughout this chapter.

[3] Genesis Rabbah 8:1.

one way of reading the plain meaning of the actual biblical account, which readily lends itself to a multiplicity of interpretations. The story is at its core a creation story, a story meant to answer the most elemental of questions. Creation stories are common to many cultures many of which perpetuate their own interpretations. The need to know where we came from, how we came into existence, and who is responsible for our creation and the world's is a universal human need. In her collection of creation stories from around the world, *In the Beginning,* Virginia Hamilton writes, "Lonely as they were, by themselves, early people looked inside themselves and expressed a longing to discover, to explain who they were, why they were, and from what and where they came" (p. xi). Stories of creation give reasons for observed and experienced realities. These elements of creation stories help human beings to feel safer and more secure. They reassure us that life is not random but happens according to the master plan of a greater being, even if we can't always fathom the plan.

The biblical text tells us that in the beginning of beginnings, God created the world. At the end of six days of creation, God created humanity. Once these first people appear, they assume center stage. Their doings and conflicts and crises are the focus of the narrative that follows their creation. They are the ultimate Everypeople, the earliest archetypes of human behavior, stand-ins for all of us as we grow from utter dependency to confident independence, experiencing the struggle of separation, growth, and suffering along the way. The biblical story of creation matters to children as it matters to us all, for their origins and their story are the blueprint for ours.

The Early Childhood of Humanity

> God said, "See, I have given you every seed-bearing plant that is upon all the earth, and every tree that has seed-bearing fruit; they shall be yours for food. And to all the animals on land, to all the birds of the sky, and to everything that creeps on earth, in which there is the breath of life, [I give] all the green plants for food."

And it was so. And God saw all that He had made, and found it very good. And there was evening and there was morning, the sixth day.

(Genesis 1:29–31)

When the first humans are created, all is perfect and well ordered. They are surrounded by beauty, and have all that they need. Their role in this environment that God has created seems well defined. As Martin Waddell writes in his 1993 retelling of the story, from the collection *Stories from the Bible,* "They were like two big babies in the beautiful garden, enjoying themselves with all the things God had made for them." Like babies, all their basic needs are met. As long as they stick to the rules that God has determined, all will be well. They will be safe, happy, and cared for.

It is not that they are entirely free from responsibilities. They have a job, part of which is to have dominion over the other creatures and to care for the earth. But these tasks are in the context of a setting within which vegetation seems to flourish without significant intervention, and in which there is peace and harmony. As imagined by several authors of retellings, it is a lush, vegetarian paradise, in which animals eat only plants rather than each other. In *The Creation*, with an original, lyrical translation of the biblical text by Stephen Mitchell and radiant art (an example of which appears on the cover of this book) by Ori Sherman, the two first humans are shown naked, reaching for plentiful fruit in the garden, surrounded by trees and animals (Sherman, 1990). A peaceful golden glow infuses the scene, in which a bear contentedly munches a leaf on one side and a crocodile eats from a tree on the other side, all under the sunny, watchful eye of God.

In his retelling of Creation in *City of Gold and Other Stories of the Old Testament* (1992), illustrated by Michael Foreman, Peter Dickinson frames the story as one retold later during the Babylonian exile. He too imagines a peaceful, inter-species herbivorous paradise, writing:

But in the garden of which my people tell, the thistle grew with the fig-tree, each in the splendor of its kind and neither the enemy of the other.

The caterpillar sucked at the juices of the lily, and the lily rejoiced in giving and was not hurt. All grew in one delighting harmony. Moreover, all beasts, wild and tame, roamed through the garden at peace with each other. The lion laired with the lamb and was not afraid. . . . [The lion] ate nectarines, and loquats, and grapes, and the trees bowed down to give him their fruits as he paced by.

In this garden, there was enough for everyone. There was no need for fighting or conflict, fear or competition. Everyone and everything worked together in perfect cooperation.

The garden was gorgeous and bountiful, and Adam lived under God's protection without any reason to worry or fear. In her 1968 version of the story, Gwendolyn Reed describes the garden as a place where not only the animals lived together in peace, but man and God also coexisted perfectly.

It was a place where God came to walk beside the man, where the man could speak to his creator. It was the earthly paradise.

Every flower, every tree, and every fruit that was beautiful or good to eat grew within Eden's walls. No bitter wind ever blew there. Frost never stiffened the grass. A river flowed through the garden with water as clear as crystal.

Nature, too, was part of this harmonious life in the garden. Illustrator Siegl's use of the woodcut technique for the accompanying illustrations is further evocation of the strong connection between Adam and the world of nature. The earth toned woodcut prints echo the idea of peace, harmony, and simplicity that existed in the garden.

God is described in Shirley Van Eyssen's *In The Beginning* like a new parent who only wants the child to be happy and fulfilled (1970). Discipline and punishment are issues that have not yet been necessary or even contemplated.

In order to make Adam happy, God created for him a most beautiful garden, called Eden—haven of trees and flowers and birds. For a while Adam was content to bask in the sunshine of God's affection and tried to please Him.

At first Adam needs only God, just as a baby needs only his or her parents. Together, they form a whole. God provides and nurtures, and Adam in turn tries to make God happy.

In Geoffrey Horn and Arthur Cavanaugh's 1980 retelling, *Bible Stories for Children*, Adam is portrayed as a good, well-behaved child. They write:

> So Adam did as God told him. He lived peacefully in the garden of Eden, taking care of the trees and eating their fruit.

Arvis Stewart's accompanying illustrations depict a world in which animals—the elephant, the kangaroo, the lion, the monkey, and the giraffe—live in peace, surrounded by lush vegetation. Only Adam, a rather undifferentiated brown-toned mass of a human, sits alone on a rock, not quite as comfortable with his surroundings as the other beings. Horn and Cavanaugh continue:

> But he had no other living creature to help him.
> Then God looked at Adam and saw that he was lonely.

Like a good parent, God is concerned with Adam's well being. God wants him to be happy and fulfilled, and so God brings Adam each animal in the hopes that one may be a good match, but all are found unsuitable.

Despite the perfection of existence within the garden, Adam needs more in his life than God and the animals. Adam needs a real peer, someone with whom he can experience the world as an equal. Horn and Cavanaugh express Adam's need for a partner.

> But later the man began to long for someone with whom to share the wonders and privileges of his new world; and so that his joy should be complete, God gave him a companion. She was the first woman on earth, and her name was Eve. Then Adam was fulfilled, for he was not lonely any more. No cold wind of unrest disturbed the lush grasses, or bowed into submission the slender stalks of the brilliant passion flower. Adam and Eve felt only the warm glow of belonging to each other, and to God.

At this point Adam is like an extension of God. It is unimaginable that Adam will disobey or rebel. But as with all parents and children, as the child grows separation begins to take place and the child begins to make independent choices and form autonomous relationships, some of which will please the parent, and some of which will not. Adam's need for Eve is the first sign that he will begin to grow and have needs that cannot be fulfilled within his relationship with God or with the animals.

Once Eve is created as a partner for Adam in Reed's retelling, life continues to be good for some time. Eve fits seamlessly into Adam's existence, shown in Siegl's woodcuts to be in as close a connection with both the plant and animal life of the garden as Adam. Reed emphasizes that everything was provided for Adam and Eve, shade to keep them comfortable, food to eat, soft moss on which to sleep at night.

> When they were hungry they plucked the fruits that hung heavy on the branches or picked the berries that crowded the bushes. In the mornings when the sun dappled the soft moss they woke with gladness. In the evenings when the moon silvered the leaves they closed their eyes in contentment.

Living under God's protection, with all their needs attended to, they lack nothing. Their existence is like that of very young children with doting, caring parents, who anticipate every possible emotional and physical requirement.

The early days of creation are similarly described as a blissful, perfect nirvana in Miriam Chaikin's *Children's Bible Stories from Genesis to Daniel* (1993). Whereas most authors of retellings for children gloss over the contradictions of the two different stories of human creation, focusing on the less ambiguous version from Chapter 2, Chaikin conflates the two versions, writing that before resting on the seventh day, God creates Adam and Eve. God breathes life into them, places them in the Garden of Eden, and charges them to take care of the Garden. The world was, at that moment, complete.

God looked at the world again. Nothing was missing. "Now it is very good," God said. Satisfied, God rested the next day, which was the seventh day.

Adam and Eve were happy in the Garden. They had everything without having to work. A river ran through the Garden, watering the beautiful flowers and many different fruit trees that grew there.

Having combined the two versions of creation, Chaikin depicts an Adam and Eve who have been created together, as absolute equals and a perfect match. Soon enough their idyll will be ruined. But for now, all is as good as it can be.

The softness of Yvonne Gilbert's colored pencil drawings echo Chaikin's evocative words. Adam and Eve are surrounded by animals and wildlife, all gloriously sharing in the wonders of the garden. Adam and Eve are portrayed as beautiful, demurely naked, long-haired, and happy hippies. Festooned with flowers, Eve's curly tresses cascade down her chest, conveniently covering her breasts, and a fig leaf covers her lap. Yet Adam's beard and Eve's curves belie the sense of youth and innocence alluded to in Chaikin's text, and hint at changes to come in their perfect existence.

Adam and Eve are shown living in peace with the animals and with each other in *Adam and Eve* by Mary Martin (1995). Bryn Barnard's bright illustrations depict a paradise filled with colorful fruit-bearing trees. The animals in the illustrations, from the elephants and the tigers to the sheep and the rabbits, are rounded and childlike themselves, with soft, open eyes and smiles on their faces. Adam and Eve appear young and innocent, satisfied to sit among the animals or swim in the bright blue waters of the garden. Martin writes:

Adam and Eve lived happily in the garden. They swam in the river and played with the animals. They cared for the trees and flowers that grew there. They always had enough to eat. They ate fruits from all the different trees in the garden. But they did not eat fruit from the tree of knowledge.

During this period, Adam and Eve live only in the present. They exhibit no signs of anxiety about the future, or even any awareness of tomorrow. They have no reason to worry about where their next meal will come from, or whether they will have shelter or protection. They do not worry about what will happen if they do not obey God. Their only reality is that of dependency on God.

Adam and Eve are initially content to remain cared for by God, and in turn to care for the bountiful garden and its inhabitants. Their basic needs for food, shelter, and companionship are being met, as are their emotional needs. Their existence reflects the period of early childhood identified as latency, defined by Erikson as "a lull before the storm of puberty" (p. 260), in which there is an unquestioning acceptance of existing family values and an expectation that the good, all-bountiful parent will always continue to protect and provide. During this period, children are free to focus on skill-building and socialization, without having to worry about adult problems like basic survival. However, the time will come for Adam and Eve, as it does for all children, when this will no longer be enough. The confines of their perfect existence within the Garden and within the limits of God's rules will no longer feel comfortable and comforting. Just as with all children when they reach adolescence, limits will have to be tested, boundaries pushed, roles challenged, and independent identities formed.

Setting Limits and Breaking Rules

> And the Lord God commanded the man, saying, "Of every tree of the garden you are free to eat; but as for the tree of knowledge of good and bad, you must not eat of it; for as soon as you eat of it, you shall die.

> (Genesis 2:16–17)

Rules and limits help a child feel secure. Unbounded existence, without any rules and expectations, is chaotic and scary for children. Even as children begin to differentiate themselves from the others around them by asserting their own needs, the rules provided by the parent give the child a safe space within which to rebel. "No," is among the first words in a child's vocabulary. As much as children want to please their parents and the other adults around them, they also want to be allowed to make up their own minds. The establishment of rules is recognition that a child is a separate being who can make his or her own choices, but who needs guidance making the appropriate choices. It is thus also the first step in the process of separation for both the parent and the child, as there is no need to set rules for something that is wholly of oneself. Now that Adam is not a lone human but has a peer of his own in Eve, the separation between God and humans is much greater than before. Adam has his own human community and God must provide rules.

Mary Martin's retelling focuses on the choice made by Adam and Eve to eat the forbidden fruit and disobey God. She focuses on obedience and the desire for knowledge rather than on punishment. Eve at first demures when the serpent tries to convince her to eat the fruit, knowing what God expects of her, but the serpent presents a compelling argument.

> "But God told us not to," Eve said. "Surely, God knows what is best."
> "Nothing will happen to you. The fruit of this tree will make you as wise as God," said the serpent. "You will know everything."

This idea of knowing all that God knows is appealing to Eve. For the first time she is faced with her own limitations and wants more. This acknowledgment is similar to that of a young child realizing for the first time that she is not omnipotent. She is suddenly unsure if God really knows what is best for her, or whether it is possible to make her own choices.

As soon as the serpent tells Eve that she will not die if she eats the fruit, she immediately gains a new understanding. "When the woman saw that the tree was good for eating and a delight to the eyes, and that the tree was desirable as a source of wisdom, she took of its fruit and ate" (Genesis 3:6). Even before she takes a bite, she begins to perceive reality in a new way and react differently to God's authority. In Waddell's retelling, one of the first things that happens after Adam and Eve eat the fruit is that they begin to doubt God's trustworthiness.

After all, God had told them they would die if they ate the fruit, and they did not. Waddell writes:

> If they didn't trust God in one thing, why should they trust Him in another? What about having no clothes, for instance?

They are no longer sure of anything. They don't know whom to trust, and they don't know what to think as they come to realize that information has been withheld from them. It is only then that they begin to feel ashamed of their nakedness. They have remained alive, but their innocence and blind trust have died, and actual death is their only sure destination.

At the same time, Waddell emphasizes a caring, parental God whose overriding emotional response to Adam and Eve's misbehavior is sadness. True, the God in this retelling of the story is angry, but God's anger is directed toward the serpent. Toward Adam and Eve God just feels sadness. Waddell writes:

> God was sad because Adam and Eve had disobeyed Him, but He loved them and He didn't want them to die. Instead He told them that because they had eaten the fruit they would have to leave the beautiful garden and go out in the world to fend for themselves.
>
> It was very sad, but it was their own fault for believing the snake, and not putting their trust in God.

Like a disappointed parent who expected better, God's reaction to Adam and Eve themselves is a commingling of sadness and unconditional love. They brought their punishment on themselves and have no one else to blame, yet having to punish them seems to pain God, similar to the parent who says, "This hurts me just as much as it hurts you," when disciplining a child.

Despite their bad behavior, God still loves them. In a note to parents in the front of her book, Martin writes, "We often consider humankind's sinfulness to be the main theme of this story because Adam and Eve disobeyed God's command. However, woven into the story is a bright thread of God's loving care for us, even when we disobey."

Martin purposefully shapes her retelling in such a way that God, while not a God of second chances, is still a caring God who wants what is best for Adam and Eve.

> Because God loved them, God wanted to protect Adam and Eve even though they had disobeyed. So God gave them clothes to keep them warm.

As in Sendak's *Where the Wild Things Are,* in which Max's mother leaves him dinner even though he has misbehaved and been sent to his room, this retelling teaches that parents still love their children even when they are naughty. When Adam and Eve misbehave, God still takes care of them, gives them clothes to protect them, and doesn't abandon them. Yet framing the story in this way does not quite work. This retelling is one of the few that includes Adam and Eve having children once they've left the garden. The last illustration in the book shows Eve holding a baby while Adam leans proudly over them. This happy conclusion is potentially in conflict with the message of obedience, for if they had obeyed God and not eaten the fruit, they would never have had to leave the garden. And if they hadn't left the garden, they would never have had to grow up and become adults. Or, rather, perhaps this version allows children to understand that ultimately being truly obedient is being true to yourself. There is a time to obey, and a time to rebel; all children must eventually leave the "garden" and go out to become decision-making adults and even parents themselves.

For children, the parent is typically all-knowing, all-powerful, and in control of the child's life. Beginning to question that knowledge and control is an important part of adolescence and is necessary to ultimately become an independent adult. This universal struggle is reflected in many well-known fairy tales. In "Hansel and Gretel," a major turning point occurs when the children realize that their father, in listening to his wife, has made a bad choice and, in abandoning his children, does not have their best interest at heart. It is then that they decide to take control over their own fate by creating a trail to find their way home. Ahead of them still lies many trials, but now it will be up to them whether they succeed or not. Their survival no longer depends on a parent. Rapunzel also comes to make her own choices; locked away in a tower and warned not to admit anyone, she finally chooses to ignore the crone's admonition and admits the prince to the tower. With this decision she alters the course of her life and, at the end, descends from her paradise-like tower, where all her needs and wishes have been provided for, to take up residence in the real world and be responsible for her own future and happiness.

In telling Adam and Eve not to eat from the tree of knowledge of good and evil, God acts like the classic over-protective parent who wants to keep the child safe. God tells them that they will die if they eat from the tree. But when they do eat from it, they don't die. Their eyes are opened, they become ashamed, and they become mortal. In eating from the tree, they begin to grow up, mature, and grow away from the parent. When they eat the fruit, they realize that there is knowledge that God has tried to keep from them.

Loss of Innocence and the Awakening of Sexuality

> Now the serpent was the shrewdest of all the wild beasts that the Lord God had made. . . . And the serpent said to the woman, "You are not going to die."
>
> (Genesis 3:1; 3:4)

Stories told to children are rife with animal trickster characters who use charm or obfuscation to lure the hero out of safety and into danger. For children familiar with this genre of stories, including such far-ranging examples as "The Three Little Pigs," "Little Red Riding Hood," Beatrix Potter's *Jemima Puddleduck*, the African spider Anansi, or the American South's Brer Rabbit, it may come as no surprise that an animal plays this kind of role in the biblical story.

The serpent is the seducer who causes Eve to lose her innocence. The serpent, a common symbol of masculinity in fairy tales and myths, uses an unspecified fruit as the vehicle of seduction (Bettelheim,

p. 212). In most retellings of the story, the fruit is thought to be an apple, which Bettelheim notes stands for both love and sex, as well as danger, in fairy tales, such as the poisoned Apple of Sleeping Beauty. So too, here the fruit is used to tempt first Eve and then Adam to surrender their innocence in exchange for adult knowledge and sexuality. In the watercolor illustrations for his retelling, *Adam and Eve: The Bible Story*, Warwick Hutton paints the serpent beguilingly wrapping himself around Eve's naked legs (Hutton, 1987). The painting shows the serpent using his phallic body as well as his smooth talk to woo Eve into breaking the rules. The serpent, armed with the fruit, is the force that pushes Eve out of latency, and into the next stage of her existence, full-blown puberty, when, as Erikson writes, "all the earlier drives reemerge in a new combination" (p. 260).

The serpent's role in the story is clear, but not so his motivation. Some authors of retellings for children try to fill in the blanks in the story in ways that will be comprehensible to young readers. Horn and Cavanaugh explain that the serpent was jealous of Adam and Eve. "The happier Adam and Eve became, the more jealous the serpent felt." In this version, the serpent plays the role of an older sibling. The serpent, who was there before the first people, resents their experience of happiness in the garden just as an older sibling resents the presence of a new baby in the home.

Also like an older sibling who possesses knowledge unknown to the younger sibling, Horn and Cavanaugh's serpent engages Eve in a conversation on the meaning of death, another complicated aspect of this part of the story of creation for children.

> "Die?" said the serpent. "Do you know what it means to die?"
> "No," Eve answered. "Does it hurt?"
> "God made you," said the serpent slyly. "Why would he want to hurt you? Surely you will not die."

Their dialogue here may be about death, but it also seems to be a thinly veiled discussion about sexual seduction, in which the experienced seducer tries to convince his prey that it won't hurt. This Eve is naive and innocent, and the serpent is able to seduce her into eating the fruit against her better judgment. Like a skilled manipulator, the serpent knows how to gain Eve's trust in order to exploit her curiosity and weakness. By doing so, the serpent enables Eve to gain knowledge that had been previously denied to her, allowing her to begin the process of growing up.

Jealousy is also a motivating factor in Peter Dickinson's retelling in *City of Gold*. Dickson imagines the serpent and Adam as close friends before God creates Eve. Eve's arrival in the garden shifts the balance of relationships and the serpent begins to feel left out and resentful.

> Of all the animals in the garden he was nearest to Adam in wisdom, so the serpent and the man had been companions until the coming of Eve, sitting together under the stars and riddling out the wonders of God's creation. . . . From this seed sprang all the sorrow of the world, for in his delight in his bride Adam forgot his long friendship with the serpent.

Unlike the jealousy of an older sibling, in this version the serpent's jealousy is more akin to that of a child's best friend once the friend discovers sexual attraction to others. Suddenly the friend is no longer the primary object of affection, behavior consistent with the social development patterns of the middle and pre-adolescent years of childhood. The Bible story also bears comparison with fairy tales, in which intimations of unresolved Oedipal conflict like that of Snow White are prevalent. Here Eve has come between the friendship of the serpent and Adam. The now deposed best friend may feel anxious or threatened, just as she or he did as a young child trying to figure out the relationship between each of the parents and him or herself. Adam's passive lack of resistance to Eve's suggestion of eating the fruit reveals a close bond between the two that eclipses Adam's bond with the serpent. The serpent, like a jealous child raging with Oedipal emotions, seeks to destroy the bond between Adam and Eve, to come between them so that he can have the undivided attention of Adam, the father figure. This is, of course, impossible, and as Adam leaves childhood behind in paradise he will form a family unit with Eve and their future children.

It is this phallic serpent that will lead Eve into the zone of danger, tempting her to do that which has been forbidden. And in so doing, she crosses out of innocence into adulthood and the world of sexuality. It is difficult to read Eve's act of defiance without the negative gloss of the "Fall" into a state of sin. Yet reading the text as a story, removed from its religious moorings, shows that Eve's experience is not necessarily all bad. There is pleasure, experienced in the taste of the fruit, and there is the emotional growth of Adam and Eve recognizing their nakedness and seeing themselves in a new way. But there is also the emotional pain of being forced to leave the garden, the safe haven of their youth, and having to enter a world in which both will have to experience the physical pain of hard manual labor or childbirth. Read this way, Eve's act of disobedience can seem inevitable. Eating the fruit does not bring only bad consequences, it brings both good *and* bad. Adam and Eve come to know both good *and* evil, not just evil; they come to pleasure *and* pain, not just pain. In other words, they grow up, as everyone eventually must.

The serpent is an integral part of the garden. In her retelling, Gwendolyn Reed makes it explicit that the serpent, just like all the good animals and just like Adam and Eve, was created by God. She writes, "Of all the creatures that God made, the serpent was the most cunning." There can be no question here that this serpent came from within the garden, from within God's realm. Yet the existence of the serpent raises questions for children. How could this evil animal exist in God's perfect garden? Why did God create the serpent if he was bad? Reed's insistence that the serpent too is part of God's creation allows for the possibility that convincing Eve to eat the fruit may have been part of God's master plan, that perhaps God actually intended for the serpent to act as the catalyst that would cause Adam and Eve to grow up and have to leave the garden.

This idea of the inevitability of growing up is found in many examples of classic children's literature. These stories reflect the ultimate conflict of childhood, wanting the privileges of adulthood without the responsibilities. In J. M. Barrie's *Peter Pan*, Peter and the wild boys don't want to grow up. They live in a perfect little boy's paradise of fun, games, no adult rules, dirty faces, and plenty of pirates and Indians to fight. When Peter meets Wendy, he is conflicted. Should he leave Neverland and grow up so that he can stay with her, or should he remain always a boy? In the end, he chooses to stay in Neverland, while Wendy grows up and has children of her own. Unlike Wendy, Eve succeeds in pushing Adam to grow up with her, so that they can share adult knowledge and experiences.

In Philip Turner's retelling of the story, "The Coming of Sorrow," found in *Brian Wildsmith's Illustrated Bible Stories,* after God instructs Adam and Eve not to eat from the Tree of Knowledge of Good and Evil, lest they die, Eve asks Adam if he knows what "die" means (Turner in Wildsmith, 1969). Turner describes Adam and Eve in a childlike way, describing them as being "snug in their bower for the night." Like a young child, Eve has heard concepts she is not familiar with, and is trying to understand them. Adam replies that he does not know. She goes on to ask him if he knows what evil is, but to that query, too, he has no answer. Eve is curious in this retelling, beginning to look beyond the safe confines of their world. She is searching, albeit tentatively, for more knowledge than she has been given up to this point, and the serpent provides that for her, telling her that if she eats the fruit she will not die, but she will gain wisdom.

In Turner's depiction of the story, Adam is a Peter Pan–like figure, seeming not to want any greater knowledge than what he already possesses. But once Eve eats the fruit, Adam, apparently understanding something of the major change in both Eve and in their existence that has just occurred, follows her.

> When Adam discovered what Eve had done he was heartbroken. But out of his love for her, and so that he might share her dying, he too took and ate the dark fruit.

Eve's act, performed in what Turner calls "a sad hour," has forced Adam to accept a new reality that he might otherwise have chosen to ignore. They both have come to recognize that the world is a dark, cold, scary place. Sadness and sorrow have entered into an existence which was previously immune from such experiences.

Whereas previously they were safe in their bower, now when God calls them they huddle "in the dark depths of a thicket," ashamed and scared. Turner writes:

> They must leave the garden and make their lonely way in a hostile world until they grew old and died.

Their age of innocence is over, and they must leave the garden and go out into the world. There is no attempt here to soften the blow for children reading this retelling, or to try to protect them from the cruel reality portrayed in Turner's vision of life outside the garden, the life to which all people thus seem to be destined once they leave innocence behind. As Horn and Cavanaugh write, "Because you were fooled by the serpent, you will know pain and sorrow for the first time."

Like the frog in Grimm's "The Frog King," the serpent makes Eve realize that there may be more to life than she has yet realized. The serpent is the herald of Eve's "call to adventure" (Campbell, p. 51), a symbol of what Campbell, based on Freud's work, calls the "suppressed desires and conflicts" that exist within. Read in this way, the serpent is a manifestation of Eve's own hidden desires and urges that lurk under the surface of her supposed contentment in the garden. The serpent appears at that moment because Eve needs it to appear. Like the adolescent princess in "The Frog King," Eve is ripe for change. As Campbell writes, "The familiar life horizon has been outgrown; the old concepts, ideals, and emotional patterns no longer fit; the time for the passing of a threshold is at hand" (p. 51). Her wish for change, for passing over the threshold of the safety of childhood into the dangers of adulthood, is beginning to break through the surface, and the serpent is the agent who enables Eve to take that desired step forward.

In the fairy tale of "Hansel and Gretel," the aspects of separation and independent decision making are vividly depicted. It is Gretel who pushes Hansel beyond the safety zone into behavior that carries with it great risk. Hansel and Gretel, like Adam and Eve, are naive innocents, and have no prior experience at making choices. Hansel has attempted to protect Gretel, first with dropping pebbles along their path and then with bread crumbs, but it is Gretel who is initially tempted by the gingerbread house. She holds Hansel's hand and urges him to eat from it with the words, "It's the loveliest house I ever saw, and it looks good enough to eat" (Gàg, 1936, p. 12). Their choice to give in to the temptation of the house may not be the wisest choice, yet it is the act that ultimately allows them to test themselves, triumph, and assure for themselves a better future.

In Van Eyssen's version of the story, the serpent is of the garden and of God, the seamy underside or hidden blemish of God's creation. The serpent represents the hidden evil that we all fear lurks deep within. The idea that if others knew what they truly thought or dreamed about, they would lose their love or be thought less of, is familiar to children. Van Eyssen writes:

> It happened that in the apple tree, coiled amid the twining foliage, there lived an evil snake, who was far too ugly and ashamed of his appearance to come out and show himself in the garden where all was beautiful. The snake was not only ugly outwardly, but inside too, and he wanted to make everyone as twisted as himself.

This serpent is like the other, hidden self that encourages making bad choices, giving in to impulse control, and specifically, the part of the self in children that begins to have sexual feelings and responses before the child is emotionally ready to handle them appropriately.

Van Eyssen's retelling acknowledges the sexual elements of the story to a much greater extent than other children's versions. In trying to convince Eve to eat the fruit, the serpent tells her, "But see how the skin of this apple swells with moist sweet juice, juice which will slake your thirst, your curious thirst, your parching, unsatisfied, wondering thirst." In this retelling, Eve is a naïf, curious about the knowledge that she does not yet have, but still somewhat cautious and afraid to push beyond her own limits. She tells the serpent, "I see what I know and I know what I see," yet she is self-aware enough to understand that there is more.

Eve's encounter with the fruit is a long, drawn-out affair in this sensual retelling, its drama and sexuality heightened by the author's careful choice of words. Van Eyssen writes:

> Eve's outstretched fingers met the blush-bloomed skin of the apple, caressed and closed about it. What harm could there be in taking one small bite? Her teeth sank sharply into its succulent fruit. The snake hissed with pleasure.

Like Gretel, once she has seen the witch's house, there can be no turning back for Eve. The one bite of the fruit has opened her eyes to possibilities she had not previously been able to fathom. Through her encounter with the serpent, she has caught a glimpse of the world of adult choices and sexuality, and must bring Adam into the world of adulthood along with her.

Reed's version of the story ends with Adam and Eve working the land, having children, and eventually dying. She makes the point that their actions in the garden had consequences not just for their own lives but for all the subsequent generations to come. Never again could the sons and daughters of Adam and Eve enter the garden: "Always on their lips was the taste of the forbidden fruit. As well as joy they knew sorrow. In their lives they knew both good and evil." It was Adam and Eve who, in eating the forbidden fruit, made the decision to be fully human. The ramifications of this choice are enormous.

Not only are Adam and Eve the first people, but they also experience the first birth and the first murder. Having been commanded by God to be fertile and fill the earth, it is only once Adam and Eve are banished beyond the confines of the garden that they can fulfill this commandment. In their earlier life in the garden, they were not yet ready or able to have children. The biblical text asserts, however, that their first act upon leaving the garden is to engage in a sexual relationship, something that has not yet been mentioned in the text (Genesis 4:1). Now that they are released from the confines of the garden and the strictures of childhood, now that they can perceive the world, each other, and themselves in a multitude of ways, they are ready to be fully sexual beings. They bring two sons into the world, one of whom will murder the other. Their new adult life outside the garden will not be simple. Pleasure will be forever entangled with pain, just as their knowledge of good will always be accompanied by a knowledge of evil.

The Transition into Adulthood

> The two of them were naked, the man and his wife, yet they felt no shame. . . . Then the eyes of both of them were opened and they perceived that they were naked; and they sewed together fig leaves and made themselves loincloths.
>
> (Genesis 2:25, 3:7)

The biblical text itself does not specify the ages of Adam and Eve, or give a clear sense through the use of language. One question that therefore faces anyone contemplating a retelling of the story of Adam and Eve for children is to decide how old to portray them. This is especially the case for illustrators, who must give a physical form to their depiction. They seem to be childlike figures, especially at the beginning of the story. Yet once they have eaten from the tree, in their new awareness of their bodies and their sexuality, and their discomfort with their new selves, they exhibit the behavior of typical adolescents, right on the verge of tremendous physical and emotional change. Before eating the fruit, Adam and Eve are content to be naked. Like very young children, they are unashamed of their bodies and their nudity. But once they have eaten from the fruit, they see the world differently. Suddenly they are ashamed to be naked. They try to hide themselves from God and fashion themselves clothes of fig leaves.

Their emotional development parallels that of typical human development, from young babies to mature adults, as described by Freud and Erickson. It might be logical to assume that in books for children, Adam and Eve would be depicted as children, but this is generally not the case in picture-book versions. Their adult attributes present challenges for illustrators, like breasts that have to be covered by hair or trees, not to mention what is demurely tucked behind leaves or hands.

Yet the common convention is to portray Adam and Eve as young adults or even fully mature adults.

The interpretation of their age provided by the illustrations is significant because it colors the way readers understand their behavior. It is one thing for a young child to disobey an authority figure and flagrantly flout a rule, but it is another thing altogether for an adult who should know better, or who is seen by the reader as an authority figure in his/her own right, to do so. How children react to the nakedness of Adam and Eve is also an issue, as children are acutely aware of the difference between the nakedness of a toddler versus the nakedness of an adult.

In her collection *Stories from the Bible*, Lisbeth Zwerger combines extracts from the King James Bible with her own original illustrations. She depicts Adam and Eve standing awkwardly under a tree, presumably the tree of the knowledge of good and evil. A dark cloud hovers at the side of the illustration, as if it is just about to come over them, and a serpent slithers by on the bottom of the page, outside of the margin of the illustration. Adam and Eve appear uncomfortable, perhaps shy, perhaps embarrassed, perhaps chagrined. It is unclear if they are about to eat from the tree, or have already done so. They look like two awkward adolescents, not like sexually self-assured young adults. They both have long hair. Adam is beardless and his chest is hairless and undefined. Eve is only minimally curved and her breasts are completely hidden by her hair. They look at each with slightly tilted heads and unsure expressions. This is a younger Adam and Eve, less sure of themselves than in many other versions of this story.

In Geoffrey Patterson's illustrations for Martin Waddell's *Stories from the Bible*, Adam and Eve are similar in appearance. They have the same dark, long hair and the same undefined bodies. Eve's green covering goes up to her chest, hinting that there is something to hide, while Adam's covers only his waist to his knees. But with no facial hair, no defined features, and no real curves or musculature, it is impossible to determine the ages that this Adam and Eve are supposed to be.

Fran Manushkin's 2001 retelling of the story, *Eve*, part of her collection *Daughters of Fire: Heroines of the Bible*, is unusual in that Adam and Eve are described as kind of proto-grownups right from the beginning. In this retelling, the "perfect trust and love" that they have for each other is a natural result of their being two sides of the same person. Manushkin blends the two versions of the creation stories from Genesis chapters 1 and 2, rather than seeing them as a contradiction or focusing only on the second version. In her version, Adam and Eve are truly one whole, God having first created one human with two faces, one female and one male. After spending some time as a two-faced creature, God casts a deep sleep upon the person and separates one side from the other, creating a man and a woman out of the original person. Right away God decides to perform a wedding for the two people. They are the perfect couple, absolutely compatible and completely happy with each other in their beautiful world that God has created for them. Even though they exist in a childlike, problem-free state, Manushkin has identified them as already being husband and wife.

The question of how to deal with themes of nakedness, shame, embarrassment, and sexuality is an important consideration for contemporary authors and illustrators attempting to retell this story for children. Shame about nudity or sexuality is today considered retrogressive and not in keeping with the current mores of child-rearing. At the same time, these themes can be very embarrassing to children. Some authors of retellings smooth out the potentially difficult nature of these elements of the story. Horn and Cavanaugh leave out the idea of shame entirely, writing:

> When they had finished, Adam and Eve stared at each other.
> Suddenly they felt cold and afraid, and covered their bodies with leaves.

This Adam and Eve are not *ashamed* of being naked, rather, they are quite naturally cold, and they are afraid. What they are afraid of is not mentioned. Perhaps they are meant to be afraid of the consequences they now face, having disobeyed God. Perhaps they are afraid of showing their naked bodies to each other. Perhaps they are afraid of what they feel when they see the nakedness of each other. Whatever the reason, Adam and Eve are people in transition at this point. There was no need before to be afraid, and thus fear is a new emotion for them.

A direct connection is made between pleasure, shame, and death in Reed's retelling. An understanding of death and, hence, one's own immortality occurs for Adam and Eve at the same time as they discover the emotion of shame. Eating the fruit has truly taught them new knowledge that they did not previously possess: a sense both of loss and self-consciousness of their place in the world.

> At first the fruit was sweet on their lips. Soon its sweetness turned to the bitter taste of dust and death. Their eyes were opened. They knew they had done evil in disobeying God. They knew shame. The man and the woman looked at each other and saw that like the beasts they were naked. This filled them with shame too. They sewed together the leaves of a fig tree and covered themselves.

Having eaten from the tree, they have lost their innocence and their ability to go through life unquestioningly accepting. They understand that the world is made up of separations and differences. They are not like the animals and must not behave like them. Knowledge of death teaches them that things change and that pain and suffering are real. Once they leave the garden, as they must, Reed writes that they come to learn "fear, and pain, and sorrow."

This is a very different description than that of Reed's portrayal of Adam and Eve's early days in the garden: "Adam and Eve lived joyously. But they did not know it, for they did not know what sorrow or suffering were. They did not know what evil was." Without eating the forbidden fruit and experiencing the knowledge of good and evil, their understanding of life is severely limited. Without understanding the bad, they cannot take true pleasure in the good. Their disobedience of God allows them to be more fully alive and to enjoy what is good in life while also opening themselves up to the capacity to suffer and feel pain.

Children don't understand death in part because they don't understand the permanence of loss, the concept of "forever." Children live only in the present. When Adam and Eve eat from the forbidden fruit, their eyes are opened to love and loss, to life and death. They will be able to be truly joyous, and they will know terrible suffering and pain. Like any caring parent, God had wanted to protect them from experiencing anguish and misery. Yet as it is for all parents, to protect children from pain is to keep them emotionally stunted. Adam and Eve leave the garden to experience life in all its permutations, the good along with the bad.

In the course of the transition into adulthood, Eve becomes aware of concepts previously unfamiliar to her. Specifically, she learns about both death and sexuality. In encountering these two concepts, she is also able to understand emotions previously unimaginable, like shame and sorrow. The blinders come off her eyes when she eats the forbidden fruit and she, and then also Adam, are able to become adults and take on their role as parents of the human race. In accepting the fruit from the serpent, Eve surrenders her innocence, but once Adam has also eaten from the fruit they are able to both gain new knowledge and form a lasting relationship.

Responsibility and Consequences

> *And the Lord God said to the woman,*
> *"What is this you have done!"*
> *The woman replied, "The serpent duped me, and I ate."*

> (Genesis 3:13)

When God asks Adam and Eve if they have eaten from the forbidden tree, they respond exactly like young children. Adam places all the blame on Eve, saying, "The woman you put at my side—she gave me of the tree, and I ate" (Genesis 3:12). And Eve blames the serpent. Taking responsibility for choices and the consequent results are understood by child development specialists as significant evidence of mature adult behavior. In Erikson's eight stages of development, taking responsibility for one's choices is an adolescent behavior that emerges first in puberty and crystallizes in adulthood, occuring usually by the time people are in their thirties. As Schaie notes, this is when they begin to seriously concentrate on real-life issues and problems that are focused on their responsibilities toward others, including spouses, older parents, children, and coworkers (1979, p. 129–38). Neither Adam nor Eve considers, even momentarily, taking responsibility for their choices and actions, nor for the consequences of their behavior; neither do they think of the effect of their behavior on their partner.

God punishes Adam and Eve for their behavior, teaching them that there are direct consequences to bad behavior. Together, they are banished from the garden and from their life of perfection and relative ease. They must now take greater responsibility for their lives, which includes pain and toil. Eve, the Ur-mother, will bear children in pain, and Adam, the prototypical provider, will have to plant his own food and work hard to bring it forth from the earth. Both of them will ultimately die, becoming once again part of the earth from which they were created.

The theme of consequences is familiar in children's folk literature from around the world. In *Why the Sky Is Far Away: A Nigerian Folktale* (Gerson, 1992), Adese and the other villagers get their food by breaking off chunks of the sky. They soon become greedy and wasteful and are warned by the king and the sky to help themselves to only as much as they can eat. They are warned not to throw unwanted pieces of the sky onto rubbish heaps. The sky complains to the king that his gifts are being wasted by the villagers and he will no longer allow such despoilment, saying, "I warn you. Do not waste my gifts any longer, or they will no longer be yours." The villagers cannot accept that there will be consequences for continuing their bad behavior. But just as Adam and Eve have to leave their paradise and work for their bread, the villagers now have to assume responsibility for tilling the soil and growing their bread. Their paradise, the beautiful sky, moves far away from the earth, out of people's reach, just as the paradise of the garden is now out of reach to Adam and Eve.

Whereas the biblical text indicates that God is angry at Adam and Eve's behavior, Martin's gentle retelling attempts to soften the story for children. As soon as they have eaten the fruit, they "felt very sorry." And when they admit what they have done, "God was sad." This is a gentle, caring God who is not angry but rather disappointed in their choice. In this version of the story the incident is shaped as a constructive learning experience. Martin writes: "Because Adam and Eve had eaten the fruit, they now knew the difference between good and evil. They knew the difference between right and wrong. They knew they had done wrong when they disobeyed God." When God makes them leave the garden, they are contrite and in tears. It can be inferred that they have learned a lesson about obeying rules and making good choices. It is too late for another chance within the garden, and they learn, too, that actions have consequences. They now see in a new way, and can never go back to a more simplistic, easier way of viewing the world.

The idea of punishment comes through forcefully in Chaikin's retelling in *Children's Bible Stories from Genesis to Daniel*. Chaikin writes "God was angry and punished them all." Adam, Eve, and the serpent all receive a personalized form of retribution from God. Adam will have to plant the earth and work hard for his food, and he will return to dust when he dies. Eve will bear children in pain. And the serpent will crawl on its belly and eat dirt. But even all this is not quite enough for God: "As a further punishment, God banished Adam and Eve from the Garden. But was that enough? Would they stay away? They had disobeyed God once; they might do so again and try to return to the Garden." This is a mistrustful God, different from Martin's caring, giving God. God here can no longer rely on Adam and Eve's obedience and must take precautions. For there is another tree in this garden that God is even more concerned about than the tree of the knowledge of good and evil—the "Tree of Living Forever." That Adam and Eve might eat from that tree is something that God cannot allow to happen. And so God places upon them this additional punishment of banishment from the garden. This God who punishes and sets absolute limits may not be the most comforting image of God. But it may be a more realistic version of the developmental model, for through their disobedience, they manage to gain responsibility over their own lives, their sexuality, and the mortality that sets them on a course toward death but, at the same time, enables them to live fully realized human lives.

The God portrayed in Van Eyssen's *In the Beginning* both punishes and protects. They must go "out into the world beyond, where they were obliged to fend for themselves." And yet they are not totally alone. God is still looking out for them and will ultimately forgive them for their disobedience: "But though they thought they had lost God's favour forever, He still watched over them, and in time showed His forgiveness by sending Adam and Eve two sons." This idea of the sons as a sign of God's forgiveness is both original to this retelling, and problematic. For of course it is not as simple as Adam and Eve receiving these two children as a gift from God. No longer living in paradise in a latent pre-adolescent stage of sexual innocence, Adam and Eve have progressed to a mature adult state of making choices and taking responsibility for their decisions. The children are a tangible sign of Adam and Eve's adulthood and an overt sign that they have reached sexual maturity, in other words, a constant reminder of their removal from the garden and the inaccessibility of the easy, perfect life that they led before. These sons are also not simply cheerful, adorable children who will brighten their parents' lives, but two opposing forces, one of whom will slay the other. They are thus a living manifestation of Adam and Eve's acquisition of the knowledge of good and evil, in which evil triumphs through the killing of Abel by Cain. Despite the sense of God's forgiveness, presenting the sons as God's gift paints a view of God as ultimately cynical and vengeful, showing compassion with a gift that will bring only more pain and suffering.

The dangers of knowledge are recognized in Chaikin's *Children's Bible Stories from Genesis to Daniel*. God is portrayed in this version as desiring punishment. God promises the serpent that he will crawl on his belly and eat dirt, Eve that she will have pain in childbirth, and Adam that he will have to work hard and suffer to bring forth food. But these punishments are not enough for God. Chaikin imagines God also concerned with not having Adam and Eve go too far now that they have some knowledge.

As a further punishment, God banished Adam and Eve from the Garden. But was that enough? Would they stay away? They had disobeyed God once; they might do so again and try to return to the Garden.

Now hidden deep in the Garden was another forbidden tree, the Tree of Living Forever. Adam and Eve now had knowledge. If they came back, they would find the Tree and eat its fruit.

In order to prevent Adam and Eve from achieving immortality and becoming like God, God blocks the way back to the garden. Adam and Eve can never come back. Their future, and the future of the human race, can only happen outside the confines of the garden.

In his collection *City of Gold,* Peter Dickinson makes the unusual choice of imagining Adam and Eve already conceiving a child while they are still within the garden. After Eve eats the fruit from the Tree of Knowledge, she hears her month-old child crying. Adam, with his new-found ability to see not only the good in the world but also the bad, sees his son in a whole new way: "Adam saw its little clenched fists striking in fury at emptiness, and knew that they would grow to be strong, clutching hands, the hands of Cain, who was first to murder a man." This Adam and Eve are not straddling the fence between childhood and adulthood, but are already sexually active parents of a child. Their disobedience thus becomes more complicated for children in this retelling, as it allows parents to be seen as people who can misbehave and be punished.

When Eve and then Adam eat the fruit from the Tree of Knowledge, they separate themselves from God irreparably. The difference between them and God is now stark. Though they obtain some knowledge, it is at a huge cost. They will now know suffering, and will eventually come to know loss and death. To die is ultimately what it means to be human, and that is the future to which, as human beings, they can look forward. But the picture is not completely bleak. Along the way, they can learn, and grow, and experience the beauty and happiness that life does have to offer.

The epic story of the first humans parallels the journey from infancy to adulthood. Existing first in a state of complete dependence and naiveté, Adam is content. Quickly though, Adam needs more from life. With the separation of humanity into distinct male and female creatures, Adam and Eve start out on the journey toward inevitable separation from the world of utter reliance upon the parental figure. Their hero's journey is not the story of a great feat accomplished, but rather the universal journey of transition that every human must make. While still protected within the safety of the Garden, they will strive for independence and self-determination, seeking greater knowledge. Their heroism lies in the very fact of having survived the journey, and in providing a model for subsequent generations.

Collections of Bible stories for children vary as to which stories are selected for retelling. Not all include Jonah or Esther, for example. They are selective about how much or what parts they tell of the Moses narratives, or the episodes of David's life. But no matter what other choices are being made, they all seem to include the story of Adam and Eve. Despite the sophisticated issues that emerge out of this tale such as sexuality and death, not to mention the inherent theological complications, this story has long been deemed a suitable story for children. It has served as a useful warning to children about the perils of misbehaving. Keeping the emphasis on the theme of obedience in retellings for children reveals both an adult desire to protect children from knowledge of sexuality and death, knowledge that is complicated and possibly even painful for children, as well as adult discomfort with these topics. But there is more to it than just the value of the story as a lesson about obedience. This story of Adam and Eve is retold over and over for children because it offers a mirror of human development, from the protected, cared-for state of early childhood, to the dormant stage of latency, into the tumultuous period of adolescence, and ultimately into fully independent adulthood. In reading their story, we begin to understand something about our own story as we ourselves grow from dependence to independence.

As much as the story of creation is often understood as a story about disobedience and the faulty nature of humankind, it is also a story about the emergence of human sexuality. Though the first people are told early on that an important human responsibility is to be fertile and multiply (Genesis 1:28), it is only after they are expelled from the garden that the biblical text makes an explicit reference to sexual activity. "Now the man knew his wife Eve, and she conceived . . ." (Genesis 4:1). There is no mention of sex or children while they are in the garden. It is only once they have eaten the fruit of knowledge and have to fend for themselves outside the garden that their emotional development is advanced enough for them to become sexual beings and then parents. This change is in keeping with the story as a model of the emotional development of children. Obedience, punishment, making choices, and having to separate and take responsibility for oneself are the themes of childhood, themes with which children can identify. Sexuality and parenthood exist outside of the garden, on the metaphoric other side of childhood.

Removed from its religious context, there is a subversive message embedded in the retellings of this story for children. Disguised as a clear-cut story with a message about obedience and the cost of disobedience, the story can also be read as the presentation of a choice for children. Obey and remain cared for but naive, lacking in knowledge. Or disobey, and gain knowledge. An argument could be made that it is God's intention all along for Adam and Eve to eat from the tree of knowledge of good and evil. Every parent knows that the best way to get children to do something is to forbid them from doing it. It is possible to surmise that God acts here like a parent shoving the baby bird from the nest, actually wanting to enable the first humans to fully separate, grow up, and leave their youthful paradise so that they can fulfill their destiny and be truly human. That growth and knowledge obtained through disobedience is accompanied by pain, suffering, and death is not likely to prevent children from wanting to choose the latter option. Rather than convincing children to behave and listen to adults, this story can serve as a comfort to children as they struggle with the conflicting inner impulses of childhood. Yes, growing up causes pain, but it also brings knowledge, pleasure, and the ability to make one's own choices.

2
NOAH

The single best-known Bible story is probably that of Noah's Ark. Over the years, it has been the most frequently published secular trade edition of a children's Bible story. A review of the standard children's catalogs[4] most widely used for collection building and maintenance in public and school libraries lists more Noah titles than any other biblical character, a fact attested to by a visit to any well-stocked bookstore or library. Catalogues of children's furnishings offer Noah's Ark themed crib sets, layettes, mobiles, lamps, curtains, and toys. It appears to be the ideal story for children, involving as it does a virtuous and obedient man and many cute animals. The first book to ever receive the Caldecott medal was *Animals of the Bible* in 1938, with text selected from the King James Bible by Helen Dean Fish and illustrated by Dorothy P. Lathrop, which contains within it two chapters related to Noah's Ark. Three other Noah's Ark themed books have been Caldecott Honor or Award Books, including *One Wide River to Cross,* with text adapted by Barbara Emberley and illustrated by Ed Emberley (1967 Caldecott Honor Book), Peter Spier's *Noah's Ark* (1978 Caldecott Award Winner), and Jerry Pinkney's *Noah's Ark* (2003 Caldecott Honor Book). Yet a closer look at this familiar story shows it to have several elements that are much more complicated than appears at first.

Reading the biblical source of the story reveals the story of Noah's Ark to be a tale about character and righteousness. Why is it that Noah is chosen for his mission of Ark-building and saving animals? The text reads, "Noah found favor with the Lord . . . Noah was a righteous man; he was blameless in his generation" (Genesis 6:8–9). It was therefore his job to save the animals while all the rest of the human race, with the exception of his family, was condemned to death for their evil ways. The next question must then be, what did people do that made God want to destroy the entire human race? What terrible thing did they do to warrant complete annihilation? The biblical text is not entirely clear on the matter. There is a reference immediately before the start of the Noah story to cohabitation between divine be-

---

[4] The Elementary School Library Collection. Williamsport, PA: Brodart, 1992. *Adventuring with Books*. Newark, NJ: NCTE, 2002.

ings and the daughters of men (Genesis 6:4). Several lines later the text tells us that there was great corruption and lawlessness on earth, but of exactly what nature is not made clear (Genesis 6:11–13).

A literal reading of the biblical Noah narrative may possibly convey the idea that if you're not good, God will slay you. This is not, however, the message of contemporary versions of Noah's Ark for children. Instead, the retellers of this story take on the task of shaping it so that the message is appropriate to both the societal concerns of the times, as well as prevailing thoughts on child-rearing, child development, and the teaching of morality. Rather than a harsh tale about behaving ethically and being righteous in order to ward off God's wrath and destruction, the story of Noah's Ark has become a somewhat sugar-coated story about animals and rainbows.

The story of Noah and his Ark is a story rich with both themes and possibilities. Most authors of mainstream trade publications downplay the issue of God killing the entire human race, and focus instead on other themes found within the story. And this certainly is a story that lends itself to many themes: what it means to be a good person, taking care of each other, taking care of the earth, ethical treatment of animals, relating to God, and making peace, just to name a few. Some of the children's book versions stick close to the original biblical text, even while modifying it for children, while others go far afield, using the story as a jumping off point. The story serves in some contemporary versions as a vehicle to teach children the names and characteristics of animals, despite the fact that the biblical text does not detail the animals at all and only briefly describes them in broad categories. Other retellers have omitted altogether the idea of Noah being somehow worthy of God's goodwill, or more righteous than his peers, in favor of a focus on the human's relationship to animals. For others, it is about our relationship to the earth and our responsibility to care for it properly. Some versions don't mention God at all, focusing only on the human aspect of the story. Issues of race and ethnicity also find a place in retellings of Noah's Ark.

At the forefront of cognitive development theories, Jean Piaget posits that young children interact continually with their environment through both direct hands-on and vicarious literary experiences in order to understand and assimilate new information about how the world works. Through such experiences they accumulate knowledge that helps them to recognize relationships and interrelationships among things in all sorts of contexts. They can then construct meaning from their experiences and the stories they hear to make sense of the world around them. Young children need motives and behaviors to be unambiguous and easily recognizable, the good are clearly good and the bad are unremittingly evil; children are very literal in their interpretations of motives and language. As children move beyond the early primary grade years they develop the ability to acknowledge other people's viewpoints and see other sides of an issue. It is at this stage of their development that children identify closely with characters in stories and are able to see themselves in someone else's role and to judge actions, behaviors, and motives. They see, side by side, that there are ways other than their own way of feeling and behaving. Because of the emphasis on Noah's goodness in most retellings of this story, it is one that has commonly been used to teach children about behavior deemed appropriate by adults.

Over the course of children's book publishing these theories of child development have greatly influenced the ways in which authors have interpreted and emphasized aspects of the Bible stories they have retold. Events at the forefront of world affairs also influence the way Bible stories are reinterpreted and retold for children; in a time of war, stories emphasize peace; stories published today reflect contemporary environmental concerns. Interpretations of the story of Noah's Ark thus vary greatly, according to both current theories of child development and reflections of societal anxiety over issues of public concern.

What Terrible Thing Did People Do?

> The earth became corrupt before God; the earth was filled with lawlessness.

> (Genesis 6:11)

Quite a few of the versions of Noah's Ark discussed in this chapter begin with the premise that people have done something wrong, something serious enough to warrant severe punishment. In some cases the authors give a vague sense of what the people had done, but often the question of what this great wrong could have been is addressed primarily in the illustrations. Peter Spier's 1978 Caldecott Award book, published in 1977, *Noah's Ark*, begins its almost wordless tale in the endpapers of the book. He tackles the question of what people are doing wrong by depicting a scene of war and destruction contrasted with a peaceful image of Noah tending a vineyard. Along the bottom are the words, ". . . But Noah found grace in the eyes of the Lord."

The only text within the book itself is a seventeenth-century Dutch poem written by Jacobus Revius. The poem details all the kinds of animals aboard the Ark, who were there whether they were "*Good and mean / Foul and clean / Fierce and tame*," rather than because of any inherent qualities they possessed. Nothing is mentioned about Noah himself, other than that his family entered the Ark as well. The purpose of the poem is to praise God, who despite all the wrongdoing of the people on earth forgave and saved them through Divine Grace. The poem concludes: "*They were killed / For the guilt / Which brought all / To the Fall. / Later on / It was done: / Back on land / Through God's hand, / Who forgave, / And did save. / The Lord's Grace / Be the praise!*"

The illustrations tell a great deal more of the story and, in fact, other than the one page of the poem and the endpapers, the illustrations are the story itself. Despite the gravity of the accompanying poem, many of the illustrations are highly humorous: a line of laundry is shown hanging from the top of the Ark; Noah's wife is shown perched on a basket as a pair of mice run past; the stubborn donkey has to be pulled into the Ark by force, while Noah has to get rid of some of the many birds and flies that try to come aboard. At the end, a huge litter of rabbits await their turn off the Ark as an elephant tries to squeeze through the opening.

Yet the ramifications of God's decision to destroy the world is removed from its off-stage setting in these illustrations, which show that whereas some animals were chosen to go into the Ark, many others were left behind. They are shown first standing on dry land, then up to their torsos in water, and then simply absent from a water-filled world. These illustrations are a wordless but vivid depiction of God's decision to destroy the world. Spier frequently uses such sequences of images to show the changes happening to the world. The crowded, busy interior of the Ark provides a sharp contrast to the empty, wet world outside.

Noah is shown to be a kind man, taking care of the animals, feeding them and visiting them. He is clearly in charge, as he is featured in almost every interior illustration, but he is a generous, caring presence. It is interesting, though, that Spier has chosen to portray Noah, for the most part, as the only human presence in the Ark. Although his family features in the initial and final illustrations, they are strangely absent from the journey itself. The book concludes as it began, in its endpapers. Noah is depicted planting new grapevines in an orchard while a rainbow shines behind him. The world is at peace, the shepherd looks after his flock and the fields are being tilled. ". . . and he planted a vineyard," reads the last line. Even for very young children, the message is unmistakable—good behavior is rewarded and bad behavior is punished.

Like children's Bible stories from past centuries, Spier's *Noah's Ark* uses illustration rather than words to depict troubling events. That cities and animals, and then presumably people as well, were covered with water and died is alluded to in the art. The first illustration in the endpapers makes a strong statement about good and bad. War, bloodshed, and destruction are the things for which the people bear the guilt mentioned in the poem, while Noah, depicted with a ray of heavenly light shining directly on him as he works, found grace in the eyes of the Lord by living in peace and taking care of his animals and his fields. No text is needed to explain more clearly why God would have wanted to destroy the world, and why Noah was different from the rest of his generation. This first spread in fact provides a summary of what this version of the story is about in terms that children can understand—a struggle between good and evil, with good and God winning out. Through the power of its illustrations, Spier's version of

Noah's Ark makes a strong statement about the destructive danger of war and violence, and serves as a reminder of the power of righteous behavior.

Noah's Ark: Words from the Book of Genesis, illustrated by Jane Ray and published in 1990, uses actual abridged biblical text from the Authorized King James Version. It is these highly detailed, primitive style illustrations that provide commentary and a contemporary point of view. On the first page, the illustrations that accompany the account of the people's wickedness shows traditional forms of harmful behavior, such as fire and physical violence. More modern forms of negative behavior are shown as well, including verbal abuse, cruelty to animals, and destruction of the environment. Having found favor in God's eyes, Noah is first depicted working in his orchards, holding a dove in his hands and looking up at God in stark contrast to the evil behavior going on around him. Again, the emphasis is on continuing to act in the right way, regardless of what others are doing.

In Barbara Reid's rhyming version of the Noah story for preschool children, *Two by Two* (1992), charmingly illustrated with plasticine figures, the focus of both text and illustrations is on the variety of animals. Unusual animals like sloths are included, sure to delight children obsessed with classifying types and classes. This is an enjoyable but bland version of Noah's Ark, devoid of almost any hint that the reason for this Ark-building and filling activity is that something has gone wrong on earth. Only in the ending is anything problematic alluded to, and then only because the problems have apparently all been resolved. *"God gave the rainbow as a sign / That after rain the sun will shine. / Seasons and days shall never cease, / And then God told them, 'Grow in peace.'"*

Noah's Ark as retold and illustrated by Lucy Cousins (1993) is another popular version that appeals particularly to young children. Its appeal can be attested to by the many ancillary products that have been developed from this book, including a board-book version and related stuffed toys based on Cousins's bright, childlike illustrations. The highly simplified text is printed in a large, easy-to-read type. The focus of this version is on building the Ark and on the animals themselves, but interestingly Cousins does not skip the beginning of the story. Intended, as noted, for young children, Cousins does tackle the question of God's displeasure. She deals with the issue of Noah's character and the people's wickedness:

> Noah was a good man, who trusted in God. There were also many wicked people in the world. God wanted to punish the wicked people, so he said to Noah, "I shall make a flood of water and wash all the wicked people away. Build an ark for your family and all the animals."

Although the language is clear and straightforward, these concepts are anything but. This is a God who punishes, severely and without forgiveness. The message of the text is in striking contrast to the bright, jolly illustrations. Despite the fear of human wickedness that Cousins introduces at the beginning of her book, though, she ends on a cheerful, reassuring note. "Then Noah and all the animals came safely out of the ark . . . and life began again on the earth."

Not all versions of the Noah story for children shy away from God's wrath. In Miriam Chaikin's retelling of the Noah story, "Noah and the Flood," from her 1993 collection *Children's Bible Stories from Genesis to Daniel,* Chaikin provides a blunt answer for the question of what the people did to anger God. She writes, "Soon the world was full of people. But the people were not good. They were violent and selfish. They stole and told lies." In naming these specific negative attributes, Chaikin has chosen behaviors for which children themselves are often reprimanded or punished. These aren't the destructive behaviors of collective adult society, like pollution or warfare, but are exactly the kinds of things that adults try to teach children not to do. Just as children are taught to make good choices about their behavior, the people's actions are examples of making individual, bad behavioral choices. God, like a parent, is "saddened and disappointed," by their poor choices. But unlike a typical parent, God therefore chooses to drown the people and put an end to their negative behavior.

One particularly terrifying example of God's fury is seen in *Noah's Ark,* written by Heinz Janisch and illustrated by Lisbeth Zwerger (1997). Though this is a picture book, its bleak view of the Noah story and the destruction of the world make it appropriate for older children. Janisch sticks closely to the biblical text, not censoring God's anger and destructive side. In this book, God is angry because the people "thought only of war and destruction." This is a God who destroys the earth and every creature in it other than those in the Ark. No rationale is provided for which creatures are to be saved and which destroyed. The illustrations echo the idea of destruction and ruin. Earth appears as a wasteland, dusty and ruined. A factory belches smoke and the land is filled with weaponry and dry bones.

There is a timeless quality to these illustrations, set in a not-too-distant past in which almost-modern looking buildings exist, and in which people uselessly carry umbrellas against the rain. Some of the illustrations were created to resemble nineteenth century scientific illustrations of animals, complete with numbers and labels. It is a fantastical past though, in which animals from medieval bestiaries like unicorns and centaurs coexist with the more usual animals, providing a contrast to the neat, rational system implied by the scientific look. It is as if to say that in spite of the many advances in science, the human race still cannot take care of itself or the world properly. This is both a powerful political and ecological statement. Challenges to the cold, rational world of science are everywhere, represented by the fantastical creatures, who do not make it onto the Ark, and by the ill-fated behavior of the people themselves. Many of the illustrations are spooky and disturbing. People are shown precariously positioned on their roofs as the water begins to fill the earth, trying futilely to save themselves. Several pages later, fish are shown swimming through eerily uninhabited buildings that are now clearly under water, with the Ark positioned safely above.

By contrast, in the Ark there is only harmony. Although crowded, the animals do not fight. The bleak, stark beginning is in contrast to the image portrayed by Janisch at the end, in which "A drying wind blew across the land. The flood was gone, and it had washed the earth clean." In the last sentence of the book, "Noah went away from the ark, in hope and trust, and his offspring peopled the earth." The earth is now green and healthy once again, and in the final illustration, Zwerger portrays the animals playfully leaping and prancing.

This is a darker version of Noah's Ark than in most other children's books, yet it too ends on a positive note. God may have been angry and destructive, but the earth is better for it, having been cleansed and healed, much as a loving parent may use punishment to change unwanted behavior. God's behavior and actions are not the issue; rather it is the people's behavior, the choices they make, that causes God to react in such a way.

Another example of a version of this story that deals with God's anger is Jerry Pinkney's magnificently illustrated *Noah's Ark*, a 2003 Caldecott Honor Book. The rich, evocative pen-and-watercolor illustrations are accompanied by a dramatic, powerful, and surprisingly direct retelling. The text begins with the majestic voice of an omniscient storyteller:

> God was not pleased with the people of the earth.
> They did not care for one another.
> They did not care for the land that God had made.
> And they did not care for God.
> God's heart was filled with pain
> to see the wickedness of humankind.
> God decided to sweep away
> all living things on the earth.

Pinkney does not mince words. Something has gone quite wrong on earth and action needs to be taken. The accompanying illustration contrasts the beauty of nature with a landscape that has been marred by violence and the neglect of those entrusted to care for it. In the background a desolate city is consumed by flames but in the foreground, a sign of hope remains in the brilliant blooming of lush watercolor flowers. In the face of all this, Noah is depicted surrounded by his family as they work together in his green fields in peaceful cooperation. Noah is an exception in his time because it is he *"who did what was right / in the sight of the Lord / and the Lord loved Noah."* Pinkney depicts Noah as a strong, sturdy farmer whose eyes reflect contentment and certainty. He obediently responds to the Lord's command and enlists the cooperation of his family. This is made unquestionably clear as Pinkney writes about Noah's wife and her bread baking, his three sons' efforts gathering food, and the efforts of his sons' wives to provide water for the family and all the creatures on the Ark. Noah is shown as smiling and pleased with everyone's efforts. As they work cooperatively with each other, neighbors come to jeer and call them fools. Yet, again Pinkney writes, "But Noah trusted in the Lord." Certain that he is obeying the command of God, Noah never falters, never questions. This is both satisfying and reassuring for young readers who are being taught at school and at home about the importance of these timeless virtues. Pinkney's own accompanying illustrations are dramatic and exciting, driving home the majestic scope of Noah's deed, reinforcing the inspirational language for children too young to read the Bible on their own. The scene on the Ark of Noah, his family, and the animals sharing their space and their food is a joyful visual reminder of the importance of cooperation, sharing, and obedience.

The Importance of Good Character

> Noah was a righteous man; he was blameless in his age; Noah walked with God.

> (Genesis 6:9)

That Noah was chosen for this mission and spared the fate of the rest of the human race begs the question of who Noah was. Or even more, *what* Noah was. The biblical text reports that he was righteous and walked with God. Yet that is hardly an unambiguous statement. What does it mean to be righteous? Biblical commentators, unsure what to make of the statement that "he was blameless in his age," ask if that means that his righteousness was only relative to those around him at that time, but that he would not have fared well compared with some of the righteous who were to come later.[5] What was it about this man, what did he do, to merit being saved at a time when the entire human race was to be destroyed? The Hebrew text raises even more questions, stating that Noah was an *ish tzadik tamim*—not only righteous, *tzadik*, but also *tamim*. The word *tamim* has various translations, including both "innocent" and "pure." The Hebrew therefore provides another layer of meaning here, that Noah is somehow unsophisticated or naive. Though it is clear that he is an adult, in that he has a wife and grown children already, the implication is that he exists in a kind of state of childlike innocence in contrast to all the evil around him. In her collection, *Stories from the Bible* (2000), Lisbeth Zwerger presents a Noah who is the pinnacle of goodness. Her version, based on extracts from the King James Bible, reads, "Noah was a just man *and* perfect in his generations, *and* Noah walked with God" [sic]. There is no equivocation here as to Noah's character. Yet the wording of the Hebrew allows for Noah's qualifications to be questioned. Is he saved by God because he is truly a man who has made good choices about how to live, or is he simply someone who is too innocent to have made bad choices?

Noah is presented as a paragon of goodness throughout the chapter entitled "Noah and the Flood" in Chaikin's *Children's Bible Stories from Genesis to Daniel*. In contrast to the badness of the other people around him, Noah's goodness stood out. After expressing God's disappointment with the people and God's plan to destroy them, Chaikin writes: "Then God noticed a certain family. A man called Noah, his wife, and their sons and daughters-in-law were good people, kind and gentle." Chaikin's implication here is that this family was chosen to survive because it was simply good, not just good relative to the badness of the other people. Yvonne Gilbert's highly detailed colored-pencil illustrations reinforce this point, depicting an elderly Noah and

---

[5] From Rashi's commentary citing Babylonian Talmud Tractate Sanhedrin 108a.

his wife as tender nurturers as they hold, feed, and care for the animals in the Ark.

The Ark by Arthur Geisert sticks closely to the biblical text, allowing the richly textured black and white illustrations to provide commentary. Geisert begins with text that sounds like a direct quote from Genesis, though which translation he uses is not identified. This quote speaks of both the wickedness of the people on earth and Noah finding favor in the eyes of God. But neither concept is explicitly addressed in either the text or the illustrations. Rather, Geisert's Noah is shown to be a man in solitary pursuit of his goals. In a desolate desert location, he works alone making the Ark, at first without help even from his sons. Only once the animals begin to arrive do the sons participate, as if driven by a new sense of urgency. The message for readers is unmistakable about the value of cooperation and completing a task when people work together with a single goal in mind. It is a forerunner of the core value of a democratic society, learned by the children of democracies first in preschool, as part of the "socialization" process, and again later in supervised team sports. The illustration is a visual paraphrasing of the cherished American ideal found in songs like "The Liberty Song" (1768) by John Dickinson that generations of American schoolchildren were made to memorize, that featured lyrics like, *"Then join hand in hand, brave Americans all! / By uniting we stand, by dividing we fall."*

Noah is the last one into the Ark, an example of his decency and leadership. In fact, his whole family is shown to be good people who care for animals and know how to cooperate. The text reads, "Watering and feeding the animals was a never-ending job. Everyone had to work to keep the ark clean." The family is depicted as hard-working and decent, the opposite of whatever lawlessness came before: "The family found time to rest only at dinner. They went to bed each night exhausted from the day's hard work." This description presents the idea of redemption through honest labor, consistent with the Protestant Work Ethic righteousness passed down from the values of the early American colonists. This is not a Noah who questions or contemplates, but rather one who takes his responsibilities seriously, gets to work, and finishes the job. Through these good qualities, he and his family merit having been saved from destruction, a-not-so-subtle lesson for young readers.

The theme of hard work as an element of good character, still a strong force in American life today, repeats in many versions of Noah's Ark. The jolly, red-cheeked, Santa-Claus-looking Noah and his family depicted by Cousins are almost always smiling, even while hard at work. One detail that Cousins adds into the text is that Noah works on the Ark for years. There is a sense of time passing as Noah prepares. Interestingly, in the illustrations she depicts Noah's three sons as children, with their wives entirely absent from the book, reinforcing the idea that the child hearing or reading the story is meant to identify personally with this family and their experience.

In *The Flood Tales,* written by Richard Monte with illustrations by Izhar Cohen (2000), Noah is depicted as a flawed human being, far from the righteous patriarch who is often encountered in children's books of Noah's Ark. He is said to have a temper and to be known to drink, something that is alluded to in the actual biblical text only after the flood is over. Monte writes:

> Why had he been chosen? Was he not as flawed as all the drowned carcasses that lay beneath the water? He was not righteous. No symbol of piety. His flaws would fill a library of parchment: drunkenness, anger, faithlessness, gluttony, fornication. . . .

These details are used in this collection of stories about Noah and the flood as a way to question what the biblical text means by calling Noah righteous. This collection allows for doubt, questioning whether or not Noah really encountered God, and if so, who or what is God, asking:

> Had Noah been duped like a gullible fool? . . . Or was he touched by flattery? Did he glow deep inside when he thought of himself as the last righteous man on earth? What human being is so righteous?

This is Noah's Ark for skeptics.

These stories have an edge of cynicism, doubt, and irreverence. Noah is old and decrepit, he has a bad back, and can't even remember the measurements that God told him. Noah's world is full of chaos. Monte's depiction of Noah at work is far from the peaceful renditions favored in most versions of this story. Here Noah is overwhelmed by his task. The animals are hard to manage. A snake eats a piglet. There isn't enough room. The long-sought behemoth is sick and might infect the other animals. The experience of trying to gather all the animals and accept that not all could be collected gives Noah a chance to ponder humanity's role vis-à-vis animals, and whether or not there really is a God who brought forth life, or whether the master hand in the universe is that of Nature.

The Role of God

> I will establish My covenant with you, and you shall enter the ark, with your sons, your wife, and your sons' wives.
>
> (Genesis 6:18)

God is a problematic concept for contemporary children's book authors in the secular marketplace. Current waves of interest in spirituality and God notwithstanding, it was long considered impolite, in our secular society, to talk about God in any but a religious setting. God was either an intensely personal matter, or alternatively, God was a primitive, superstitious concept. It seemed that God had been superseded by science and rationality. The books produced for the religious market, in which God is a given, are different from the trade books produced as children's literature for a broader, nonsectarian market. What to do about God's role in the story is therefore a significant challenge for the author and illustrator wanting to reach this market, as well as for the publisher.

Bowing to the Judeo–Christian prohibition against depicting the likeness of God, most children's picture books leave God in the text but do not provide a visual portrayal. One exception is Jane Ray's version of Noah's Ark, which shows a physical representation of God. God appears in several illustrations at the top of the page in the sky, an oversized human face encircled by a wreath of flames, hair, or rays of light.

In some of the contemporary retellings of Noah's Ark, though, God is glossed over or absent altogether. In *A Stowaway on Noah's Ark,* written and illustrated by Charles Santore (2000), the focus of the story has nothing to do with a relationship between Noah and God, or the human race and God. Rather, it is a story of Noah's Ark as told from the point of view of a mouse named Achbar, not incidentally the word for mouse in Hebrew. Noah, on the other hand, is never named. Rather, he is described as a "kindly old man" who speaks to the sky, and is depicted in classic Western–patriarchal style, with a white flowing mane and beard, and wrapped in white robelike clothing. Instead of God, the sky itself speaks to Noah one day, and tells him to build the Ark because "the people have become wicked and evil."

Santore presents a sweet, richly illustrated version of Noah's Ark that works hard not to scare its readers. It tells a positive story of a good, old man, an almost godlike figure himself despite the fact that God is never mentioned, who takes care of all the animals under his protection and delivers them safely into a better future. The warm cast of the watercolor illustrations provides a comforting sense of hope for a sunny future. Santore takes liberty with the biblical text beyond the issue of writing God out of the story and creating the character of Achbar. Instead of sending first a raven and then a dove (Genesis 8: 7–8), Santore's old man sends the same dove twice. Whereas in the biblical version of the story, God is in firm control of the events and their sequence and Noah simply does as he is told, here the "old man" is in charge. As the animals begin to depart, he announces to his family members, "Go forth and prosper and lead righteous lives." The story continues: " 'We were blessed from the very beginning,' the old man said, looking up to the sky. At the moment, the sun lit the earth and a glorious rainbow appeared."

It is as if God and Noah have merged into one in Santore's humanistic retelling. Santore has also added elements not found in the Bible to enhance his version. The rainbow is not God's promise to people never to destroy the earth again. Rather, nature, some supernatural force, or his own inherent righteousness, has conferred this gift upon the old man, who speaks like a prophet. This is a retelling that suggests to children that they can have control over their lives, that outcomes in life are ultimately based on behavior.

The opposite approach to God is seen in John W. Stewig's alphabet picture book, *The Animals* (2005). This version relies completely on divine intervention. Noah does not appear in this picture book at all; rather God speaks directly to each of the pairs of animals pictured on each page. The animals are able to communicate with God directly just as young children frequently believe they are able to do. In keeping with the cognitive development of young children, God is not portrayed here as an omniscient being but, rather, a literal, unambiguous presence in their lives. Just as children believe they can talk to their teddy bears, they believe animals can speak to them and to each other. It is not unusual to overhear four-, five-, and six-year-olds speaking out loud to their toys and conversing with God as they interact with the environment and try to make sense of the world.

In his tall-tale style retelling, *Washday on Noah's Ark* (1983), author–illustrator Glen Rounds chooses a relatively contemporary setting. Noah is depicted in overalls, listening to weather reports over a gramophone. It is because of reports of severe rain and flooding that he decides to build his Ark. As in *A Stowaway on Noah's Ark*, there is no mention of God in this book. Nor is there any issue of ethical behavior or righteousness, other than the fact that Rounds's Noah seems to be kind to animals and enjoys spending time with his grandchildren, helping to keep them amused during their time on the Ark by telling them stories and building them a kite. This is a version of the Noah story completely removed from its biblical framing, but is in keeping with the can-do tradition of Rounds's folktales set in the American

West, such as *Ol' Paul the Mighty Logger* and *Casey Jones, the Story of a Brave Engineer*.

In most retellings of the Noah story, God is either clearly present or conspicuously absent. Monte's Noah, however, spends some time in an internal struggle about the very idea of God. He is torn between a belief in God and religion and a belief in the rational, scientific theories put forth by his son Ham. He has time on the Ark to ask the big questions:

> Was there such a thing as divine punishment? Had this been brought on by the wickedness of the human race? Or was it some colossal natural disaster brought on by climatic changes, and the melting of ice at the edges of the world? Noah was confused. How could he believe in God—the work of a divine hand—when these rational thoughts crowded in upon his mind. . . .

Toward the end, the book does seem to present a real anti–God bias, or at least the stereotypical Old Testament God. A scientific explanation is given for the rainbow, and Mrs. Noah cries out against the kind of God who requires animal sacrifices, saying:

> How can you bow down before a brute like that? The devil take your lord of the skies. Give me a God who is the sap oozing through a blade of grass, the blood pumping in our veins, the water babbling through a brook. . . .

In contrast, Pinkney is not afraid to deal with issues of God and faith in his *Noah's Ark*. Pinkney's Noah is a man who "did what was right in the sight of the Lord." Because of this, God speaks to Noah and entrusts him with the task of creating an Ark and filling it with two of every kind of animal, promising safety to his family and the animals. Although other people jeer and doubt, Noah has faith in God and continues in his task. While the water fills the earth, covering houses and cities, Noah, his family, and the animals are safe inside the Ark. As they disembark, Noah and his family "turned their faces up to the sun and sang praise to God." Throughout their whole ordeal, they have not lost their faith. In the final double-page illustration, Pinkney shows Noah resolutely continuing to care for the earth that God has preserved. He and his wife once again plow the land and plant the seeds for a new harvest even as they witness the rainbow sent as a sign of Noah's faithfulness and God's promise to Noah and his family.

This interpretation of Noah's Ark is a story about the gift of faith, and about second chances. Although humankind has lost its connection to God and to each other, God has not given up on them. Pinkney's is a compassionate God, who destroys the world not in anger, but in pain, and who, as an act of faith or promise of redemption, sends a rainbow as a pledge to let people try all over again. The rear endpaper is used as a vivid illustration of God's assurance to the faithful and the obedient through Pinkney's use of a stylized, hand-lettered text of God's promise and a swirling earth awash with rainbows.

Chaikin offers an interesting twist in her version of the Noah story, "Noah and the Flood." In the end of the story, it is not just people who may have learned something from the experience, but God as well. She writes:

> God watched them, these people who would continue the world. Humans are not perfect, God thought. There is an evil corner in their hearts. Perhaps they will learn goodness one day. In the meantime, I made them, and must accept them as they are.

God has come to the realization that to be human is to be imperfect, and God must learn to live with that. Just as people aren't perfect and must continually learn and grow, Chaikin presents a God who is also not perfect, and who continues to evolve. There are important messages of reassurance for children in Chaikin's version of the story. Chaikin stresses that it is human to slip up and make mistakes, an essential idea for children to learn and absorb. They are not expected to be perfect, they are just expected to try their best. Even God must learn to accept that perfection is unattainable, rather than hope for it and thus be continually disappointed. If God can come to learn this, then surely the adults in their lives can understand their occasional lapses into bad behavior and forgive them. Moreover, they do not need to be in fear that their bad behavior might cause, or contribute to God destroying the world yet again, as God has learned to exercise greater self-control.

The Role of Animals

You shall take two of each into the ark with you. . . .

(Genesis 6:19)

In literature for children, animals are often the main characters. Sometimes they are realistic animals, but it is also common to see animals playing human roles. As noted, Piaget maintains that young children learn primarily through direct, hands-on experience between ages two to six. They do not readily distinguish between fantasy, make-believe, and reality; they talk to their stuffed animals, the moon, and imaginary friends. Monsters, giants, and ogres are real threats, and characters in their picture books are as familiar as parents and siblings. They like stories about children just like themselves, but stories in which animals behave like real children, wear clothes, and behave in easily recognizable ways are perennial favorite choices.

The first two Caldecott books that deal with the Noah story focus primarily on the theme of animals. *Animals of the Bible,* the first winner of the Caldecott Medal in 1938, uses text from the King James Bible selected by Helen Dean Fish, accompanied by Dorothy P. Lathrop's black and white illustrations. The two chapters that deal with Noah are "The Story of Animals Saved in the Ark," and "The Dove who Served Noah." The animals are used in these chapters and throughout this collection as a way to introduce and connect children to biblical text. In *One Wide River to Cross,* adapted by Barabara Emberley, the text is the traditional African American spiritual that names individual animals as it counts from one to ten. Ed Emberley's black inked woodcuts against the bright, celebratory colored background provide a strong visual tie to the words of the text, emphasizing both the variety of animals and the triumph of making it through a long and difficult journey.

Like many of the other versions of this story created for children, a great deal of attention in Geisert's *The Ark* is focused on the animals. They are shown arriving in an orderly fashion, and cooperating nicely just as young children are supposed to do. They line up in even pairs and wait their turn boarding the Ark. There is a great amount of wonderful detail shown in Geisert's cross-sections of the Ark. No doubt children enjoy closely examining these illustrations. However, there is also something distinctively instructional about Geisert's retelling, in which the animals present role models for child readers: "The animals learned to live together in almost perfect harmony." If people could do the same, Geisert seems to say, God will not have need again to flood and destroy the world.

Using Achbar the mouse as his main character, Santore is able to achieve two goals. He can both describe the story from the viewpoint of a small and overlooked narrator, one that is easy for a child to relate to, and at the same time he can sensitively address one of the fears of a child hearing the story of Noah's Ark: the fear of being left behind. For whereas two mice are chosen to board the Ark, Achbar himself is slated to be left behind. Like a typical child, Achbar's curiousity gets the better of his distress. Being a mouse, he is not noticed as he follows the line of animals on their way to the Ark. From his vantage point, he describes with wonder and amazement both the sight of the Ark itself, and the incredible variety of animals in their pairings.

Like a child, Achbar is frightened by the idea of the flood. As the rains continue to rise, Achbar finds different hiding places. He hides in the mane of a lion, the ear of a rhino, and in the wool of a sheep. Each affords him some amount of comfort or safety, but none is just right. Achbar is there when the rains cease to fall, and sees the old man sending the dove to search for dry land. And Achbar is there, very happy, when it is time to leave the Ark and go back onto dry land, running off to "join the others of his kind in the brand-new world." Having survived, Achbar provides comfort and reassurance for young readers.

Some versions of Noah's Ark use the biblical story as a backdrop to introducing children to different animals. In these versions, the animals are the primary focus, and the story itself is secondary. *On Noah's Ark,* written and illustrated by Jan Brett (2003), is an example of a Noah story concerned mainly with animals. Brett's busy, highly detailed and textured watercolor and gouache style is captivating to children and works well in bringing the animals to life. There is much to look at and wonder about on these pages. One interesting aspect of her text is the choice to make the main character not Noah, but a child. This child is referred to as Noah's granddaughter in the description of the book, though both Brett's illustrations and text keep the gender of the child ambiguous. However, Brett's choice of this child narrator enables young readers to imagine themselves in the central role in this story, helping to fill up the Ark with food, caring for the animals, and getting to know all the different species while the Ark "rocks back and forth like a giant cradle." This is a version of Noah's Ark told from a young child's perspective, in which what is interesting is the animals, not the bigger questions of why the journey was necessary in the first place.

Noah as the Father of Many Nations

> *These three were the sons of Noah, and from these the whole world branched out.*

(Genesis 9:19)

The majority of illustrators portray Noah in traditional, patriarchal fashion, as an old, white-skinned man with a flowing beard. However, some contemporary artists have chosen to break this mold and reenvision Noah. Since Noah and his family were the only humans to survive the flood, it is not a stretch to view Noah as the progenitor of the entire human race. This idea is in fact embedded in the biblical text itself, which imagines Noah as the Father of many nations. Some authors and illustrators have used this idea to question the assumption that Noah and his family has to be white, giving new layers of meaning to a familiar story.

In Jane Ray's aforementioned *Noah's Ark*, Noah and his family are portrayed as being racially mixed. They have a wide spectrum of skin colors and hair types, and Noah himself is quite dark-skinned. Although using a traditional biblical text, the author–illustrator provides a definite viewpoint on the story through illustrations alone. Not only are all types of animals represented in the Ark, but the continuum of the human race is as well. Just as representatives of all the animal types were saved to repopulate the animal world after the flood, so was the full range of human types in order to repopulate the human world. Implicit in this depiction is the idea that righteousness is not tied to one particular race, and that God does not favor one race over another.

Noah, written by Patricia Lee Gauch and illustrated by Jonathan Green (1994), also uses a black-skinned Noah. In the endnotes, the illustrator writes that his art for this book is inspired by his experiences growing up as part of the Gullah community of Hesbah Baptist Church of Gardens Corners, South Carolina, where Bible stories were part of the oral tradition of the community. Gauch's text begins: *"Here is Noah, with grace in his eyes, / Here are his sons / right by his side. / But the people on earth / are not good at all."*

Noah and his family are depicted as African, wearing cloth wraps and carrying sticks, and living in a rural environment close to animals. The women walk with baskets on their heads, and both men and women have their heads covered from the sun. Although Noah himself is black-skinned, the members of his family range from black to brown to yellow. The ocher-skinned daughter-in-law has blue eyes, indicating that the full range of races are included in Noah's family.

Like so many of the versions of Noah's Ark for children, the emphasis of this version of the story is on the animals and on the flood itself. The text takes great delight in both listing all the kinds of animals that enter the Ark, and in the details of the flood. In the end, Noah is happy to be able to leave the Ark and go back onto land, where he and his family get to work planting fields and caring for the earth.

Illustrated by Pam Paparone, *Who Built the Ark?* (1994), like *One Wide River to Cross,* is a Noah-related book that has as its text the African American spiritual of the same name. The song is entirely about the building of the Ark and the animals, with no reference to Noah's character or God's reason for destroying the earth. Paparone notes in the front matter of the book that, "With its playful references to the animals and its counting game, this version seems to have been designed for the children in the rural churches where it probably originated." The book begins with an illustration showing the inside of an African American church, full of congregants in pews, a choir and piano player, and a preacher at the front. As the story progresses, the preacher becomes Brother Noah, first building the Ark and then welcoming the animals aboard. Each time the chorus is repeated, the members of the choir and a dancing child appear next to the main illustration.

The tone of this book is joyful and celebratory, both of life on earth and its possibilities in general, and of the African American Church–going community. The song and the book end with the rain just starting. There is no sense of what will come next for Noah and the animals. But the last two illustrations speak of a happy and hopeful ending. The penultimate illustration takes place back in the church. The congregants are up on their feet, clapping their hands and singing along, enjoying their community and their time together. The very last illustration takes place outside the church, as friends and family interact as they say their good-byes and start for home, ready to begin another week. Although the song ends before the rain stops and harmony is restored on earth, it is clear from the illustrations that life is continuing and that there are once again good people in the world. Paparone uses this song as a metaphor for survival of a community under God's protection, even under the harshest of conditions. Like the world in which Noah lived, which was filled with bad people and violence, this community too has suffered and survived, managing to make spiritual communities that call for the best that is in each one of them and in every person.

Environmental Themes

> So long as the earth endures,
> Seedtime and harvest,
> Cold and heat,
> Summer and winter,
> Day and night
> Shall not cease.

(Genesis 8:22)

Contemporary authors have found the story of Noah's Ark to be a useful framework for modern themes. In *The Flood Tales*, the traditional story of Noah's Ark is used by Richard Monte as a vehicle for exploring contemporary concerns such as the environment, faith, gender issues, and the treatment of animals. Each chapter in *The Flood Tales* takes on another modern concept and clothes it in the garb of the familiar biblical tale. The flood provides Noah the opportunity to learn what it truly is to be human. He comes to understand what differentiates human beings from the other animals. As he, his family, and the animals begin to re-create civilization as the sole survivors of the flood, he learns that with freedom comes responsibility. The relationship between animals and humans is explored, with concern voiced about the potential abuse and exploitation of animals and fears of their future extinction. One chapter deals with the beginning of art, exploring the human capacity for self-expression. The importance of human language, and the potential for its misuse is discussed, as is the human propensity for racism and preoccupation with skin color.

The chapter entitled "The Vegetarian Supper" in *The Flood Tales* is a modern parable about the environment disguised as a biblical story. Realizing that they have not been careful about disposing of their waste and have managed to pollute the water around the Ark, Noah wonders:

Is this . . . what happens near cities? The accumulated waste of the population is distributed unevenly in the surrounding areas, intoxicating the countryside; seeping into the rivers and the land, until fish begin to die in the stale waters, plants cannot grow in the famished soils. And he began to wonder whether the swollen populations of the cities had played a part in the coming of the flood waters. Perhaps the careless disposal of waste products had altered the natural balance of the land.

Another contemporary interpretation with a similar theme is offered by Sting, former member of the rock band the Police. *Rock Steady* (2001) is the Noah's Ark story in verse based on Sting's 1987 music and lyrics. Hugh Whyte's illustrations, in bright-crayon colors, feature angular-geometric shapes that complement the contemporary rock verse. Here, a couple notice a newspaper ad seeking volunteers "To commune with Mother Nature / On a big wooden ship." They take camel taxis to see if there is vacant space for them. Once aboard the Ark, they are kept busy washing and feeding the animals. As it continues to rain for forty days and nights and the Ark is pitched about in rough seas, the nervous couple is reassured by Noah that the Ark is "Rock Steady":

> *He's God's best friend,*
> *He's got a seat on the board,*
> *And life may be tough,*
> *But we're sailing with the Lord.*
> *Rock Steady, Rock Steady.*

Is the Ark as steady as a rock? Is Planet Earth a firm rock on which to anchor civilization? Does belief in God and living by his precepts keep us on course/rock steady? Or, simply, can we learn about the environment from rock music? *Rock Steady* offers an unequivocal *Yes!* as the answer to these questions. Noah is depicted as a fatherly figure determined to obey God's command as he has heard it on the radio. The message is that political divisions are not relevant. Preserving the environment is what is important. The earth is big enough to support all living creatures as long as we take care of it; it is "rock steady." Proceeds from the sale of the book are donated to Sting's nonprofit Rainforest Foundation, thus carrying the theme of the work to its ultimate conclusion.

God is not present nor is any reason given for the flood that destroys all humanity and desolates the earth in Ann Jonas's *Aardvarks, Disembark!* (1990). The focus in this version is on the animals themselves. On the forty-first morning, the rain ends, the Ark rests atop a snow-capped Mount Ararat, and a rainbow appears without any explanation of who causes it to appear. Noah sends only one dove which returns with the symbolic olive leaf signifying it is time to leave the Ark. Noah calls: "Aardvarks, disembark! Adders, disembark! Albatrosses, disembark!" and so it goes through the letter Z. The book, which features double-page spreads, is held vertically. One spread shows the Ark resting on Mount Ararat on the top of the page, while an elderly Noah rests on a cane urging the animals to leave. At the bottom of the illustration, in the right-hand corner, two zebras are shown going on their way. Noah calls to them all to disembark as he descends the mountain. The spare text relates Noah's dismay that he doesn't know the names of many animals still left in the Ark. Over the next fourteen double-page spreads, dozens of pairs of animals are named in reverse alphabetic order, ending with Noah's admonition to "Take good care of yourselves. Take good care, everyone" to the assemblage at the foot of the mountain. Pairs of animals are shown dispersing in all four directions as Noah with his wife and their sons with their wives go off to settle and populate the earth. The book concludes with the words, undoubtedly reassuring to young children, that "life began again."

The last page highlights the central theme of this retelling, that life endures but, over time, many species have become extinct and others are now endangered and facing extinction. Just as Noah contributed to the conservation of numerous species, we should do no less today. Jonas invites children to be part of the solution by including them in her final words that "we" need to work to protect endangered species. One hundred thirty-two animal species are then named in alphabetic order, with marks indicating which are endangered and which are already extinct.

The Unnamed Wife and Gender Roles

*Noah, with his sons, his wife, and his sons' wives, went into
the ark because of the waters of the Flood.*

(Genesis 7:7)

Like many biblical women, Noah's wife is not named. In the original biblical story, Noah's wife has no role at all, other than being included in the list of people who can enter the Ark and be saved, along with Noah's named sons and unnamed daughters-in-law. She is mentioned entering the Ark, and she is mentioned coming out of the Ark, but that is all.

Feminist biblical scholarship and feminist theory has taught that the lack of women's names, roles, and duties in biblical text does not mean that women were not there or were not important, but that centuries of male-controlled writing, editing, and scholarship have written women out of the text. For many contemporary retellers of the Noah story, this presents a problem, as today's children know that men are not the only movers and shakers in the world, and that both men and women can run households, and businesses—even Arks. Several contemporary retellings have therefore created roles and even names for Noah's wife.

Noah's wife is named "Mrs. Noah" in Monte's *The Flood Tales,* in which she is depicted essentially as a shrew. She does not believe in her husband, she constantly criticizes him, scolds, nags, and acts as the foil for Noah's naiveté. Nor is their relationship described in positive terms, so much so that "Noah thought he saw his wife mirrored in the orang-utan [sic] cage and began disputing the theory of spontaneous creation once more." As the story continues though, she is shown to have another side. She cares and worries about the animals, and is even affected enough by her relationship with the animals aboard the Ark to become a vegetarian. She has a practical, efficient sensibility regarding the work to be done on the Ark, in contrast to Noah's more bumbling nature.

Despite the negative way in which Noah's wife is first introduced in *The Flood Tales,* the issue of food preparation on the Ark is used by Monte as an opportunity to discuss gender roles. The women are shown in the kitchen cooking the first vegetarian meal, where:

> A conversation began between the kitchen staff as to why there was only a single male in the room, and the women lavished praise on young Japheth for making no distinction between men's and women's work and finding himself just as much at home among the pots and pans as among the hammers and nails. They determined to make Noah and his two elder sons wash up after the meal.

There is also a running commentary on the use of the term "Ms." versus "Mrs." Shem's wife takes on the feminist term, becoming Ms. Shem, which she sees as a large step up from being Mrs. Shem. In her words, " 'The Mr is the male part. When we add the s to it, we are admitting to being the servant of that man.' She believed that, by removing the r, a woman could become master of herself—the M for madam." However, since Monte is already taking such liberties with the text, if he had really wanted to make a feminist point he might have given the women their own names entirely, instead of just giving them a feminized version of their husbands'.

In Arthur Geisert's *The Ark,* the women remain nameless. Yet they are assigned an important role in both the text and the illustrations, caring for the animals before entering the Ark, and then together with the men, tending to their needs while aboard. In Jane Ray's *Noah's Ark,* the women are depicted as working alongside the men first in their fields, and then creating the Ark itself.

Glen Rounds calls Noah's wife Mrs. Noah in *Washday on Noah's Ark* (1985). Despite the fact that she is assigned a name and a central role in this modernized version of the story, she is still relegated to a traditional female realm, that of taking care of the laundry. At the end of the forty days and nights on the Ark, Mrs. Noah is thrilled to see the sun, since she hasn't been able to do the wash for all that time. She and her daughters-in-law spend the day doing the family laundry, after which she goes to make everyone peanut butter sandwiches and tea. The book concludes:

> It had been a long and busy day for Mrs. Noah. But that night at supper, when she saw how nice her family looked after they'd all taken baths and put on clean clothes for the first time in forty days and forty nights, she figures that it had been well worthwhile.

Despite the updated framing of the story, it works to reinforce the same stereotypical gender roles portrayed in the Bible itself.

There is one retelling of the Noah story that allows Noah's wife to come into her own, providing a stark contrast to the other stories available for children. In *A Prayer for the Earth: The Story of Naamah, Noah's Wife,* written by Sandy Eisenberg Sasso and illustrated by Bethanne Andersen (1996), the wife has a name, a personality, and a story of her own. Sasso calls Noah's wife *Naamah,* a name found in an ancient rabbinic interpretation of Genesis. Based on the explanation for her name provided by the anonymous rabbinic writers that connect the name Naamah with the adjective *neimim,* meaning "pleasing," Sasso has created a parallel story to that of Noah. In this version, both Noah and Naamah are good and both "walked in God's ways." In this tale, when God instructs Noah to build the Ark and collect the animals, God also gives Naamah instructions. She is to:

> Walk across the land and gather the seeds of all the flowers and all the trees. Take two of every kind of living plant and bring each one onto the ark. They shall not be for food, but they shall be your garden, to tend and to keep. Work quickly. The rains begin tomorrow.

Sasso's tale allows Noah and his wife Naamah to be partners in all that is about to unfold. Both Noah and Naamah care for the animals aboard the Ark. They are partners too in helping to save the best of the world, both the animals and the plant-life, and to make sure that not everything in God's creation is destroyed in the flood. Just as

Noah repopulates the animal world after the flood, Naamah replants the earth. Naamah is portrayed as caring, capable, strong, and smart. In this story, it is Naamah who comforts a reluctant raven and gives him an olive seed to let fall to earth wherever he sees a spot of dry land. And again, later, it is Naamah who gently tells the dove to look for the olive tree and bring back a branch. She is a woman who can think ahead and plan: "In a few days, the dove returned. Just as Naamah had hoped, the dove carried an olive branch in her beak. 'Dry land!' shouted Noah. 'God has planted an olive tree for us!' Naamah just smiled."

The enduring popularity of Noah and the Ark clearly corresponds with the child-rearing concerns of parents, caregivers, schools, and the wider community, and is an enduring adventure story for children. The emphasis in stories about Noah and the Ark have changed over the years in keeping with the public's perception of children, their development, and world events. An example of the adaptability of this story can be seen in the recent retellings in which Noah responds with sensitivity to environmental concerns, a trait recognized as desirable by contemporary parents and communities. There is no single "correct" or universal interpretation of the biblical Noah story. The many examples of children's books based on the tale of Noah's Ark are multilayered stories about people's relationship to God and to the world around them. The concept of obedience is a central element to the story of Noah as it is central to the child-rearing concerns of many parents. In these picture book retellings of this story, Noah follows God's directives much as an obedient child would do. The primary question, whether about Noah or one's child, is how much obedience is essential to make someone a "good person."

The corollary to that question is whether there can be such a thing as too much obedience. Does being a good person require absolute, unquestioning obedience, as in Peter Spier's *Noah's Ark*? Or can one maintain a more contemporary, nuanced sense as seen in the Monte and Charles Santore editions in which Noah wrestles with the idea of obedience to God? If Noah is to be presented to children as a heroic figure or role model, these versions of the Noah story then beg the question of whether obedience is truly one quality of a hero, or whether obedience is simply a quality adults desire in children because it eases the task of child-rearing and education. In the model presented in Sting's *Rock Steady,* it could be argued that this trait helps develop leadership, valor, and bravery, thereby helping to develop the trait of cooperation so necessary at home, at school, and in community settings. All the Noah picture books show, however reluctantly, that Noah provided leadership by organizing the Ark and providing for its inhabitants for forty days. Yet they do not tell children whether Noah was a leader due to his obedient character *before* God chose him for his task, even as they all provide fine examples of the noble way Noah responded to the situation in which God placed him.

Of significant importance for young readers is the recognition of the responsible behavior shown by Noah's unquestioning readiness to obey God's command to build an Ark and prepare for the destruction of his known world. The development of Noah's ability to do what he thinks is right regardless of the opinions or behaviors of others in the community makes the story of Noah powerful beyond the fun of seeing all the animals in a picture book setting. This theme, recognizable in many folk and fairy tales from "The Frog Prince" to *Robin Hood,* is consistent with commonly accepted developmental theories. In particular, Schaie delineates the stages of cognitive development in adults. He writes that there is a stage of responsibility, usually occurring when people are in their thirties, when they are concerned with the practical problems of daily existence and their responsibility for family members and those very close to them. This is followed by what Schaie calls an "executive" stage when people look to the larger society and feel a responsibility for the extended group.

The story of Noah also parallels Erikson's stages of personality development, from early childhood through to the full maturity exemplified by Noah as he is commonly depicted with a flowing white beard. When God appears before Noah and commands him to build an Ark in preparation for the destruction of this world, Noah trusts

God enough because his life experiences up to this moment have inspired an attitude of "basic trust" from infancy onward. Noah has lived, the text tells us, an exemplary life that has allowed him to develop self-confidence and trust; thus, he is able to accept God's command despite its prediction of dire consequences. The story of Noah thus represents Erikson's outline of the stages of personality development in consecutive order. According to Erikson, children have to pass through this order of stages to reach self-fulfillment in their own lives and become adults who care about others as well as their world. The first instance readers see of Noah's basic trust is when he is approached by God and told to build an Ark in preparation for the earth's destruction. The second event children see is Noah's acceptance of his own role in God's plan and his decision to do as he is commanded; Erikson calls this stage "autonomy." It is followed by the development of "initiative," represented by Noah's immediately setting to work, planning what is needed to build such a gigantic vessel. The fourth stage, "industry," is clearly apparent to children as they observe Noah's labors in building the Ark and enlisting the aid of his family in a cooperative venture. Finally, there is the revelation of Noah's "identity" as the patriarch of his family and savior/preserver of all living species. This pattern of development is seen in many fairy tales; Bettelheim presents an interpretation of the Cinderella story that follows a similar trajectory of development and self-knowledge similar to the story of Noah.

The challenge of introducing the story of Noah and the Ark to children lies in the inherent question of how to interpret Noah's obedience and his character. It is ultimately a question of parental, educational, or community values. Is Noah to be introduced as a perfect hero who rises to a challenge and comes into his own? Just as Noah was able to do the right thing, so can any right-minded child when given the opportunity. A problematic situation therefore becomes a potential opportunity to save the day by acting righteously. Or is Noah to serve as a model of a hero despite his imperfections, a man who acts blindly without questioning or arguing? No person is perfect, and it is often hard to know how to act in complicated situations. This model allows for questions of how much responsibility one should take for one's actions, and whether or not it is right to challenge authority figures. Whichever version of the Noah story is used, it is a tale rich with possibility for further explorations of the ideas of obedience, goodness, and how to act under difficult circumstances.

3
JOSEPH

The image of the biblical Joseph that first comes to mind is that of the famous multicolored coat. This familiar story of Joseph focuses on him as an eternal youth, the beloved son among many brothers. Yet this incident is only one moment in the extended arc of the biblical Joseph narrative. Joseph's story begins long before his birth with the narratives involving his parents, Jacob and Rachel, providing much background to the birth of this longed-for son. The biblical text introduces Joseph at birth, and continues to chronicle important moments in his life up until his death. So central is his character that even after death he continues to figure into the ongoing story of his family, as seen when his bones are carried by Moses out of Egypt (Exodus 13:19).

Much of the Joseph narrative contains material about family relationships that still feel all too familiar to contemporary readers. Joseph is the second youngest of twelve brothers and one sister. He is, though, the first son of his mother, his father's favored wife. The two connected strands that run through the Joseph narratives are that of sibling relationships and parental favoritism. Joseph's brothers are both jealous and resentful of the attention that Joseph receives. The coat of many colors is just one of their perceived injustices. Yet, a close look at the biblical text reveals that Joseph himself may not have been the most sympathetic of victims. He comes across as perhaps arrogant, somewhat smug, or at the very least, naive. When he tells his brothers his dream, reporting that in his dream his brother's sheaves of wheat bow down to his sheaf (Genesis 37:5–8), can he really not know the effect this will have on them? And yet he goes on to tell of still another dream, in which the sun, the moon, and eleven stars bowed down to him (Genesis 37:9–11).

It is of course normal for siblings to resent each other and to claim that a parent favors one over the other. Yet this story goes a step farther. One day Joseph's brothers have had enough, and they hatch a plan to kill him. At the last minute one brother, Reuben, persuades the others just to throw him in a pit, planning to come back later and save him. Joseph is thrown into the pit, but before Reuben can save him another brother, Judah, talks them into selling Joseph to traders going down to Egypt. They dip the coat of many colors in the blood of a goat and bring it back to their father Jacob, telling him that Joseph has been killed (Genesis 37:18–25). Though fantasizing about doing away with bothersome brothers or sisters is a normal part of childhood, this biblical tale allows the brothers to live out their fantasy. Though for many children the fulfillment of this fantasy will be delightful, this wish come true isn't the part of the story that is generally stressed in retellings for children.

Sibling rivalry is a struggle for equal parental affection, a struggle to be loved as much as other siblings, and is a story as old as humankind. Bruno Bettelheim notes that sibling jealousy is a universal element of fairy tales as well as many Bible stories. As in the story of Cinderella and her evil stepsisters, this rivalry is often depicted through the relationship of step- or half-siblings. Similarly, Joseph and his older brothers are half siblings vying for the affection and respect of their father. The brothers deeply fear that, despite their hard work and filial devotion, Jacob cannot love and care for them as deeply as he does Joseph. Bettelheim writes that it is not Joseph's ability to interpret dreams and predict a future of domination vis-à-vis his brothers that leads to their effort to first kill him and then sell him into slavery, but rather it is their jealousy of Jacob's unremitting affection and marked preference for Joseph, as evidenced by his splendid coat. In *The Uses of Enchantment*, Bettelheim notes further that Bible stories are not sympathetic to instances of sibling rivalry, but rather serve as warnings of its "devastating consequences." For example, Cain kills Abel and then must bear his guilt for the rest of his life. Joseph's father, Jacob, tricks his brother Esau out of his birthright and then lives in fear of Esau's retribution for many years of his adult life. When Joseph confronts his brothers years later in Egypt, they confess how they have lived in agony and remorse ever since their heinous deed.

The Joseph story also offers the opposite kind of wish fulfillment though, as Joseph, the bullied victim, gets his revenge. For children who feel themselves to be picked on and tormented by their siblings or other kids, the Joseph story becomes one of ultimate victory of the underdog. Bettelheim writes:

> Telling a child who is devastated by sibling rivalry that he will grow up
> to do as well as his brothers and sisters offers little relief from his present

feelings of dejection. . . . If he could believe more in himself, he would not feel destroyed by his siblings no matter what they might do to him, since then he could trust that time would bring about a desired reversal of fortune. But since the child cannot, on his own, look forward with confidence to some future day when things will turn out all right for him, he can gain relief only through fantasies of glory—a domination over his siblings—which he hopes will become reality through some fortunate event. (p. 238–39)

After an initial rough start in Egypt that includes working as a house servant, being accused of attempted rape, and spending time in jail, Joseph winds up on top. He earns a reputation as an interpreter of dreams, and comes to be a trusted advisor to Pharaoh, playing the role of second-in-command over all of Egypt. Eventually, due to a severe famine, Joseph's brothers come down to Egypt looking for food. They do not recognize their brother, and Joseph is not forthcoming. The choice is Joseph's at that moment. He now has power over them. He can trick his brothers, he can condemn them to poverty and starvation, or he can forgive them. Ultimately Joseph does reveal himself to his brothers and shows that he can take the moral high ground. The brothers reconcile, and the whole family, at Pharaoh's invitation, comes down to live in Egypt (Exodus 45). It is the perfect conclusion to Joseph's childhood wish of supremacy over his brothers. Now that they are at his mercy, he can show his moral superiority by forgiving them and saving their lives. As Campbell writes, "The conclusion of the childhood cycle is the return or recognition of the hero, when, after the long period of obscurity, his true character is revealed."

Parental Favoritism

> *Now Israel [Jacob] loved Joseph best of all his sons,*
> *for he was the child of his old age; and he had made him*
> *an ornamented tunic.*

> (Genesis 37:3)

The family dynamics of this story are straight out of today's daytime dramas of dysfunctional families. The biblical text states clearly that his father "loved Joseph best of all his sons, for he was the child of his old age" (Genesis 37:3). How does a book intended for children deal with this injustice, this blatant example of poor parenting, the result of which is jealous, resentful, and angry siblings? Like "Cinderella" or "The Three Feathers," classic fairy tales of jealousy over parental favoritism taken to an extreme, Joseph's half-siblings want nothing to do with him and would much prefer if he would just go away.

In many retellings of this story for children, including *Joseph and His Brothers,* by Mary Auld and illustrated by Diana Mayo (1999), this frank statement of parental favoritism is not prettied up or ignored. It is simply presented as fact. In Marcia Williams's sunny version of the Joseph story, *Joseph and his Magnificent Coat of Many Colors* (1994), the language is blunt and to the point: Jacob had twelve fine sons, but the one he loved best was Joseph. Similarly, in *Joseph,* author and illustrator Brian Wildsmith writes, "Joseph was Jacob's favorite son. Jacob gave Joseph a coat of many colors to show him how much he loved him. Joseph's eleven brothers knew that he was the favorite, and they hated him for it." For children whose parents work hard to assure them that they do not love one child more than another, this clear statement of favoritism may come as a shock. Or then again, it may be received as confirmation of what they had always suspected. Despite the oft-repeated parental claim that they don't love one child more than another, this story presents hard evidence that it is possible to do so.

The words describing the garment that Jacob made for Joseph are unclear in the Hebrew. The phrase, which could be translated literally as a "striped garment," is translated alternately as an ornamented tunic (New JPS), a long robe with sleeves (New Revised Standard), or, the most familiar in English, a coat of many colors (King James). The majority of the books for children in the secular market that deal with the story of Joseph focus on this garment. Like Noah and his animals, this colorful coat is perceived as a way to connect children to biblical text.

That this coat is one of the timeless elements of the Joseph story that continues to resonate today can be seen in *Coat of Many Colors,* written by the singer and actress Dolly Parton and illustrated by Judith Sutton (1994). In this version, a contemporary story based only loosely on that one element of the Joseph tale, the pastoral watercolors evoke the clichéd industry, thriftiness, and wholesomeness of American farm life. The main character in this book is a girl who, for lack of money, does not have a coat to wear. Her mother lovingly sews her a coat stitched together from rags, telling her about the biblical Joseph as she sews. The girl is immensely proud of her special coat, and is therefore puzzled when the children at school make fun of it. Because she knows that her coat was made with love, she feels rich and is able to bear the taunts of the other children. One message of this story is the importance of being happy with one's lot. This is a story about seeing the glass as half-full, no matter what is in the glass. The author makes the connection to Joseph, his coat, and the theme of jealousy, but she shapes these elements of the original story into something else altogether. Whereas Joseph's experiences are painful, like those of this little girl, over many years and at great emotional cost they ultimately enable him to learn and grow, but this little girl already seems to have all the answers. In most retellings of this biblical story, Joseph's coat serves as a plot device to highlight Jacob's favoritism, Joseph's arrogance, and his brothers' resentment; in *Coat of Many Colors* the coat instead helps the child learn to appreciate parental love, which enables her to stand up to the teasing of her classmates and remember that love is more important than money. Parton has used the biblical character and his coat to frame quite a different story.

Marcia Williams's *Joseph and his Magnificent Coat of Many Colors* uses the coat as the focal point of the title. Yet this comic strip version of the story actually covers, in highly abbreviated form, the whole Joseph narrative, from his childhood to his reconciliation with his brothers and their move down to Egypt. The coat itself is only in fact a bit player in the Joseph drama, though it is the detail that gets the story going on its course. She writes, "Jacob had twelve fine sons, but the one he loved best was Joseph. Jacob gave Joseph a magnificent coat of many colors, which made his brothers sick with jealousy." Even with the highly simplified language she uses throughout the book, Williams has managed to convey the extent of the brothers' envy and resentment of Joseph. In the brightly colored, comic-strip style illustrations Joseph is portrayed as being self-centered, oblivious to his brothers' feelings or reactions.

The fact that Joseph is the son of Jacob's beloved wife Rachel is given as a reason for the favoritism shown him in "How Can You Forgive?" from *Let My People Go* by Patricia and Frederick McKissack. They write:

> Poor Israel [Jacob] mourned the loss of his beloved Rachel, and he poured all the love he had for her on Joseph, Rachel's firstborn. The boys grew jealous of this favorite son, even though Joseph loved them. Israel made matters worse when he gave Joseph a fine cloak of dazzling colors—red, orange, green, yellow, and blue. Joseph put the cloak on and paraded 'round in front of the others. Father Israel was pleased that his son loved the gift, never once noticin' that his older sons were angry.

This retelling points out that Joseph was the favorite due to an accident of birth, not because he merited this status in any way. However, the brothers are not shown in a good light themselves. Joseph had good intentions, but was foiled in his attempts to get along with his brothers because of their dislike of him. Some of the blame for the situation is placed on Jacob's shoulders in this version as well. He is guilty both of favoring one child over the others, and also of not noticing the distress of his other sons in the face of Joseph's happiness.

Yet none of these stories explains why Joseph was most beloved, other than because of what he was. He was the child of his father's old age, he was the first son of his father's favorite wife, but not because of anything intrinsic to his character. Kirk Douglas addresses this question in his *Young Heroes of the Bible: A Book for Family Sharing* (1999). In this retelling, Douglas puts a contemporary gloss on the story so that today's children can better identify with Joseph. In this version, Joseph is Jacob's favorite because of his academic accomplishments.

. . . from the time Joseph was very little, he was the best at everything he tried. He was very smart and he always learned everything quickly. He got A's on his tests in school. He won prizes for best scholarship and best penmanship and best this and best that. He always raised his hand first whenever the teacher asked a question.

When I was growing up, there was a kid like that in my school, and I hated his guts.

This Joseph is a "teacher's pet," the kind of child other children love to hate. Douglas is trying to create a character for whom children will immediately feel antipathy and therefore better understand the brothers' feelings. Yet in explaining Joseph's offensiveness as a result of his success at school, he removes the textured complexity of the biblical story, and winds up trivializing both the brothers' jealousy and Jacob's favoritism.

In another attempt to update the story, Douglas envisions the special coat that Jacob makes for him as a "really terrific jacket" that is "made out of the same kind of a shiny material that Superman's and Batman's capes are made out of." In giving him this gift, Jacob is thus elevating Joseph as a superhero above his brothers, who must therefore just be ordinary kids. All of this goes to Joseph's head, and he thinks he is better than anyone else. Here Douglas is able to introduce more subtlety into his retelling. Joseph's delight in his costume reinforces his extreme youthfulness and naiveté, while also allowing for the possibility that Joseph is in fact not so strong and mighty, but rather is in need of a masquerade to help him camouflage his weaknesses. The image of Joseph in a superhero costume calls to mind the common penchant of many boys between the ages of three to six to dress up on a daily basis as superheroes, cowboys, knights, and pirates, armed to the teeth with plastic swords, Lego guns, and sticks in an attempt to cover up their vulnerability in a big, scary world. Douglas's retelling asks whether Jacob gave him the outfit because of favoritism, or in order to help Joseph compensate for his youth and innocence in the face of his older brothers' strength and worldliness.

Whatever the reason, Joseph has been a source of much ill will on the part of his brothers. His presence in their midst is for them like a

fun-house mirror that reflects their worst fears about their own weaknesses and shortcomings. Who Joseph himself will become is still to
be determined—he has a great deal of growing up to do and many
choices to make. When his brothers sell him into slavery his story is
only beginning and his character is just being formed.

Joseph's Culpability

> *And Joseph brought bad reports of them to his father.*
>
> (Genesis 37:2)

What, if anything, is Joseph's culpability for what goes on between
him and his brothers? Is he simply a mistreated youngest son, unable
to stand up for himself? Or does he bear some responsibility for the
negative relationships between himself and his brothers? The biblical
text hints that Joseph may bear some responsibility, stating "Joseph
brought bad reports of them to their father" (Genesis 37:2). Was he a
tattletale who got his brothers in trouble with his father? Was he simply a naive child, trying to obey a parent, or a scheming young man
trying to outshine his brothers in his father's eyes? His forthright manner of telling his dreams (Genesis 37:5–11) makes him look arrogant,
like a braggart. He tells his brothers his dreams, and when they ask if
he means to rule over them, the silence in the text is loud. He does
not confirm, but neither does he deny. Joseph is presented as a flawed
and unfinished human, in need of growth and maturity. He is no perfect hero, no role model of brotherly love; rather, he has years of work
ahead of him.

Auld's 1999 version immediately identifies Joseph as a talebearer,
stating, "Joseph worked alongside his brothers and told Jacob what
they did wrong." As with this version's approach to parental favoritism,
and in keeping with the manufactured editorial neutrality of this series,
there is no explanation given or value placed on this information.

According to both Erik Erikson and Jean Piaget, tattling is a behavior typical of children of about six or seven as they become aware of

their parents and of their older siblings as people distinct from themselves. At this age children become aware of "rules" and want consistency in the prevailing social structure at home, in school, and on the playground. As they work to establish their own autonomy they strive to develop "rules" for all situations and are usually inflexible in how they want the "rules" enforced. They understand people on a superficial level, and form judgments of people and events on the basis of appearances. Only gradually, as they become more independent, do children understand and appreciate that their own behavior may be in opposition to others' expectations. This is the period in children's lives that Piaget labels "concrete operational." Joseph's behavior in the books mentioned above show that he is in his concrete operational period, initially unable to distinguish the difference between how his dreams appear to him and how they will be perceived by his brothers. At this point in his story, Joseph is still a young egocentric child. He is responsive only to his own thoughts and desires, unable to see events from another's point of view. Going back to his father to report on his brothers' behavior in the fields is consistent with this stage of child development. Joseph wants people and events to be just exactly as he thinks they should be and as the dominant adult in his life, Jacob, has requested them to be. It is not unreasonable for a young child who is aware that he cannot yet influence events to return to the adult authority who has ordered the events and report that things are amiss. This behavior is called "tattling," but to Joseph it is a developmentally appropriate attempt to make the world follow the rules he perceives his father has ordered.

The reason that Joseph is sent after his brothers in Williams's version is because Jacob wants them to "make peace." Having heard Joseph's dreams about ruling over them someday, and their father's belief in these dreams, the brothers have taken the sheep and stormed off in anger. In addition to the formal text lines, Williams uses speech bubbles in the illustrations. The brothers are saying things like, "Stupid dreamer," "He's quite pleased with himself," and "Our brother a ruler . . . ridiculous." When Joseph approaches his brothers in the field, he is depicted as surrounded by a golden glow. His brothers are not pleased, to say the least. The light-hearted illustrations belie the seriousness of what is transpiring. Within the illustration, the brothers say to each other, "Who does he think he is?" "I want his coat," "Shame there are no lions around today," and "Do you think he'd taste good?" In the main body of the text, the brothers then come up with their plan first to kill him, so that "our father will pay some attention to us," and then, when stopped by Rueben, to throw him into the pit and then sell him to the Ishmaelites. The idea that Joseph had some part in fostering his brother's negative feelings for him, implied in the line, "And Joseph brought bad reports of them to their father" (Genesis 37:2) is completely absent here. Joseph remains blameless, unfairly treated by his mean and jealous brothers. The problem in this version is purely parental favoritism, while Joseph is an innocent. His lack of good judgment in telling his brothers about his dream is less a result of his own arrogance and more the fault of his father's misguided encouragement. The illustrations reinforce this sense of Joseph as a naïf. When Joseph is stripped of his coat, he is revealed to be naked underneath, and covers himself up with his hands like an embarrassed child.

Brian Wildsmith, in his gorgeously and extravagantly illustrated *Joseph,* also plays down Joseph's culpability in his brother's resentment of him. Joseph is depicted as a young, clean-shaven boy compared to his brothers, who are all bearded. He is portrayed as being perhaps naive in telling his brothers his dreams, but it is his brothers who act with malice. He simply tells them his dream, after which they hate and resent him even more. As in Williams's version, Joseph is not described as being responsible for his brothers' bad feelings toward him. The idea that Joseph had some part in fostering his brother's negative feelings for him, as understood from verse Genesis 37:2, is completely absent here. Later, Joseph goes out to his brothers in the fields, having been told by Jacob, "Go and see how your brothers are and how the flocks are faring, and bring me back word" (Genesis 37:14). This line can be read as Jacob asking Joseph to spy on them, or at the least to bring back further reports, to be a tattletale. This being the case, it is no wonder that his brothers are resentful. Yet again Wildsmith leaves out the motivation for Joseph's visit, putting the full responsibility on his brothers. They see him coming and immediately plot to kill him, restrained only by Reuben who insists that they can't kill their own brother. But they can throw him in a pit, and this is what they do. In Wildsmith's version, Joseph is purely the victim of his vicious, resentful brothers.

Joseph's brothers are all grown men with their own families in "Brothers Got Bad Heart for Joseph" from Lorenz Graham's *How God Fix Jonah*. Even so, his favored status and his arrogance still bother them. They have married and had children, but their lives still revolve around Jacob, whose heart is bound up not with them, but with Joseph. Graham writes:

> *He be strong*
> *He be clean*
> *He be quick.*
> *Joseph be fine young man.*
> *He mind him pa's word.*
> *He make him pa's heart lay down.*
> *Joseph have plenty brothers.*
> *The brothers be old past Joseph.*
> *They got the womens*
> *They got they picans.*
> *They no live in one house together*
> *But all live close by.*
> *All mind the old man's word*
> *But they no love Joseph.*

They have not been able to get over their jealousy and resentment of this favored brother. Their feelings are so strong that, "Them brothers got bad heart for Joseph." In this version, instead of placing him in a pit, they beat him and he cries. They then decide to sell him to a "Mandingo trader" so that he will pay the price for his conceit. The brothers in Graham's retelling want vengeance on Joseph. Their goal is not simply to get rid of this annoyance; they want him to suffer.

The Pit

> *They saw him from afar, and before he came close to them they conspired to kill him. They said to one another, "Here comes that dreamer! Come now, let us kill him and throw him into one of the pits, and we can say, 'A savage beast devoured him.' We shall see what comes of his dreams!"*
>
> (Genesis 37:18–20)

The pit into which Joseph is thrown by his brothers is what Campbell calls "the representative of that unconscious deep . . . wherein are hoarded all of the rejected, unadmitted, unrecognized, unknown or undeveloped factors, laws, and elements of existence" (p. 52). What Joseph encounters there in the pit is all that he has been avoiding in his attempt to remain his father's protected, favored son who does not have to grow up, become independent, and take responsibility for his own actions. Like Jonah's stay in the belly of the fish, it is through this encounter with the deep unknown that he can come through to the other side and begin the necessary journey to maturity and selfhood. Joseph's stay in the pit is the first stage of his hero's journey, in which he has been forced to leave his metaphoric, or in this case real, comfort zone, and go out into the unknown wilderness, symbolized here by Egypt.

The pit into which Joseph is thrown is imagined differently in various retellings. Sometimes it is a raw, naturally occurring hole in the ground, part of a landscape that is, in Chaikin's words, a "rocky, thorny wilderness." In *Joseph, King of Dreams,* the pit is described as a "parched hole" with "rough dirt walls." This pit is part of the untamed natural world, a sharp contrast to the safety to which Joseph has been accustomed at home under Jacob's protection. Joseph's companion in the pit is a scorpion. This detail, not found in the biblical text, is borrowed from classical Midrash, which imagines a pit filled with snakes.[6] This detail lends an element of danger beyond simply that of dying of thirst. Alone in the pit, abandoned by his brothers, Joseph

---

[6] Genesis Rabbah LXXXIV:16

faces an unknown, terrifying future, filled with potentially malicious creatures.

On a symbolic level, there is also a sexual element to the presence of snakes, as Joseph begins his journey toward manhood. Bettelheim notes that Adam and Eve are young and innocent in Eden until the appearance of the snake. In *The Uses of Enchantment*, he writes, "It was Eve who was tempted by male masculinity, as represented by the snake" (p. 212). In the story of Adam and Eve, the snake symbolizes sexual knowledge. Once Eve encounters the snake and gains knowledge, she can no longer go on living in a childlike state in Eden where she will never have to make choices or think for herself. Similarly, before being thrown in the snake-ridden pit, Joseph is young and innocent. He acts impulsively, without understanding the consequences of his behavior. Indeed, his stay in the pit is the beginning of his journey from naive youth to adulthood, which enables him later to make the mature choice to avoid a dangerous sexual encounter with Potiphar's wife.

In Douglas's *Young Heroes of the Bible* (1999), the possibility that there are snakes in the pit is mentioned. One of Joseph's brothers maliciously hopes aloud that the snakes in the pit will bite Joseph and he will die. But Douglas immediately pulls back from this idea, writing, "Little did they know that there were no poisonous snakes in the pit. I'd like to think that the skinny angel who had saved Eliezer was doing his job again and had scared the snakes away." The chance that there might be snakes is presented just long enough to both illustrate the meanness of Joseph's brothers, and to cause the reader to sufficiently worry about Joseph's welfare. But reassurance is immediately offered. Just as children often fantasize that there is an unseen protective hand watching over them, Douglas imagines that Joseph is protected from harm by an unknown force, perhaps even an angel.

In other retellings, such as *Let My People Go*, the pit is a man-made well that has gone dry. In Wildsmith's *Joseph* (1997), the illustrations show an empty well lined with neat stonework. A sophisticated mechanism used to pull a jug up and down hangs above Joseph, tantalizingly out of his reach. Rather than the wild, untamed image of the natural hole, this kind of a well is a symbol of civilization. To some extent, this kind of a pit is even scarier, in that it is symbolic of the way that the rules and behavioral norms of a neatly ordered society or family structure cannot always protect us from harm.

The Accusation Against Joseph

> After a time, his master's wife cast her eyes upon Joseph and said, "Lie with me." But he refused. He said to his master's wife, ". . . How then could I do this most wicked thing, and sin before God?" And as much as she coaxed Joseph day after day, he did not yield to her request to lie beside her, to be with her.
>
> (Genesis 39:7–10)

Many of the children's books based on the Joseph narrative conveniently skip over the disturbing episode between Joseph and Potiphar's wife. This is understandably a difficult section to read to children, and the flow of the story is not egregiously interrupted by skipping it entirely. Yet viewing the Joseph story as a whole, this is an important piece in that it signifies another one of the many trials that Joseph, like Moses after him, must pass through before the end of his hero's journey. The importance of this episode lies in the fact that it gets Joseph where he needs to be next, in prison, in order to become known to Pharaoh as a dream-interpreter.

Joseph comes to be trusted in the House of Potiphar, where he serves as a personal attendant in charge of the household. The biblical narrative mentions that Joseph is well built and handsome (Genesis 39:6), and he soon attracts the interest of Potiphar's wife. She tries to seduce him, but he refuses to succumb, insisting that he could not do such a wicked thing to Potiphar and sin before God. Ironically, a piece of Joseph's clothing again plays an important role in determining his fate (Genesis 12–18). A close reading of the biblical text shows why it is no mystery that children's books tend to skip this section and proceed right to Joseph's stay in prison, as if after having been sent down to Egypt as a slave he was sent directly to prison. Angry at being rejected, Potiphar's wife makes it look like Joseph had tried to rape her (Genesis 39:1–18). Sue Kassirer's simplified *Joseph and His Coat of Many Colors,* part of Simon and Schuster's Ready-to-Read series, is an example of this type of shaping of the story, in which the narration moves quickly from the brothers tricking Jacob to Joseph being in prison while ignoring completely the contretemps between Joseph and Potiphar's wife:

> *Jacob cried and cried.*
> *Was Joseph really dead?*
> *No!*
> *He was alive in Egypt.*
> *But he was in prison.*

In Marcia Williams's highly simplified version of the Joseph story, the incident with Potiphar's wife is mentioned, but only in a sanitized, offhand way. Regarding his early days in Egypt, she writes, "But God took care of Joseph, and he fared well, until the day when he upset Potiphar's wife. She had him arrested and locked up." Auld's version sticks closely to the biblical text. Potiphar's wife is shown lying on a chaise in a provocative pose, while Joseph has his back to her, only his face turned slightly toward her. The story goes so far as to say, "He was very handsome and she wanted him to be her lover." Yet this retelling loses courage when faced with how to explain exactly what Potiphar's wife has accused Joseph of doing, stating, "She went to her husband and told him that Joseph had tried to kiss her and more." Despite trying to stick closely to the biblical text, like most of the retellings of this episode it misses an opportunity for making a connection between Joseph's multicolored cloak and the garment that Potiphar's wife uses to try to prove his guilt.

Wildsmith's *Joseph* does not skip over this episode, but does tone it down significantly. Joseph and Potiphar's wife are shown in a colorful, flower-filled, lush, Egyptian courtyard. Unlike Auld's retelling, they are both vertical, in full standing position. Potiphar's wife is shown to be holding Joseph's cloak, evoking in its colorfulness the one made for him by his father, while Joseph reaches out for the cloak with one hand, as if hesitating. Cloaks play a role in two pivotal moments in Joseph's life. Jealousy over one cloak has gotten him thrown into a pit and convinced his father that he is dead, and now another cloak and a jealous husband will convince the Pharaoh that Joseph has betrayed him and get him thrown into prison:

> Potiphar's wife fell in love with him, and one day she caught Joseph by his cloak and begged him to return her love. But Joseph refused. "How can I betray my master and my God?" he asked her.
>   Potiphar's wife was furious. She rushed to her husband and accused Joseph of attacking her. Potiphar believed his wife's story and had Joseph thrown into prison.

There is no mention of love in the biblical narrative relating the incident, only physical attraction. But Wildsmith makes this episode of seduction and betrayal more palatable for children by putting love into the equation.

In Dandi Daley Mackall's *Joseph King of Dreams,* a version of the story related to the Dreamworks animated film of the same name, this incident plays a part but in a most oblique way. Potiphar's wife, named Zuleika[7] in this version, "observed Joseph, now strong and handsome." She comes secretly to him in the night and asks him to "betray Potiphar's trust." What has in fact happened here is sure to escape the notice of all but the most sophisticated children. The episode simply serves as a way to get Joseph into the jail cell, from which he can later be rescued. In this version, it is Potiphar himself who, some years later, comes to take Joseph out of the cell. Joseph's internal growth is shown in part by his forgiveness of Potiphar, foreshadowing the way in which he will later be able to treat his brothers.

---

[7] Potiphar's wife is called Zuleika in the medieval Midrash Yashar Va-Yeshev 86b, cited in Ginzberg's *Legends of the Jews,* vol 2.

Responsibility for Joseph's Gift

> *And they said to him, "We had dreams, and there is no one to interpret them." So Joseph said to them, "Surely God can interpret! Tell me [your dreams]."*

(Genesis 40:8)

Joseph is a gifted child, and later a gifted young man. He has the ability to interpret dreams, even as he first misuses this gift. Joseph's evolving relationship with this gift can be seen as symbolic of his emotional growth. The first time Joseph talks about his ability to interpret dreams, he makes no mention of the source of this gift, rather, he speaks of it with arrogance, taunting his brothers with his special ability (Genesis 37). The next time that his gift is mentioned, he is in prison and interprets the dreams of the chief cupbearer and the baker. In this instance, Joseph, now older and wiser, gives full credit to God for his gift, saying, "Surely God can interpret" (Genesis 40:8).

Whereas Auld's retelling follows the original biblical source, other versions of Joseph's story remove God from the equation or downplay God's role. God is not mentioned at all in Sue Kassirer's *Joseph and His Coat of Many Colors* (1997), which states, "Joseph kept busy in prison. He told the other prisoners what their dreams meant." In so doing, the stories are made more palatable for a secular audience, but the significance of Joseph's character development, as seen in the contrast between Joseph's younger, arrogant self and his older, more humble self, gets lost.

The only connection between God and Joseph's ability to interpret dreams in *Joseph and his Magnificent Coat of Many Colors* comes after Joseph has already interpreted Pharaoh's dream. Joseph tells him the meaning of the seven ears of corn and the seven cows, and only when advising Pharaoh how to deal with the problem does he invoke God, saying, "As God has told you of his intentions, you should appoint a wise man to store food during the years of plenty." The emphasis here is not on God as the source of Joseph's dream-interpreting ability, but rather on God as the source of the dream itself. Joseph's ability to understand it correctly appears to be simply a result of his own skill or good luck.

Wildsmith, however, does not shy away from God's role in the story, writing, "But God was with Joseph in prison." It comes as no surprise then that in this version, when Pharaoh summons Joseph from prison to interpret his dream, Joseph immediately credits God with his ability to do as Pharaoh requests, saying, "God has revealed what he is about to do." Once Joseph has interpreted the dream, Pharaoh answers, saying, " 'Since God has revealed all this to you, it is clear that you are the man we need.' So Joseph was made Governor of all Egypt, second in power only to Pharaoh himself." Joseph has learned some humility since his earlier days with his brothers. By acknowledging God's role in his life, he then goes on to achieve astounding success in his new country.

What Joseph is guilty of early on in Douglas's *Young Heroes of the Bible* is thinking that he was responsible for being so good at everything he attempted. Instead of remembering that God is the source of his success and being humbly grateful, he lets it go to his head. Douglas writes:

> I learned in Sunday school that God gives us all special gifts. Some people are really good at playing the piano—and of course they get better if they practice. And some people are good at math—and they get better if they work out a lot of difficult problems. And some people are good at sports—and the more they play, the faster and stronger they become. But the original gift comes from God. So you can't take all the credit yourself. And you have to remember that other people have special gifts too. You are *not* better than everybody else.
>
> Well, Joseph forgot that. He started to think that he was *too* good.

In being able to later credit God as the source of his gifts, Joseph shows evidence of having grown and matured since he left home. He has learned that God plays an important role in his life and his success. His humility will serve him well as he flourishes in Egypt, and will ultimately allow him to rebuild his relationship with his brothers.

That God is with Joseph comes across clearly in Mackall's *Joseph King of Dreams*. When Joseph is thrown into jail, he immediately calls out in anger to God, asking why God is doing such a thing to him. This version of the story introduces an original element that does not appear in the Bible or other retellings, that of a plant growing inside the prison cell. This plant gives Joseph hope, and in caring for the plant he comes to see that God is caring for him as well, even if he doesn't understand how or what God has in mind. The plant, reminiscent of Jonah's vine, comes to be a symbol of Joseph's character growth while in jail. The plant has grown and flourished, as has Joseph himself. When he is taken out of the cell by Potiphar, the illustrations show a serious, bearded man in place of the scared, clean-shaven boy who had originally been placed in the cell, standing next to a full-size healthy tree. When Pharaoh asks him about his ability to interpret dreams, he states right away that his ability comes from God, not himself. His time in prison has served to mature him as well as to humble him. Interestingly, this version adds a more overt connection to God than what exists in the biblical text. Later, when Pharaoh appointed Joseph to be his second-in-command over Egypt, Joseph still did not give in to pride and self-importance, but rather "looked to heaven and praised God."

Can Joseph Learn Forgiveness?

> *Then Joseph said to his brothers, "Come forward to me." And when they came forward, he said, "I am your brother Joseph, he whom you sold into Egypt. Now, do not be distressed or reproach yourselves because you sold me hither; it was to save life that God sent me ahead of you. . . ." He kissed all his brothers and wept upon them; only then were his brothers able to talk to him.*
>
> (Genesis 45:4–5, 15)

The theme of forgiveness is central to the story of Joseph. When Joseph at last meets his brothers again, they don't recognize him. The choice is thus his: he can send them on their way, or he can reveal to them his identity. After all these years, how much anger does he still feel toward them? While they did not take his life, they may as well have killed him, sending him away from his homeland and his family, and lying to his father. Yet so many years have passed, and life has not been bad to Joseph. Joseph's encounter with his brothers becomes the real test of his character. With all that he has experienced since his last meeting with his brothers, will he act differently than he did years before? How much has he really grown and learned in the intervening years?

Kassirer's *Joseph and His Coat of Many Colors* emphasizes both his anger and his power. In Danuta Jarecka's illustrations, Joseph is depicted sitting on a raised, throne-like chair, looking down at his brothers, whose heads are bent in deference. She writes, "Joseph was still angry at his brothers. What should he do? Should he hurt his brothers? Should he punish them? Should he let them starve? He could do anything—anything he wanted!" These many years later, Joseph is in quite a different situation vis-à-vis his brothers. He can do to them what they did to him. But he doesn't. He takes some time to think, and finally reveals himself to them, hugging them and weeping. He welcomes the brothers to his adopted land, invites them to come live there permanently, and is reunited with his father. This is the rare biblical story with a happy ending.

The lead-up to Joseph's dramatic revelation to his brothers is related in broad strokes in *Joseph and His Coat of Many Colors*. Because they don't recognize him, he manipulates them, planting stolen goods in their bags, and threatens to put Benjamin, the most beloved son after Joseph, in prison. But the brothers respond differently now than they did years ago with Joseph. This time they rally to Benjamin's defense, trying to protect him and unwilling to cause their father additional heartbreak (Genesis 42–43). Through their reactions, Joseph is able to see that they too have changed and grown. In this version of the story, it is this care for both Benjamin and Jacob that causes Joseph to forgive them and disclose his identity. The happy ending is evidence that Joseph has grown up and overcome his arrogance, anger, and resentment.

Once Joseph tells his brothers who he is, they worry about what he will do to them. But this is a changed Joseph, and there is no need to worry. Miriam Chaikin's Joseph tells his brothers, "Don't blame yourselves. . . . It was all for the good. God brought me here to save you from starvation." Sticking even more closely to the biblical source, Mary Auld's Joseph is able to forgive and move on, telling them, "Don't worry, God has wished it this way." The brothers shouldn't feel bad about what has happened, because by putting Joseph into the pit and selling him to the traders, they were actually putting God's plan into effect. If it hadn't been for their actions, they would have nowhere to turn now in this time of extreme famine. That Joseph casts God as the central figure in the events of his life is also a sign of Joseph's maturity and humility. He is only a small player on a big stage; his success in Egypt is not due to his own special nature but is part of God's bigger plan. The problem with this version is that in order to stick so literally to the biblical text, Joseph isn't allowed to become a three-dimensional character, but rather comes off as a stick figure of righteousness.

As in Marcia Williams's book, Brian Wildsmith uses the illustrations to show that Joseph is in a higher position of power than his brothers. He stands on a grand staircase, looking down on his brothers, who kneel on the floor before him. Wildsmith's account of Joseph's dealings with his brothers closely follows the biblical text. Yet unlike Auld, Wildsmith introduces certain elements that are not in the original. When Joseph makes known his true identity, he actually tells his brothers that he forgives them. Although forgiveness is certainly implied in the biblical account, Joseph does not ever actually say that he forgives them. He simply hugs his brothers and they all weep together while Joseph excuses them for what they did by saying that it was God's will (Genesis 45:3–15). But forgiveness is clearly an important theme for Wildsmith, as it is for the writers of other children's versions of the Joseph story. That it is all right to be angry but that we must also learn to forgive is an important lesson for children. Children want to be forgiven, and adults want children to learn how to forgive. Part of becoming an adult is learning that even the people we love the most are fallible and can make mistakes.

In intriguing contrast to the story of Joseph and his brothers, *A Time to Love: Stories from the Old Testament,* by the father-and-son team of author Walter Dean Myers and illustrator Christopher Myers, and with a preface by another brother, Michael Dean Myers, represents the cooperative work of a father and his sons. The illustration on the cover of their book depicts a white-robed Joseph with his arms stretched wide enough to hold his eleven brothers in a close, protective embrace. It is repeated again within this collection in the chapter entitled "Reuben and Joseph." This version of Joseph's story is told from the first-person perspective of Joseph's oldest brother, Reuben, and opens with his brief declaration, "My brother lives." The devastating repercussions of sibling rivalry are immediately established by Reuben's realization that the joy of Joseph's reappearance "from the ashes of memory" is ultimately painful news for the family because it is a reminder of the terrible way they had behaved earlier. Joseph's first response upon being reunited with his brothers is to direct them to return home and tell their father that he is alive. But Reuben's response to the joyous news is to think about what the results of the brothers' jealousy and rivalry really mean. Once Jacob learns what they have done, there will be "disgrace for the messengers" of this news. How, he asks himself, will he and his brothers confront the deed they committed so many years ago while they were young and all living in their father's household, answerable to his commands? Thinking about the likelihood of an angry response to their confession, Reuben speaks about how his "grief and fear sit in the pit of my stomach like two huge rocks." As the oldest of Jacob's twelve sons, Reuben is particularly attuned to the possibility of his father's anger and thoughts of retribution. In a continuation of their childhood rivalry, he acts in response to the potential loss of his father's love. He lies awake trying to find a coherent thread in his brother's story, but like a child still looking for assurance that he is the favored son, Reuben remembers that his father reprimanded Joseph for telling his brothers that one day they would be his servants. He recalls his brothers discussing what to do to silence Joseph's apparent bragging and sees himself as Joseph's attempted savior, even though he failed in the effort.

Despite his brothers' fears of what he may do to them in retribution for their jealous behavior toward him, Joseph tells them: "Come to me" and holds out his arms (Genesis 45:4). In Myers's retelling, Joseph then tells his brothers, "There is no vengeance in my heart for those I love." And so Myers's version becomes a powerful story to share with children, teaching them that loving the other people in your family is the most important lesson of all and that familial love is stronger than familial conflict. Even as the brothers accept Joseph's embrace and are relieved of the guilt they have borne for many years, Reuben finds no solace; he is aware that his behavior was motivated by jealousy and that he did not try hard enough to save his brother. Cognizant of his agony, Joseph assures Reuben that he does not need Joseph's forgiveness. All the brothers are humbled by Joseph's graceful pardon and express the childlike wish to be able to go back in time and undo their jealous action. They are astonished that Joseph accepts them as brothers and seeks only the love and approval of their father. In this retelling, they have learned an important life lesson and moved on to the final stage of maturity delineated in both Erikson's and Piaget's developmental theory, as Reuben notes: *"Innocence is a road that burns behind the traveler—there is no return, only the ashes of what might have been."* Having found each other, reconciled, and reunited with their father, the brothers can now continue on with the rest of their lives, settling down to a quiet and calm life in Egypt.

The story of Joseph and his brothers is a moral tale about what happens when people act impulsively on their anger without regard for obligations and values determined by family relationships and the community. Jean Piaget refers to "mutual respect" and "moral realism" as necessary developments on the road to maturity. Moral realism is determined independent of one's intentions and relationships. As Joseph's brothers knew, but chose to ignore, it is not negotiable. They return home to their father with heavy hearts and later confess to Joseph how they lived for so many years with the guilt of their action; time did not make their guilt easier to bear. The story of Joseph illustrates for children what happens when family and community values are ignored.

When attempting to understand the story of Joseph and his eleven brothers in order to introduce it to children, it is necessary to also look at the character of Jacob. Was there anything in his behavior and attitude toward his sons that fostered such markedly aggressive, hostile behavior toward one of their own? Each storybook retelling of Joseph indicts Jacob for his inconsistent behavior toward his sons as manifested by his favoritism toward Joseph. That only Joseph is singled out to receive a magnificent multicolored robe results in frustration among the brothers, and they are further insulted when Joseph reveals his dreams to them as Jacob listens passively. Jacob's tacit approval of Joseph's behavior is made all the more intolerable in each of the above books when no reference is made to Jacob's ever complimenting his other sons for their hard work and productive labors.

The themes of jealousy, resentment, and sibling rivalry in the Joseph story are interwoven with themes of forgiveness, redemption, and growth. Joseph's horrific experience of being abandoned by his brothers and sold into slavery is redressed by their subsequent need of help that only he can provide. They atone for their past actions toward Joseph through their care and concern for Benjamin and Jacob. Though Joseph does at first manipulate his brothers when given the chance, and does temporarily cause his father pain, he chooses in the end not to abuse the power that he has over his brothers and father. That Joseph's brothers mistreated him is not a reason for him to do the same to them. Along with the universal themes of sibling rivalry and parental favoritism, this is also a story of generosity, compassion, humility, and sensitivity as seen through the forgiveness of Joseph toward his brothers. His wish in the end is not for revenge but reconciliation. His actions show that he has learned to conquer his impulsivity and can now take the time to think and reflect before acting.

In one sense, Joseph is a hero because he is able to overcome personal adversity and use his gifts to help a whole nation avoid starvation and death. But on another level, it is Joseph's growth of character that makes him a hero. By having the inner strength to learn and develop, he acquires the ability to see beyond himself and thus be able to help others. In so doing, he comes to understand the importance of acknowledging and overcoming his character weaknesses, and is then ready to forgive the failings of others. He also learns along the way to make good choices rather than acting selfishly or impulsively, and to take responsibility for his actions. By not giving in to anger and vengeance, but by trying to use the best that he has inside himself, he saves himself from a life consumed by hurt, hatred, and rage.

The story of Joseph is an important story for children, enmeshed as they are in their own family situations, struggling to grow up. Joseph's story is complicated and, despite the coat of many colors, not always pretty. But children already know that life is just that, complicated and sometimes downright ugly. This is a story that acknowledges their reality, that tells them yes, sometimes parents are unfair, sometimes siblings do terrible things to each other, and sometimes life itself isn't fair. But it is not a story that leaves children in despair. Rather, this story shows that the struggle toward maturity is worth the hard work. Joseph's hardships notwithstanding, the story presents a positive model for children. Children do grow up, find their purpose in life, and sometimes even achieve greatness. Family rifts can be healed. Jealousies and rivalries can be overcome and forgiven. Parents and children can be reunited. This is a basic story of both family relationships and the pain of growing up. All the brothers learn, grow, and come to appreciate the importance of family, despite its complications. But the story of Joseph is, in the end, a story of hope.

4
MOSES

Moses is one of the greatest biblical leaders, revered by Judaism, Christianity, and Islam as a prophet and teacher. He is absent entirely from Genesis, as his birth is recorded only in Chapter 2 of the Book of Exodus. But he is the central character in the Books of Exodus, Numbers, Leviticus, and Deuteronomy. Moses is so essential to the Bible that the first five biblical books, which make up the Torah, or the Pentateuch, are known in Jewish tradition as the Five Books of Moses.

The narratives related to Moses and his life are plentiful. These stories span his childhood years, his youth, his coming of age, the years of his great leadership and maturity, and go all the way to his death. Through these many tales, Moses comes to life as a multidimensional character. Despite the reverence with which he is treated by later tradition, the Bible allows Moses to be portrayed as someone who can sometimes be angry, unsure of himself, impatient, and even slip up. He is a great leader who, with God's help, performs miracles and enables the Israelites to leave the slavery of Egypt. He is allowed to draw close to God as no other human is allowed to do, yet he is never shown to be perfect. He is always a flawed human being, never a romanticized ideal.

Though Joseph also represents a biblical character who is allowed to mature and change, the arc of Moses' life is even bigger, and the stories in which he appears are much more extensive than those of Joseph. The biblical stories about Moses are therefore all the richer because he is allowed to be imperfect and ever-changing. The implication here for children is that perfection is not expected or required, not even in great leaders; rather that it's more important to learn and grow from one's mistakes.

Moses comes into the world under a cloud, the evil Pharaoh having decreed that any baby boy born to a Hebrew woman must be thrown into the Nile. His mother hides him for the first three months of his life, and then puts him into a basket in the Nile. His sister keeps watch and sees that he is taken out of the water by the daughter of Pharaoh, who adopts him. Moses' clever sister then arranges for their mother to be his nursemaid. When Moses grows up, he sees an Egyptian beat a Hebrew slave to death. He strikes the Egyptian, thinking that no one has seen him, but upon realizing that his deed is known, runs away to the land of Midian to escape Pharaoh's wrath. While there, he encounters the daughter of a Midianite priest, Zipporah, who becomes his wife, and they have two sons (Exodus 1:22–2:23).

A major turning point in Moses' life occurs when he is out shepherding his father-in-law's sheep and encounters a bush that burns but is not consumed. Through this bush, the God of the Hebrews speaks to him and tells him to return to Egypt. He is to convince Pharaoh to let the Israelites go, and bring them to a land flowing with milk and honey. Though Moses demurs and tries to talk his way out of this task, he winds up accepting this responsibility and returns to Egypt to become the leader of his people. Some of the Bible's most dramatic episodes thus ensue, involving Moses' negotiations with Pharaoh, the ten plagues, and finally the parting of the sea as Moses leads his people out of Egypt (Exodus 5–14). Moses then leads the people through the desert for forty years, continuing to deepen his ongoing relationship with God. In another well-known biblical scene, Moses ascends Mount Sinai to receive the Ten Commandments, an act he must repeat after the episode with the golden calf (Exodus 19–34). Moses eventually gets a glimpse of the Promised Land before he dies, but is not permitted to enter the land himself (Deuteronomy 3:23–27).

The stories about Moses involve a great deal of drama, invoking as they do the themes of good and evil, rebellion, growth, revenge, and triumph. These are stories of a child, an adult, a family, and a people, which include themes and motifs familiar from many other hero legends. Like the heroes in so many fairy and folk tales, Moses is a classic hero figure who must struggle, endure difficult tests, and grow to be a mature adult as well as a leader. Campbell delineates the difference between the heroes of fairy tales and those of myths, writing:

> Typically the hero of the fairy tale achieves a domestic, microscopic triumph, and the hero of myth a world-historical, macroscopic triumph. Whereas the former—the youngest or despised child who becomes the master of extraordinary powers—prevails over his personal oppressors, the latter brings back from his adventure the means for the regeneration of his society as a whole. (p. 37–38)

Moses has much in common with the heroes of both of Campbell's categories. His ultimate triumphs are both microscopic and macroscopic—he is both a familiar character who could be any child hoping to someday prove his worth, and he is the great leader of his people who will bring them from slavery to freedom.

The symbol of a baby found floating in a basket in the water is another familiar element that the story of Moses shares with other myths and fairy tales, one of the most familiar of which is the Mesopotamian tale of Sargon. Otto Rank interprets this as an allusion to the birth process that allows the baby's rebirth in preparation for his role as a hero. Moses may have been born as an ordinary baby, but in being spared death and reborn as a member of Pharaoh's household, he is refashioned as a hero. Yet despite Moses' role as a hero figure, the stories about Moses offer a quite human perspective on the developmental process toward selfhood: a model of communal leadership, and the narrative of an ongoing, ever-evolving relationship with God, Moses' protector, teacher, and partner. It is plain to see why the stories about Moses are told and retold to generation after generation of children. Yet how to do so presents the thoughtful storyteller with complicated challenges.

The Baby Moses

> The woman conceived and bore a son; and when she saw how beautiful he was, she hid him for three months.
>
> (Exodus 2:2)

There are serious hurdles involved in recounting the story of Moses for children. The question then of how these stories should be retold and shaped becomes quite significant. A major theme of the Moses stories revolves around the purposeful harming of children, specifically boy children. Children's lives are endangered by powerful authority figures who want to kill them, first by Pharaoh who wants to kill all the newborn Hebrew boys, and then by God who kills the first born of the Egyptian families. The narrative also offers a compelling story about a baby in danger who is saved by the love of his mother, the ingenuity of his sister, the care of a foster mother, and the assumption of a different identity.

Though the idea of a baby in great peril, at risk of losing his life or identity because of a powerful evil force, might not seem like appropriate content for children, this theme is familiar from the folk tales of cultures all around the world. In Greek mythology, for instance, Zeus's mother, Rhea, uses trickery to save him from being swallowed and destroyed by his father Cronus. The story of King Arthur is another example of a child's identity being hidden until it is safe and appropriate for his true identity to be revealed. Jane Yolen writes about Arthur as the classic quest fantasy featuring a child-hero with a hidden identity.

> Consider this: the story of Arthur begins with a foster child, orphaned, unsure of his own background and worth. This small, insignificant fosterling actually has unknown power coursing through his veins—the blood of kings, the lore of magicians. (p. 66)

Bettelheim considers a similar character in fairy tales. "The fairy tale . . . offers the story of the unnoticed little boy who goes out into the world and makes a great success of life" (p. 111). In this example it is a disregarded young boy, rather than one whose identity is actually hidden, but the result is the same—a child who has been overlooked and underestimated but who will someday be able to prove who he really is and of what he is truly capable.

These themes found in the story of Moses continue to be prevalent in modern children's literature. One popular example can be seen in J. K. Rowling's Harry Potter series, in which Harry narrowly misses being killed by the evil Voldemort as a baby. One reason why Voldemort is unable to kill Harry is because he, like Moses, is protected by his mother's strong love, which acts as a counterbalance to Voldemort's evil magic. Orphaned and sent to live with relatives who don't like him, Harry spends the first years of his life in obscurity, an example of both Yolen's "insignificant fosterling" and Bettelheim's "unnoticed little boy." He only comes to learn his true identity years later, when the time is right.

Another feature that these stories all share is the involvement of a wise, all-knowing adult figure, who guides the hero through his adventures and with whose help the hero is able to succeed. Campbell writes, "The first encounter of the hero-journey is with a protective figure . . . who provides the adventurer with amulets against the dragon forces he is about to pass" (p. 69). For Harry Potter, that figure is Dumbledore, for Arthur, it is Merlin, and for Moses, it is God.

Though they may certainly be scary for children, these universal elements of the Moses story are thus familiar from fairy tales, mythology, and legends. It is up to the individual writer to stress or minimize certain elements over others. Depending on how the story is framed, these themes can even serve to emphasize the life-affirming power of love, particularly mother-love, in overcoming the forces of evil.

In *Baby Moses,* written by Linda Hayward and illustrated by Barb Henry (1989), the focus is on Moses' birth and babyhood. The simple language of this Step-Into-Reading book offers a gentle, abridged version of the biblical story. The tender watercolor illustrations depict a family that looks poor but not miserable, trying their best to care for their beloved newborn baby. The mother is caring, loving, and ready to do anything to save her son, including making him a "basket out of bulrushes."

The actual peril to the baby's life is not made clear at first. Hayward writes only, "His mother had to save him from the wicked Pharaoh." Why Pharaoh was wicked, or what he planned to do to Moses, is not explained until pages later, and then only once Pharaoh's daughter has decided that she wants to care for this baby, in other words, when a positive resolution has already been determined. Hayward writes, "Pharaoh found out. He said the baby must die." The cruelty of this is balanced by the illustration showing Pharaoh's daughter holding the baby in a protective, loving way. The story continues, "Pharaoh let her keep the baby because he loved his daughter. Then was the baby safe? Yes! Baby Moses was as safe as a prince in Pharaoh's house." Parental love wins out again—because Pharaoh doesn't want to go against the wishes of the daughter *he* loves, he spares the life of this baby whom *she* loves, who has now been saved yet again by the all-powerful love of a parent.

Other than an oblique reference right at the end there is no mention at all in this version of the Moses story of ethnic or religious strife being at the core of the problem. Nowhere in this version is Moses or his family identified as being different than Pharaoh and the other Egyptians. Why Pharaoh wanted to have Moses killed is not explained. Only the last page hints at these elements of the story, stating, "And when Moses grew up he saved his people from the wicked Pharaoh." Nor is there anything about God, or what role God might have played in keeping Moses safe. Rather, this story of Moses' babyhood presents a strong and affirming message for children about the awesome power of parental love to keep them safe.

Similarly, mother-love triumphs again in Brad Kessler's *Moses in Egypt*. Kessler writes, "Yet this one woman resolved to save her son from Pharaoh's soldiers, for her heart would break from sorrow if harm were to come to the child." This mother's love is stronger than Pharaoh's hate and fear, stronger than all of Pharaoh's armies. This love keeps the baby Moses safe, so that he can grow up and fulfill his role as the savior of his people.

Warwick Hutton's *Moses in the Bulrushes* (1999) also emphasizes the birth and youth of Moses (Hutton, 1992). Unlike Hayward's version though, Hutton introduces the idea of Pharaoh's evil ways right at the beginning, writing:

> The Pharaoh, king of Egypt, was alarmed. "Behold the people of Israel are more numerous and mightier than we are," he said. To reduce their numbers, he decreed that all boy babies born to Hebrew women must be killed.

There is no question as to what is the driving issue behind the story about to unfold in this retelling. There is also no question as to the identity of Moses and his family, who are identified right away as a "Hebrew" family. Here too mother-love is stressed. The illustrations show a mother in bed with her swaddled newborn, looking at him adoringly. This mother will do everything she can to save her child, first hiding him under the bed, and then carefully constructing an ark for him. When the ark is found by Pharaoh's daughter, she realizes immediately that this baby is a Hebrew child, which allows Moses' sister to reveal herself and offer to find a Hebrew nurse for the child. The issues behind this exchange, such as how she would have known he was a Hebrew child (was he circumcised in the Hebrew way?), and why he would have needed a nurse (because Pharaoh's daughter couldn't have breastfed him?) are left unexplained, as they are in all retellings for children. Instead, what is important here is that Moses' sister is able to get Pharaoh's daughter to hire Moses' own mother to be his nursemaid—a rather clever example of fancy footwork, good planning, and the triumph of familial love.

Hutton's book emphasizes not just mother-love but the importance of the whole family and the influence of being part of a people. In this version, Moses' life is saved first by his mother and then by Pharaoh's daughter, his substitute mother. But his identity is saved by his sister. Moses' mother now gets a chance to raise her own son without fear of harm coming to him, and Moses gets a chance to be raised within the bosom of his own family and people. Due to her quick thinking he can be raised within his family and people long enough to form an affiliation and attachment, so that by the time he goes back to live in Pharaoh's house he knows who he is and where his loyalty lies. Without that help from his sister, he might not have been able to assume his role as, in Hutton's words, "a man of God." This positive portrayal of a sibling relationship is yet another theme that emerges from the story of Moses' youth. This theme will be repeated again later, when it is only with his brother Aaron's help that Moses can fulfill his role as a leader. The book ends with a brief summary of Moses' later years, in which he grows up to see the persecution of the Hebrews and then lead his people out of Egypt at God's command.

In his 1946 book cited earlier, *How God Fix Jonah*, Lorenz Graham retells a selection of Bible stories from the oral tradition he first encountered as a missionary in Liberia in the 1920s. One whole chapter is devoted to the dramatic retelling of Moses' birth and his mother's plan to save him. In this narration, Graham explains that Pharaoh's reason for his murderous decree is his fear of the Hebrews growing too numerous and rising up to overthrow their slave masters, even as they are overcome by harsh working conditions. Pharaoh explains that the Hebrew mothers must kill their own baby boys, saying:

> . . . *The boy picans* [babies] *in every Hebrew house must die.*
> *The Hebrew mommies self must kill them*
> *Else soldiers go and break the house*
> *And kill all people in it.*
> *This be my law!*

Graham then asks, "You think so law can make a mommy kill she child?" Just because Pharaoh told them to do it doesn't mean they will, regardless of his power. The love of a mother is even more powerful than Pharaoh's laws. Twice in this narrative, Moses' mother exclaims, "Not nobody going kill my child." She also says, "Not no soldier going kill my child," and then as she hides him in the river grass, "Not nobody going kill my child." There is no clearer, more reassuring statement of a mother's selfless love for her child.

Moses' mother is representative of the all-giving mother often found in fairy tales whose existence revolves around satisfying her child's every wish—and no wish is greater than the wish to live. This image of the mother is separate from the dark aspect of the mother as witch. She never turns away from Moses, remaining all-giving, all-satisfying in emotional sustenance as well as nourishment, never taking part in what Yolen calls the "contrapuntal dance." Instead, Moses' conflict will develop later with his adopted father figure, Pharaoh, who, in contrast to his mother, wants Moses to be killed.

Pharaoh's wish to enslave the Israelites is explained in Miriam Chaikin's *Children's Bible Stories from Genesis to Daniel* as a result of his fear that they were growing too numerous. If they were made to work hard enough, they would not have the strength to have children. But even with all the hard work, the Israelites continue to have children, further angering Pharaoh. He comes up with a plan, ordering the midwives to kill newborn baby boys. However, they do not do so, telling

Pharaoh that the Hebrew women have children so quickly that the midwives don't even have time to arrive. This version makes the point that it is not only mothers who save babies, but that there are also other benevolent adults who are able to intervene and save children from evil. In retelling this story, Chaikin also addresses a question that begs to be asked: Why only the boy babies? "Now in those days sons were more highly prized than daughters. And the pharaoh said to the midwives, 'If you see a boy born, kill him. If it is a girl, let her live.'" This version raises uncomfortable ethnic and gender related issues. Chaikin does not sugarcoat what exists in the biblical text—that Pharaoh fears not just the Israelites but Israelite males in particular. This idea is often overlooked in retellings for children. But it underscores the tension that is to come between Moses and Pharaoh, which is not only hostility between two opposing peoples, but a classic story of conflict between a young man and his father-figure.

The story of Moses' childhood, as retold for children, is generally in stark contrast to the familiar fairy-tale depictions of family relationships. In "Hansel and Gretel," a parent willingly abandons his children at a time of crisis. Rapunzel's parents, albeit tearfully but without undue pressure, hand her over to the old crone with whom they have made a bargain, choosing to sacrifice their parental relationship. And the unnamed father in "Rumpelstilskin," for his own potential gain, cheerfully sends his daughter off to the castle to spin gold for the king all the while knowing she would surely be punished for her certain failure to please the king. In the retellings of this biblical story, however, children are given reassurance that their parents will go to any length necessary to protect them, something children universally want to hear.

The Leader of the Hebrews

> She took pity on it and said, "This must be a Hebrew child."
>
> (Exodus 2:6)

Leonard Everett Fisher's *Moses* (1995) begins with baby Moses being placed in the river by his mother and sister. But unlike the versions of this story cited above, Fisher focuses on Moses as the emblematic leader of a specific people. In giving the reason for Pharaoh's evil decree, he writes:

"These Israelites do not worship our gods, only their own god. And their numbers keep growing. This is not good," he told his court. "One day they will take this land and this throne. We must kill their newborn sons. Now!"

This explanation sets the stage for a battle that pits one people against another, one set of religious beliefs against another. This is not merely evil, but evil that is motivated by racial, ethnic, or religious differences.

These differences, and the problems that accompany them, are highlighted again when Pharaoh's daughter finds Moses. She tries to comfort the crying child, but cannot, saying that she is unable to nurse him, as it is "forbidden for us to nurse Israelite babies." This explanation is not found within the biblical text. Rather, the biblical narrative simply assumes that she is unable to nurse, without providing a reason: "When she opened it [the basket], she saw that it was a child, a boy crying. She took pity on it and said, 'This must be a Hebrew child.' Then his sister said to Pharaoh's daughter, 'Shall I go and get you a Hebrew nurse to suckle the child for you?'" (Exodus 2:6–7). The explanation provided by Fisher overlooks the simple biological presumption that, having not given birth, she was unable to produce any milk with which to nurse him. Instead, it emphasizes the ethnic/religious difference between Moses and his foster mother, and hints at how wide that gulf really is, despite the Princess' sincere willingness to take Moses in.

Whatever reason is supplied for why Pharaoh's daughter needs a wetnurse, the fact remains that this problem provides a way for Moses to be cared for by his biological mother. From her, he learns about the inherent dissimilarities between himself and his foster family. Fisher imagines Moses' mother reminding him who he is, and connecting him to his people and his God. She speaks to Moses of his family lineage so that he should never think he truly belongs in Pharaoh's house. Through her teachings, he is meant to see himself as an outsider. There is an important message for children here about being a minority. In these retellings, differences between people matter greatly, and knowing one's ethnic and/or religious identity is a critical piece of knowing oneself. The place where one belongs is with one's own family and by extension, one's own people.

A friendship between two boys, one a Hebrew boy named Aser, and one, Gamiel, an Egyptian, is imagined in Walter Dean Myers's "Aser and Gamiel," from *A Time to Love: Stories from the Old Testament*. The two boys are devoted best friends who don't let the divisions between the adults tear them apart. Gamiel had once saved Aser's life in a swimming accident, and now his parents consider Aser another son. Though these characters do not exist in the biblical text, they evoke for the reader Moses being saved from the water by Pharaoh's daughter, and how Moses grew up in Pharaoh's palace as a welcomed member of the family. Yet Myers repeatedly emphasizes the differences between them. One is enslaved and made to work hard, while the other is free to roam and play. The boys acknowledge that they are part of two separate peoples, and that Pharaoh's actions impact upon them differently. Yet Gamiel, like a typical child, naively maintains that the leader he believes in will turn out to be a good guy in the end, telling his friend: " 'Aser, Pharaoh is wise and knows what to do,' Gamiel said. 'He will free your people when the time comes. Believe me.' " Aser, however, has his own leader, Moshe (Hebrew for Moses), and it is in him that Aser puts his faith. Myers writes,

> But it was Moshe who led us, and whom I believed. Moshe—sometimes distant in his manner, sometimes strange in his speech, but always with a passion in his bosom that lifted and rose like the tide. When I heard Moshe speak, he was a raging sea, a flood. To imagine him standing up against the great god of Egypt filled my heart with pride.

Moses becomes the leader of his people not just because God has appointed him, but because he comes across as a leader to the people themselves. In Moshe, Aser has found a role model, a leader in whom he can believe. His youth may allow him to overcome what separates him from Gamiel, but he is not so naive as to believe that Pharaoh will help his people. He knows in his heart that he and Gamiel are different. Like Moses in some of the retellings, he knows that he does not truly belong in Egypt and that he will not ultimately be protected by Pharaoh. At the same time, by showing Gamiel as a sympathetic character, Myers adds a nuance absent from the biblical story that may be reassuring to the contemporary child—not all Egyptians were bad, and genuine friendships across ethnic lines are possible. In creating these characters, Myers is able to show Moses from the perspective of a witness to the story, allowing the child reader an eye level view in as well.

The contrast between Moses' adoptive home and the family from which he came is emphasized in Brian Wildsmith's 1998 *Exodus*. Wildsmith depicts a Moses who is acutely aware, despite his upbringing in Pharaoh's house, that it is not truly his home. Like Myers's Aser, he knows that his allegiance is ultimately to a different people. Wildsmith writes:

> Moses grew up as an Egyptian prince, surrounded by the riches of Egypt. But he never forgot that he was a Hebrew, and he hated the cruel way his people were treated. One day he saw an Egyptian guard whipping a Hebrew slave. Moses was so angry that he leaped at the guard and killed him with his bare hands.

The intricately detailed illustrations show an even deeper contrast between the riches and excesses of Pharaoh, and the hordes of oppressed Hebrew slaves who worked tirelessly to support Pharaoh's building projects. Against this backdrop Moses stands out, dressed in Egyptian finery but aligning himself with the slave being beaten.

Brad Kessler's *Moses in Egypt* (1997) is focused primarily on the themes of slavery and freedom and thus, much is left out about Moses' early years and his connection to his people. No mention is made in this version about Moses being nursed and spending his early years

Adam and Eve. From *Children's Bible Stories from Genesis to Daniel,* retold by
Miriam Chaikin, pictures by Yvonne Gilbert (1993), Dial Books for Young Readers.

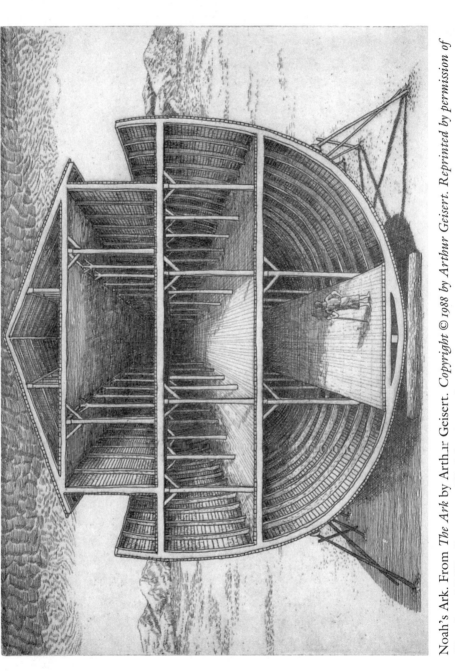

Noah's Ark. From *The Ark* by Arthur Geisert. Copyright © 1988 by Arthur Geisert. Reprinted by permission of Houghton Mifflin Company. All rights reserved.

Noah's Ark. From *Noah's Ark*, adapted by Heinz Janisch, illustrated by Lisbeth Zwerger. *Copyright © 1997 Nord-Süd Verlag AG, Gossau Zürich, Switzerland. Used with permission of North-South Books.*

Jonah. From *How God Fix Jonah* by Lorenz Graham, illustrated by Ashley Bryan. *Copyright © 1946, 1974 by Lorenz Graham; Revised edition copyright © 2000 by Ruth Graham Siegrist; Illustrations copyright © 2000 by Ashley Bryan. Published by Caroline House, Boyds Mills Press Inc. Reprinted by permission.*

David and Goliath. From *How God Fix Jonah* by Lorenz Graham, illustrated by Ashley Bryan. *Copyright © 1946, 1974 by Lorenz Graham; Revised edition copyright © 2000 by Ruth Graham Siegrist; Illustrations copyright © 2000
by Ashley Bryan. Published by Caroline House, Boyds Mills Press Inc.
Reprinted by permission.*

When Goliath saw David he burst out laughing. "Isra-elites! You insult me," he bellowed. "You have sent a boy to fight a man. His flesh and bones will feed birds and beasts."

David and Goliath. From *David and Goliath*, adapted from the Bible and illustrated by Leonard Everett Fisher. *Courtesy of Holiday House.*

Joseph. From *Joseph and His Magnificent Coat of Many Colors* by Marcia Williams. *Copyright © 1990 Marcia Williams. Reproduced by permission of the publisher Candlewick Press, Inc., Cambridge, MA., on behalf of Walker Books Ltd., London.*

"Tonight, the eldest son of each family in the land will die . . . ."
From Exodus, *Written and Illustrated by Brian Wildsmith*
Copyright 1998 Published by Eerdmans Publishing Company (800)
253-7521 www.eerdmans.com/youngreaders. Used by permission, all
rights reserved.

within the community of his birth. Instead, Kessler adds details that emphasize the luxury in which Moses was raised in his adopted home:

> . . . Moses grew up in Pharaoh's court surrounded by silk and sandal-wood and roasts of meat and fine spices from the four corners of the land. He grew strong and tall and his tutors taught him to read and write and his bearers bathed him in lavender and rose water.

One day, when Moses is walking in the area where the Israelites are being made to toil, he "saw his people, their mud-stained bodies bent and twisted from the weight of their bondage . . ." The question is raised then in this retelling, how did Moses know these were his people, and what was his connection to them? When Moses sees the slavemaster beating the Israelite, Kessler writes that "he could bear the injustice no longer." The impression then is that Moses is motivated not by impulse, and not even so much by connection to his people, but rather by the basic injustice of what he has witnessed. What is at issue in this version is the universal injustice of the whole system of slavery, as well as the necessity of responding to injustice by being more than merely a passive witness. How can someone live in luxury and enjoy freedom when others are enslaved and suffering? How can anyone witness cruelty and injustice and not intervene? That Moses reacts as he does shows him to be a young man who cares deeply about justice, a man therefore well suited to help the slaves achieve the freedom they so desperately desire.

Moses was a young man when this event occurred, poised between adolescence and adulthood. He is old enough to make his own choices, and yet young enough to still be unencumbered by adult responsibilities. His behavior in this incident, though extreme, is consistent with the observations of child development research regarding the development of a sense of morality and justice in adolescents. Piaget argues that a sense of moral judgment develops as the child matures. In adolescence, young people begin to be able to see beyond a rule-bound morality that allows for no exception. They move from an adult-imposed set of rules to an emergent concept of morality based on the ability to make mature judgments and to empathize with the experiences of others. The concept of slavery is thus an anathema to Moses, repugnant and morally unjustifiable in every sense.

Lawrence Kohlberg, who continued to explore Piaget's theory about the development of morality in children and adolescents, notes that young children progress from a sense of obedience and punishment to a level of maturity that includes conforming to community-based behaviors designed to maintain law and order, and acknowledging the rights of others. This level of moral behavior, evident in late adolescence, is governed by individual conscience. Through Moses' response to the overseer's beating of the Hebrew slave, young readers are introduced to the concept of responding to events in terms of ethical principles rather than the rules of the governing group. The imperatives of the universally acknowledged "higher authority," which include the ideals of respect for others and the equality of all humanity, are exemplified in this example of Moses' act of courage and leadership. The story of Moses therefore stands out as an example of ethical behavior for children.

When he then sees the Hebrew slave being mercilessly beaten, Moses responds age-appropriately to the injustice he has witnessed. He is able, at that age, to identify with the slave and assume his point of view, while intuitively becoming aware of his relationship within his own family, his adopted royal family, and the Hebrew community of which he knows he is a member. At that moment, as each retelling shows, Moses makes an irrevocable choice regarding the community to which he belongs. Joseph Campbell writes that "the passage of the threshold is a form of self-annihilation" (p. 91). When Moses responds to the beating of the Hebrew slave, he passes over the threshold. He can never again return to his former state of innocence, protection, and privilege, enjoying the luxuries of Pharaoh's household. By making the choice of identifying with the slave and not with the power of the taskmaster, he has made his first step into independent selfhood, identifying himself as other than the family in which he was raised, and doing away with his former identity as the adopted son of Pharaoh's household. As Campbell writes, "For the mythological hero is the champion not of things become but of things becoming; the dragon to be slain by him is precisely the monster of the status quo" (p. 337). In killing the taskmaster, he kills his former self. Things are now going to change dramatically for Moses. He has taken a step that permanently alters what will be written in the next chapter in his life. Though he is not yet a leader, he has made his first move toward leadership.

The establishment of identity is cited by Erik Erikson as the significant achievement of adolescence. Moses is surely attached to members of the royal household who have raised him in love, but he is just as surely attached to his natural mother who has also had a hand in raising him. By striking the guard, he immediately acknowledges his cultural identity with the Hebrew slaves and rejects his upbringing as the adopted son of Pharaoh. In each of these retellings, readers see Moses align himself through this act as a member of a specific group and community as well as an individual.

The act of slaying the guard brings Moses' dilemma of cultural identity into sharp focus. A hallmark of contemporary childhood is the struggle over whether it is going to be parent or society that exerts the greater influence on children. Moses' conflict is therefore familiar to today's children, exposed as they are to an ongoing battery of often contradictory influences from home, school, and the media. With so many competing influences and choices, children today, like Moses, have to make difficult choices about their identity in order to achieve their potential and become the heroes of their own life journeys. Until Moses is able to secure his identity, he is not able to set out on the road that will lead him to his hero-journey and his future as a leader of his people.

Moses the Reluctant Leader

> But Moses said to the Lord, "Please, O Lord, I have never been a man of words, either in times past or now that You have spoken to Your servant; I am slow of speech and slow of tongue.
>
> (Exodus 4:10)

Children are often asked to do something that they are not comfortable doing, from writing answers on a blackboard, to reading out loud, to singing solo in music class. The feeling of "why me?" and of not being up to the task is one to which most children can relate. In

Chaikin's *Exodus,* when Moses encounters God at the Burning Bush, Moses asks: "Who am I, that I should speak to the pharaoh? . . . And who am I that the Israelites should obey me?" God tells Moses to cast his rod onto the ground, where it turns into a serpent. Even after turning the serpent back into a rod again, Moses is still not convinced, and continues to argue with God, saying that he is "slow of tongue." This whole dialogue from Exodus 4:6–17 is recounted faithfully by Chaikin, without any elaboration to further explain Moses' diffidence. Moses has been presented with, in Joseph Campbell's words, his "hero-task" (p. 31). Like many heroes in fairy tales and mythology, he has a "symbolical deficiency," which could theoretically render him incapable of fulfilling his task. For King Arthur it is his lack of strength, for Jack of beanstalk fame it is his naiveté, for the young David it is his size, and for Moses it is his speech. While God may know that Moses is ready for the task, Moses himself is not sure at all.

Fisher (1995) gives additional details for Moses' hesitation, citing first his age, and asking God for proof through a sign. Fisher emphasizes this sense of doubt, allowing Moses to be less than a perfect model of faith and belief. Just like contemporary children who read Bible stories and ask for proof that it's true, Moses needs to have tangible proof of God to show the people. Interestingly, Fisher also allows for God to be less than perfect. After Moses continues to protest, citing his stutter, Fisher writes: "God grew impatient with Moses' excuses." The image of Moses presented here is that of someone who will not blindly do what God asks of him, and who has a close enough relationship with God that he can have an impact on God. This kind of relationship is in keeping with Moses' ongoing developmental process. Scholars of child development note that it is typical for young adults to come to see their parents and other authority figures in the community as distinct from themselves, and having now developed their own moral judgments and standards, no longer need those figures to be perfect. Moses has reached the developmental level at which he can begin to use his own judgment, and can form a new kind of relationship with God that would not have been possible when he was younger. The relationship, as portrayed in Fisher's retelling, is not one of absolute obedience, but rather more one of partnership, albeit not between equals. The implication is that complying with the demands of an authority figure can be an opportunity for dialogue rather than just a time for submission to the will of another.

Kessler's Moses is more humble. When he hears the voice from the bush, he says, "Who am I . . . that I should challenge Pharaoh and lead the Israelites out of Egypt." Whereas in the biblical text God answers Moses' concern about his stuttering by telling him that his brother Aaron will help him, Kessler takes God's answer in another direction. "Who makes a person swift or slow in speech, Moses? Is it not I, the Lord? I will be your eloquence." This is a fitting response for a book that highlights the aspect of the story connected to slavery and freedom. Freedom will ultimately be achieved not through the help or intervention of another person, but through the help of God. Similarly then, it will be God who helps Moses speak and lead the people.

This retelling presents a truncated version of the entire incident at the Burning Bush. Moses' reluctance is omitted, so that unlike Fisher's version the story becomes one of immediate obedience. God speaks out of the flames to Moses and tells him to go back to Egypt. Then God speaks to Aaron, telling him to go meet Moses, who will be arriving shortly. Aaron does so, and the two brothers set off for Pharaoh's court. An entirely different picture of Moses emerges, in which he appears much more obedient than in versions in which he is reluctant or even argumentative with God.

In Lorenz Graham's *How God Fix Jonah*, God is firmly at the helm, directing the action. God chooses Moses and instructs him to go to Pharaoh, saying:

> *Moses,*
> *You the one*
> *To go fore Old King Paraoh.*
> *You the one to carry him My Word.*
> *Tell King Paraoh that I say*
> *"Let My people go!"*
> *Tell him,*
> *"Let My people go!"*

Though his side of the discussion is absent here, the text conveys a sense of Moses' reluctance to cast himself as the savior of his people. At this point he is not yet a leader, but only a leader in formation. Mindful of his hesitance, God reassures him that he is "the one." When Moses goes back to Egypt, the people are willing to follow Moses to freedom. Yet later, they come to protest his leadership, saying:

> *Who be this man Moses?*
> *What he think he be?*
> *We no be in Egypt land*
> *And he no be we master.*

Having just left the shackles of Egyptian slavery behind, the people are neither ready nor willing to be told what to do by anyone. And Moses himself, despite his bold defense of the Hebrew slave, is still only in the process of becoming a leader. But God commands Moses repeatedly to assert himself and continue to lead his people. God explains the Hebrews' reluctance, saying:

> *Moses, hear My Word.*
> *Them people savvy nothing*
> *They be slaves too long*
> *So hear Me good:*
> *Call you brother Aaron*
> *Let Aaron lead the people*
> *While you come set down by My hand*
> *And I make law.*

In this version God teaches Moses that different kinds of leaders can reach the people in different ways, that there is no one way to be a leader. There are certain skills that Aaron can bring to the task, different from those of Moses. Moses becomes a hero not only by leading the slaves out of Egypt, but by learning how to delegate responsibility and share leadership. And when Aaron's leadership results in the creation of the golden calf, Moses is able to use his particular set of leadership skills to successfully intercede before God on behalf of his people, pleading with God to forgive them.

Though some of these retellings mention Moses' claim that he should not be the one to speak to Pharaoh due to his speech problem, none of them focuses specifically on this. Moses is one of the few biblical leaders reported to have a disability. What it is exactly is not clear from the biblical text. "I am slow of speech and slow of tongue," says Moses (Exodus 4:10). Is this simply a lack of self-confidence? Is this a language problem, in which Moses, the product of two cultures, can speak the language of neither one well? Or does Moses have a real disability, like a stutter? The text does not elaborate. The rabbis of the Midrash create a story to explain Moses' speech problem, imaging that he put hot coal in his mouth as a baby and thereby damaged his ability to speak properly.[8] This is, however, just legend, an example of a gap in the story filled in through the imagination of its readers.

Despite Moses' perception that he does not have what it takes to do what God asks of him, with the help of both God and his brother Aaron he is able to overcome his disability and become a great leader. How often do children feel that they are not up to the task before them? Whether it is simply a matter of self-confidence, size, or an actual physical disability, children face stumbling blocks and the fear of embarrassment all the time. How reassuring it can be to see Moses as a model of a man who succeeded, in spite of his own doubts and disability.

Moses as a Human Being

> As soon as Moses came near the camp and saw the calf and the dancing, he became enraged; and he hurled the tablets from his hands and shattered them at the foot of the mountain.
>
> (Exodus 32:19)

A note at the beginning of *Exodus* (Chaikin and Mikolaycak) states that "The author consulted the *King James Version of the Bible,* the

---

[8] Exodus Rabbah 1:26

Revised Standard Version, the *Bible of the Jewish Publication Society, The New American Bible,* and other English translations." In her re-telling of the Moses story, Chaikin is concerned with creating an accurate retelling of the biblical text that remains faithful to the source. At the same time the earthy, highly expressive illustrations by Charles Mikolaycak provide their own form of commentary. There is a marked contrast between the finely detailed gold and jewels of the Egyptians, and the coarse, simple textiles worn by the Israelites. By both the expressions on his face and his muscular physique, Moses is shown here to be a determined, strong young man.

Campbell writes that the "adventure of the hero normally follows the pattern of . . . a separation from the world, a penetration to some source of power, and a life-enhancing return" (p. 35). Moses' experience on Sinai fits this pattern well. He has separated himself from the community, gone up to Sinai where he has encountered God beyond the experience of any other human, and has returned with the Tablets of the Law to share with his people. These tablets represent what Campbell calls the "life-transmuting trophy" of Moses' hero-quest, the object that is supposed to have been the goal of all his trials. Imagine, then, his frustration at being greeted with the sight of the people worshiping the golden calf that they have created in his absence. It is clear at that moment that his quest is far from over, that there are many more trials still ahead. He may be a hero, but he still has his own negative and positive qualities, his own human hopes, aspirations, and disappointments.

Moses' moments of doubt, anger, and impatience have a prominent place in Chaikin's work, just as in the Bible itself. When the people rebel and complain about the lack of water, Moses cries out to God, saying, "What shall I do with this people?" Later, when Moses comes down from the mountain and sees that the people have created a golden calf, he cries out in anger and throws down the tablets, breaking them (Exodus 32:19). But in a sign of his increasing maturity and wisdom, when the moment has passed Moses is able to reflect on what has happened and find a better solution (Exodus 32:30–32). Chaikin writes, "When his anger had cooled, he returned to the mount to ask

God to forgive the people." Though Chaikin's order of events does not exactly parallel those within the biblical text itself, she has created an image of Moses as a strong-willed man who tries his best. Although he does at times act impulsively in anger, he is also able to calm down and act with the compassion of a true leader.

Fisher's Moses (1995) is a man with a temper. When Moses sees an Egyptian slavemaster beating an Israelite, he kills the slavemaster "on the spot." In Midian, when Moses comes to a well and sees some shepherds mistreating a group of sisters, "Moses was so angry, he drove the shepherds off." A picture emerges of Moses as an impetuous, impulsive man, one who tends to act before he thinks. These are not generally thought of as the qualities found in a great leader, the image of which summons instead the ideals of wisdom, thoughtfulness, righteousness, and strategic thinking. Instead, Fisher's portrait of Moses is of a man in process, someone who still has some maturing to do and some work required on his flaws. At the same time, these glimpses also show him to be a compassionate man with a strong sense of justice. In both of these examples, his acting hastily in anger was on behalf of other, weaker people. Though impulsiveness is not a typical characteristic of a leader, coming to the defense of those in need certainly is.

When Fisher depicts Moses standing in front of the burning bush on the very next page, it is clear that some time has passed. Moses is now portrayed as an older man. Fisher writes that he was forty at the time that he killed the slavemaster and fled Egypt. When he encounters the burning bush in this retelling he is eighty years old. Moses asks God, "Why have you picked me?" He continues detailing all the reasons that he is not the right person for this job. But Fisher highlights the difference in Moses' age between these two incidents, details not found in the biblical text, to show that Moses has matured, that he is now ready for his encounter with God, ready to assume the mantle of leadership that God is demanding of him.

And yet, even as Moses continues to age in the striking and evocative illustrations, he remains a human being, and as such, never achieves perfection. When the people complain to him about their hardships in the desert, his complaint to God, "What should I do with these people?"(Exodus 17:4), reveals both his frustration and his impatience. When Moses comes down from the mountain with the two Tablets of the Law and finds the people worshiping a golden calf, he is "outraged" and smashes the tablets (Exodus 32:19). This is not simply more evidence of Moses' temper though, as Fisher connects Moses' reaction to God's expression of anger as in Exodus 32:9. Moses' rage then is only an echo of God's, and is clearly the right response to the behavior of the people. And Moses' sense of compassion and justice plays a role here too, as he pleads with God to forgive the people. A fuller, more multidimensional picture begins to emerge in this retelling of Moses as the fitting human partner for a God who can also be temperamental. When God begins to lose patience with the people, it is Moses who now intervenes to calm God down, again pleading with God to forgive them.

Fisher has chosen to include in his book an episode that has confounded sages and scholars for generations, the story of the striking of the rock at Kadesh from Exodus 20. This story is used to explain why God does not let Moses live to step foot in the Promised Land but must be buried outside it. Yet, it is not entirely clear from a literal reading of the biblical text what Moses has done wrong. Is it that he is doubting God? Is it that he speaks disrespectfully to the people? Is it that he uses physical force when he should have used words? Is it that he acts in anger? Fisher writes:

> God told Moses to speak to a rocky cliff and water would come out.
>
> Moses doubted that water could be had from the dry, stony wall of a cliff. He shouted to the Israelites, "Here now, you rebels, are we to bring forth water out of this cliff?" Whereupon, instead of speaking to the rocky cliff as God had commanded, Moses rapped it twice with his staff. Water poured out. God did not think that Moses should have shown such little faith.
>
> He said to both Moses and Aaron: "Because ye believed not in Me, therefore ye shall not bring this assembly into the land which I have given them."

Thus, Moses and Aaron could never set foot in the Promised Land.

Fisher uses both the incident and God's reaction to it to further underscore Moses' humanity. Even with his unique relationship to God and his role as the leader of the Israelites, he was still only a human, prone to mistakes. Fisher further uses this episode to show that in the end it is both Moses' doubt in God and his temper that are his undoing. Fisher's inclusion and interpretation of this incident imply that there are always consequences to actions; even the great Moses could not escape the consequences of what he did. At the very end of his life, Moses tries to renegotiate with God, hoping that after all he will be allowed to enter the Promised Land. But like a firm and consistent parent, God refuses to give in (Deuteronomy 3:26). As Fisher writes, "It was not to be." God only allows Moses to see the Land from afar.

In contrast, Wildsmith (1998) includes instead a different biblical story about Moses obtaining water for the people. In this version, from Exodus 17:1–7, a calmer, less-conflicted Moses is depicted, and the relationship between Moses and the people is less contentious. When the people complain to Moses about food, God rains down manna and quails. When they complain about the lack of water, God tells Moses to strike the rock to get water. There is no evidence of anger or frustration on the part of Moses, only on the part of the people. In this story of striking the rock, there is no sense that this is a turning point for Moses or a significant moment in his relationship with God. The story that Wildsmith has chosen to recount is a simpler, softer story than that told by Fisher. Wildsmith writes:

> As the Hebrews went deeper into the desert, the sun beat down on them, and there was no water. They began to quarrel with Moses. "We should have stayed in Egypt!" they cried. "We will all die of thirst here." God told Moses to strike the rock with his staff. Suddenly fresh water gushed out, and they all had enough to drink.

The art that accompanies this text shows a pleasant, pastoral scene, with Moses releasing water from the rock and goats happily drinking against the backdrop of a clear, blue sky. Wildsmith does indicate at the end of the book that Moses is allowed to see the Promised Land but not to enter. It is not mentioned though that this was a punishment for his earlier behavior. The only time that Moses' anger surfaces in Wildsmith's telling is when Moses comes down from the mountain with the tablets and sees that the people are worshiping a golden calf. Also in this retelling, there is no mention that God's forgiveness of the people was motivated by Moses' intercession on their behalf. Wildsmith's Moses is thus presented as a less fully developed character than in some of the other versions. By not allowing him to express the full range of emotions that come through in the biblical text, Wildsmith also does not allow for Moses to grow and learn from his experiences.

A Story of Slavery and Freedom

> Now the cry of the Israelites has reached Me; moreover, I have seen how the Egyptians oppress them.
> Come, therefore, I will send you to Pharaoh, and you shall free My people, the Israelites, from Egypt.

(Exodus 3:9–10)

The story of Moses and the enslavement of the Hebrew people has resonated eloquently throughout African American literature and music. The story has served as a beacon around which African American slaves have rallied, giving hope and encouragement to an enslaved people. This connection is reflected in particular in the music of the slave experience, the spiritual. Spirituals were first sung by evangelical Protestant choirs in the northeast but soon were adopted by slaves in the south who heard them at camp revival meetings. They spoke directly to the experience of a people held in bondage, longing for liberation. Spirituals have a strong emotional content and powerful energetic rhythm. They are often accompanied by rhythmic clapping of hands, making it easy for slaves and newly emancipated blacks, who often could not read, to remember the words without printed lyrics or songsheets. Sung with great emotional feeling, spirituals are based on characters and events from the Old Testament. The most popular of all spirituals is the song "Go Down, Moses":

> When Israel was in Egypt's land,
> Let my people go!
> Oppressed so hard they could not stand,
> Let my people go!
> *Chorus:*
> *Go down, Moses,*
> *Way down in Egypt's land*
> *Tell old Pharaoh*
> *To let my people go!*

This spiritual, and others like it such as "Deep River" and "Swing Low Sweet Chariot," show great faith in liberation from their oppressive bondage by a leader arising from the slave population. American slaves identified with the ancient Hebrews and their abiding faith that God watched over them in their struggle to be free, as recounted in many Old Testament stories. The power of spirituals such as "Go Down, Moses" is so strong that these songs are recognized worldwide as a uniquely American music form that expresses the hope for freedom from slavery for all people through stories of well-known heroes.

Let My People Go: Bible Stories Told By a Freeman of Color by the McKissacks uses the line from the spiritual "Go Down, Moses" as the title of their collection. These stories are intended to inspire hope and determination, despite the harsh circumstances of slavery. They also emphasize the slaves' belief that one day God would send a hero to lead them out of bondage. The stories are recounted as first-person narratives set in the context of a confrontation between Price Jefferies, a former slave, and people and events in pre–Civil War Charleston. Jefferies uses each incident to illustrate for his daughter the parallels between the suffering of the Hebrews in biblical times and the suffering of the pre–Civil War American slaves. As the Hebrews eventually won their freedom, so will the slaves.

Jefferies tells his former slave master that one day slavery will end, and that all slaves will be free with or without his help. When Jefferies' daughter asks him how he can be so sure of this, he replies: " 'Cause God created all people free and equal. Slavery's wrong,' he answered. 'And God will not hold with wrong, never mind how right folks think they be.' " In additional support of his belief, Jefferies responds that it is all foretold in the biblical story of Moses. This provides the setting for telling the story of Exodus, during which the parallels in the two peoples' stories are pointed out. In showing readers that righteous be- havior is always expected of people, at all times, in all circumstances, Jefferies carefully explains to his young daughter how it is possible to find courage and strength in adversity. His careful depiction of Moses as a man who is unsure of his ability to lead his people out of slavery and who frequently questions God helps young readers know it is all right to proceed cautiously, but always to put forth one's best possible effort in proceeding toward the righteous and moral way.

In his own words, Jefferies explains to his daughter the Hebrews' response when Pharaoh's chariots followed them to the Red Sea:

> "I wasn't there, but I imagine that it was a scary sight: all the might of Egypt comin' after them, and comin' fast. The people were terrified. "Look what you're done to us, Moses!" they shouted, "We should have stayed slaves in Egypt rather than die like this."
>
> "You will not die," said Moses calmly. "Don't fret. The Lord has and always will provide for and protect us."

He goes on to tell her that God will not stand for evil and misconduct no matter how long it takes to correct the evil: ". . . in the end the power of the Lord will bring things to right side up. That was the hard lesson Pharaoh had to learn." The parallels with American slavery could not be more clear. The story ends with Jefferies telling his daughter what is the most important part of the story for him: that people will be free when they are able to claim their freedom not only over their bodies, but just as importantly over their minds and souls. This is what it is to be truly free and what God intends for all people.

The subtitle of *Moses in Egypt,* written by Brad Kessler and illustrated by Phil Hunting, is "Liberation from Slavery." In this retelling of the biblical Moses narratives, the focus is the attainment of freedom by a subjugated people led by a man named Moses. When the people cry out to God, they "prayed for a liberator who would lead them out of Egypt." This retelling is a story about slavery and freedom. The muted, textured illustrations portray a people pushed beyond any normal human limit, bound with actual chains and crying out in their misery. This is another example of how the slavery of the Israelites and their subsequent liberation through the intervention of Moses was often used by slaves in the United States as a metaphor for their actual lives. Kessler's book, which includes a CD of the actor Danny Glover reading the story and The Sounds of Blackness singing songs such as "Go Down, Moses" and "Free at Last" is part of that tradition.

This oppressed people get their liberator in Moses. When Moses encounters God at the burning bush and argues that he is not the right person to be sent to Pharaoh, God answers: "It is you, Moses, whom I shall send to Pharaoh as my messenger; you who shall lead the Israelites as liberator out of Egypt." Although the biblical text stresses that Moses is simply the agent of God in effecting liberation, Kessler's version of the story puts the responsibility for liberation squarely on the shoulders of Moses himself.

Moses in Egypt ends as the Israelites make their way out of Egypt. They "cast off their shackles and set forth" into freedom. Much still lies ahead, for they have not yet even crossed the Red Sea, but they are free. Kessler ends his story with these words:

> Little did they know what hardships lay ahead, or how long it would take to get to the land promised them. But for a brief moment that day, it did not matter. They drank the cool draught of freedom; they inhaled the sweet smell, the succulent foretaste of the Promised Land. And on their tongues it tasted, that morning, of milk and honey.

By ending the story here, Kessler keeps the focus squarely on his central theme of slavery versus freedom. Slavery is painful but freedom has its own hardships, too. There are choices to be made and responsibilities to be met. Nevertheless, the ecstasy of the newly freed people is made palpable by the language and the accompanying illustrations. The poetry of his language and the sensuality of his imagery make freedom something attainable, reviving, and utterly delicious. This is not a story about parents and children, the character development of an individual, or the forming of a nation. This is a story about the hopes of an enslaved people to one day be free. Because of one man who believed in justice and the intervention of God, this people was able to achieve its goal.

In Lorenz Graham's *How God Fix Jonah*, the dramatic retelling of Moses' birth and the Exodus are tales of compassion for an enslaved people infused with solemn dignity, despite the circumstances of their enslavement. He emphasizes the emotional strength of the Hebrew slaves when he writes:

> *King Paraoh make hard law for slaves*
> *But they still be strong.*
> *The masters make the Hebrews work too much*
> *But picans* [babies] *keep on borning.*

As Graham proceeds with the retelling he too echoes the language of "Go Down, Moses," when God responds to the Hebrews' plea, "How long, O God, How long?"

Wildsmith also ends his book with the idea of freedom. He writes, "After all their wanderings and struggles, they were a free people at last. They had finally come home." This freedom happens not in the wilderness, immediately after having left Egypt, as it does in Kessler's version. Instead, this is a freedom earned not only by the exodus from Egypt, but also by the hard years that followed in the desert. It is only upon entering their Promised Land and establishing a home that they can truly be a free people.

There is a completely different version of freedom depicted in Lisbeth Zwerger's *Stories from the Bible,* based on extracts from the King

James Version. To accompany the section of text entitled "The Pharaoh Lets the Israelites Go," she provides an illustration of an Israelite on his way out of Egypt. This bearded Israelite is a modern-looking man, dressed in typical Western style, wearing a brown overcoat, trousers, and black shoes. In one hand, he carries a baby, in his other hand is an old-fashioned suitcase, and on his back is slung another piece of luggage. His eyes are downcast and his back is bent under his burden. Zwerger's unusual depiction calls to mind the countless refugees of twentieth century Europe, people made to cross borders and change nationalities in the pursuit of safety and peace. While she uses a standard English language text of the Bible, her illustration makes another point altogether, reminding readers that the struggle for freedom is not just an issue of the past but is still very much part of the modern human condition.

The Killing of the First-Born

> *Thus says the Lord: Toward midnight I will go forth from among the Egyptians, and every first-born in the land of Egypt shall die, from the first-born of Pharaoh who sits on his throne to the first-born of the slave girl who is behind the millstones; and all the first-born of the cattle.*

(Exodus 11:4–5)

As discussed above, one of the most difficult aspects of the Moses story is that it involves both a baby condemned to death by an adult who is himself a father, and the killing of children by the decree of God. How can either of these aspects of the story be told appropriately for children? Yet, how can they be skipped altogether without having the story lose its power?

There are many myths, folk, and fairy tales, in which children are to be killed by evil forces such as witches, demons, fairies, stepparents, and even parents. Stories like "Sleeping Beauty," "Snow White," "Hansel and Gretel," and "Little Red Riding Hood" are just some examples. As Bettelheim notes, the mother gives birth to the child, nurses him, and is involved in all aspects of his life. On the other hand, the father traditionally is out of the house working and involved in important societal affairs rather than child-rearing. The nurturing parent with whom the child bonds and learns from is therefore most often the mother. The child's relationship with his or her mother determines whether his or her view of the world will be trusting or suspicious.

In fairy tales, the mother figure is often split into two: the good mother and the evil stepmother/witch. Bettelheim argues that splitting the mother into these two figures is not only a literary device but also a psychological survival tactic. The good mother allows the child to develop a sense of basic trust and a positive attitude toward the world, while the evil mother allows the child a way to make sense of the aspects of the mother that the child finds objectionable. Instead of having to reconcile diverse aspects of one person, by creating this fantasy division the child is able to attribute the different sides to actual different people (p. 67–69). But as a child matures, in order to become a fully integrated adult, the child should be able to become emotionally secure enough to heal the rift and come to accept that the mother is not all good, and that it is occasionally all right to get angry or frustrated at the mother without risking her love.

From the day he is born, Moses is exposed to two opposing cultures—one vowing to kill him, and his own people eager to see him reach manhood. As in the fairy-tale paradigm, he comes to have two mothers, his biological mother and his stepmother, each representing one of his two cultures. Both Bettelheim and Erikson relate how this dichotomy thwarts Moses from developing a mature, integrated personality, as seen in many of the descriptions of Moses as self-effacing, unsure of himself, stuttering, or slow of speech. Yet for Moses, his two mothers do not easily fit into the typical fairy-tale division of the good, protective mother and the evil, harmful mother. Both of his mothers save his life, each in her own way, and tacitly work as a team to do so. At no time in the biblical story or any of the retellings does a conflict develop between Moses' two mother figures, and in fact they work together for his benefit. Rather, it is Pharaoh, Moses' father figure, who fills the dualistic role often given to mothers in fairy tales.

Pharaoh's daughter simply wants a baby, and knows at once that the baby she has found is a Hebrew baby condemned to death by her father. Nothing is written in the biblical text about Pharaoh's reaction to his daughter's new baby. All that is mentioned in the text itself is that Moses is taken in by Pharaoh's daughter, nursed by his own mother, and is assumed to be a member of Pharaoh's household until he flees after striking the slavemaster. The void in the text allows for the creation of imaginary scenarios regarding Pharaoh's acceptance of his daughter's wishes and each reteller handles the details differently. The overriding sense in the versions for children is that Pharaoh, perhaps ambivalent at first but wanting to please his daughter, benevolently treats Moses as a son while knowing that Moses is a Hebrew child condemned, like all Hebrew–boy children, to death. This would have likely created tremendous conflict in Moses: his life has been spared by the very person who has ordered all other Hebrew boys to be slain.

In contrast to his perilous beginnings, Moses' boyhood is by extension steeped in the luxury of palace life, fulfilling every child's fantasy of having whatever he or she could desire. But, of course, something is not quite right with this seemingly happy picture. What kind of father figure is Pharaoh really? Twice Pharaoh has condemned Moses to death, first at his birth, saving his life only to make his daughter happy, and later for slaying his overseer. Looking at "Hansel and Gretel," for example, shows readers a similar father image; twice the father leads his children into the woods in hope of their not returning. Until Moses asserts his independence and leaves Pharaoh's house for good, whether he will live or die is in Pharaoh's hands.

The eternal conflict between fathers and their sons is another common fairy-tale theme. Bettelheim writes that many fairy tales and legends about boys have a similar plot of a little boy, ordinary and unremarkable, who grows up, goes out to make his way in the world, and becomes a great hero. In fairy tales and quest stories the plots are similar: dragons and giants are slain, great problems are solved and the hero comes to accept his own leadership and skills. Right before "happily ever after" the boy receives his ultimate prize, the beautiful princess's hand in marriage, his royal heritage is revealed, and he claims the kingdom. "No little boy has ever failed to see himself in this starring role," Bettelheim writes (p. 111).

A disciple of Freud, Otto Rank talks about the births of mythological heroes such as Oedipus and Hercules, as well as biblical heroes, including Moses and Jesus. Rank writes that the births of all these heroes follow a similar pattern, wherein the birth of a baby boy, often to a royal couple, involves difficult circumstances. A dream prophesizes the hero's birth and warns of danger to the father. The baby is either left to die or is cast out of the family, put in a basket and left floating in the water. The baby is then rescued and reared by a loving parent substitute, often of a lowly caste, until the time comes when he can learn the true circumstances of his birth. The hero then takes revenge on his father, generally slaying him, and is received as a hero among the people or the gods (Rank, p. 2–63).

The story of Moses closely illustrates Rank's theory about the birth and personality of the hero that he describes in *The Myth of the Birth of the Hero* (p. 13–15, 62). In the story of Moses, it is his adoptive father figure, Pharaoh, upon whom Moses takes his revenge and symbolically slays. According to Rank, this is a universal story of parent-and-child conflict, and the need to assert oneself. In childhood, parents, especially the father, are seen as faultless, whereas in adolescence their shortcomings become all too apparent. The story symbolizes the teenager's wish to return to the time when parents were accepted as perfect and all knowing. The hero's revenge releases him from the anger at what he perceives to have been his mistreatment and allows him to assume his rightful place of leadership in the community as a mature adult with a well-integrated personality.

In Bettelheim's reading of fairy tales, the dragon or giant slaying motif is a metaphor for a boy's jealous slaying of his father, having his mother to himself and living "happily ever after," as in Jack and the Beanstalk (p.111). In the epic story of Moses, the parallels with classic fairy tales occur on a grander scale. Moses, described in many of these stories as shy and quiet, strikes out at injustice, the horrific beating of a slave, and slays the overseer, a representative of Pharaoh who has reared him as his own son. Many questions are raised here: is this a matter of retribution for Pharaoh's order to kill all first-born Hebrew boys, or is this the awakening of morality and a sense of justice on the part of Moses, foreshadowing his impending role as leader of his people and deliverer of God's commandments? Children may also wonder, upon hearing this story, about the death of Pharaoh's son as a result of Moses' invoking the tenth plague.

In *Moses in Egypt,* what finally moves Pharaoh to give the people their freedom is the death of his own son. Kessler writes: "And when he saw that his own son was dead, he too became undone and his hard heart was pierced at last." In Wildsmith's *Exodus* there is also a great sense of anguish over what has come to pass. Wildsmith describes the scene from the point of view of the Egyptian people as a whole, writing, "A great cry rose up from Egyptians, a cry of grief for their dead sons." The artwork also focuses on generalized grief, rather than the personal grief of Pharaoh, showing a partly mummified body laid out on a bed with women grieving and crying over it. It is only in the face of these deaths and the ensuing sorrow that Pharaoh calls Moses and Aaron to him and tells them to leave before more lives are lost.

One issue highlighted by this plague is what it must have been like for Moses, as a former member of Pharaoh's household, to know that people *he* knew were going to be killed by order of his God. Walter Dean Myers uses his characters Aser and Gamiel to imagine a possible allegorical scenario. Aser runs to tell his friend Gamiel about the tenth plague as soon as he hears about it. Gamiel quickly realizes what this means, as he himself is a firstborn. Aser then comes up with a plan to save Gamiel's life, which involves making his house look like a house of the Hebrews. And yet his plan does not work, because in the end, Gamiel cannot go against his father. The friendship and love between the boys is strong, but not strong enough to defy the wishes of a father or the command of God. Unlike Moses, Gamiel is unable to defy his father and save his own life. The lines have been drawn and the Hebrew boy and the Egyptian boy are on different sides, despite their friendship. Ultimately their familial and ethnic connections are stronger than their emotional bond, as it must have also been for

Moses. But Myers concludes the chapter with Aser acknowledging mixed feelings, as a child might imagine Moses had also done. He thanks God for the freedom given to his people and "for the promise of a new life" as he also thinks fondly of his friend Gamiel.

The same scene is told from a different perspective in Fisher's *Moses*. In this version, the main protagonist is God. Fisher writes:

> God lost patience with Pharaoh. Now He would slay every firstborn child and beast in Egypt, including the king's oldest son. . . . At midnight, God killed every firstborn Egyptian and Egyptian beast. Pharaoh was terrified. Now he begged the Israelites to leave, and they did.

Through this terrible act, Pharaoh has been humbled not by Moses but by God. Rather than ordering the Israelites to leave, in this version Pharaoh is "begging" them to go. It is significant that in Fisher's version the responsibility for this violence rests with God and not Moses. Against ultimate evil, only an act of ultimate horror has an effect. But it is not within Moses' human power to do such a thing. It can only be God who causes such a thing to happen. Similarly, in Chaikin's *Exodus*, when Pharaoh refuses to give in to Moses or acknowledge the power of his God after the ninth plague, God warns him of the tenth. But still Pharaoh does not listen, and God sends the tenth plague, the killing of the firstborn of the Egyptians and their cattle. Closely following the biblical text, Chaikin writes, "And the son of the pharaoh also died. A great cry went up in the land, the like of which was never heard before and will never be heard again." Mikolaycak's art offers a chilling depiction of what has happened, with an image of a limp body of a child held in Pharaoh's arms.

The art by Diana Mayo in Auld's *Exodus from Egypt* (2000) tends to be rather literal and illustrative. However, the spread that deals with the killing of the firstborn reveals a reluctance to depict what is going on in the text. Using details based on those provided in the biblical text, Auld writes:

> And at midnight on that day, God struck down all the firstborn sons of Egypt, from the firstborn of Pharaoh, who sat on the throne, to the

firstborn of the prisoner, who was in the dungeon. A loud cry rose up from the Egyptians, for there was not one house without someone dead.

Although Auld has added many details from the biblical text, the art that accompanies this section is strangely silent, not even abstract but simply absent. What Mayo has shown here is the fronts of houses, without any people, and with only the blood on the doorposts of the Israelites to hint at a connection to the text. It is as if a graphic depiction of the killing would be more difficult for children than a verbal description.

In all of these retellings, the thing that will most upset an adult, that will cause an adult to "come undone" and will most be able to pierce their hard shell of stubbornness or meanness is the death of their own children. This is a powerful message for children about their importance to their parents. Though parents can behave in ways that upset or even harm their children, this story suggests that in the end, parents always love their children.

The story of Moses is a tale about the birth of national identity, the bursting forth out of slavery and into peoplehood for the Hebrews. Out of these elements of the story comes the holiday of Passover and the resultant theological implications. At the same time, the story of Moses is also about a person born into a tragic situation who triumphs over adversity to lead his people into a better future. Along the way, the Moses narratives also recount a tale of a man struggling with his personal identity.

Moses' birth, his very entrance into the world, is itself problematic. His early years are full of oppression, death, and violence. He bears the burden of his troubling dual identity as a Hebrew growing up in Pharaoh's household. Moses' struggle to fit in and find his place, to define who and what he is and what really matters to him, is something children can relate to. The theme of power versus powerlessness is one that is all too familiar to children. While Moses' struggle with these issues takes place on a grander scale than most children's, it is a struggle with which they can identify. Who do they want to be? What identity is hiding inside themselves, waiting for the right opportunity to emerge? When are they going to get the call that will send them on their own life journey, searching for their true purpose?

This is also a story of parents and children. Though the brutality of his early years, as well as the subsequent horror of the killing of the firstborn, may be troubling to children, the fierce love of Moses' mother is in stark contrast to the violence running through this narrative. Mothers, whether biological or adoptive, are shown as being protectors of their children. The story also acknowledges that the parent-child relationship is complicated and fraught with the potential for difficulty, especially as the child matures. In keeping with established paradigms of identity development, as Moses gets older he must rebel against his father figure Pharaoh. By doing so, he is able to claim his identity and begin to make his own choices about right and wrong.

Justice is another important theme for children in this story. The idea of one person standing up for what he believes is right is exemplified here, an important message for children to hear. Moses models the idea that one person can make a difference when he takes a proactive position against violence and oppression, and stands up to the taskmaster beating the Hebrew slave. Significantly, Moses is not a superhero who arrives on the scene fully formed, but a mere mortal who is constantly evolving and continuing to learn. Like a child, his impulse to help is right, but his action of killing the taskmaster is not. He is a hero who is unfinished at that point in the story, a hero who still has a lot to learn before he can emerge as a true leader. That this process of learning and refinement must take place is a crucial important message for children to hear.

Moses emerges from his hero-journey as a leader, but one who continues to learn under the guidance of a higher authority for the rest of his life. He is never a model of blind obedience, as he constantly questions and even argues with God. But he is never completely free from the authority of another outside himself. As Moses comes into his own, he is expected to take greater responsibility for his actions, a lesson that he must transmit to the people as well. Moses leads the people out of slavery and oppression, but not into absolute freedom. He presents them with laws and rules about how to live in order to create a just and ordered society. As children wrestle with the question of obedience and begin to make more of their own choices, they must learn that even adults are required to obey certain laws and norms and are accountable to authority outside of themselves. The story of Moses teaches that freedom from tyranny is far different from freedom from responsibility.

That Moses is a great leader but never a perfect person is another important piece of the lesson to be learned from the story of Moses. Despite their self-perceived flaws, like Moses' speech defect, all children have the potential to be great leaders. Children can learn from this story that they need not hold themselves to impossible standards. Becoming oneself is a long, slow, and sometimes painful process.

5

DAVID

David is a dramatic, bigger-than-life character. Like Moses, he is a colorful leader whose stories carry him from childhood to death. Within the canon of the Hebrew Bible, David is a King Arthur-like figure, about whom many tales arose. Narratives related to David are woven throughout several biblical books. His adventures are detailed throughout the books of I and II Samuel and Chronicles, and the Book of Psalms is popularly attributed to him as well. As a hero figure he is complex, first appearing as a young underdog in his well-known battle against Goliath, then alternately as a brave warrior, a noble king, a wise leader, a renowned poet and musician, a womanizer of dubious ethics, and finally as a lonely old man. There are stories that emphasize his bravery, as when he battles Goliath and triumphs (I Samuel 16), his success as a warrior in defeating army after army (II Samuel 8), his lust and his underhandedness, as when he sleeps with Bathsheba and then arranges to have her husband killed (II Samuel 11), and those that show him looking foolish, when he dances and exposes himself (II Samuel 6:14–20). As Barbara Cohen writes,

> More words are devoted to David's life than to any other figures in the scriptures of both the Old and New Testaments, except for Jesus. Jews pray for the coming of "Messiah, son of David." For Moslems, Da'oud is the greatest king who ever lived. And Christians, who believe that the Messiah has already come in the person of Jesus, trace his descent back a thousand years to David. (p. xviii)

Since David's story begins in his childhood, he is a natural subject for children's books. It is these early parts of the David narratives that are most often found in retellings for children, though they generally include a vague allusion to his later years. The themes that are found most commonly in renditions for children concern his youth, his bravery against Goliath, and his relationship with his family members. The story of David becomes a universal story of heroism, bravery, emotional development, taking charge of one's own life, and growing up.

The story of David has much in common with fairy tales, myths, and legends from around the world. David is the classic underappreciated youngest son who must prove himself in order to become a fully integrated, mature adult. Like the hero-character in many familiar stories, he must undergo several trials in order to prove himself, one that entails slaying a fantastical creature, the exaggerated strength, size, or power of which far surpasses his own. Along the way, he will become an admired warrior and leader, and win the hand of the king's daughter. The story of David is also a story of a child separating from parental figures, first from his real biological father, Jesse, and then from King Saul, a powerful father figure, so that he can become his own person. Like Moses, David is not shown to be a perfect character. He has his character flaws, and throughout the span of his life he uses poor judgment on occasion, angering God and those around him. But perhaps because of this, and because the biblical text allows David to be a real human being, blemishes and all, who has many different sides to his personality, the story of David, like the best of fairy tales and legends, can provide a prototype for young children seeking role models.

It has been pointed out that in fairy tales, the figure of a giant or dragon traditionally represents one aspect of the father's personality (Bettleheim, p. 190; Yolen, p. 58). Battling with a giant and defeating him is the resolution of a boy's journey to emotional maturity. It allows the child to face reality, no longer forced to live in his imagination and dream of invoking magic as a solution to his problems. Jane Yolen identifies characters in children's literature who, like David, are small or young, but must fight their metaphoric dragons in order to grow up.

> There seems to be no end to dragons, and the only way to conquer them is—to grow up. . . . In the great fantasy stories it is the same. We meet Ged in *A Wizard of Earthsea* as a boy who at first misuses power and then, in seeking for the released shadow side of his magic, tries to integrate himself. Young Arietty in *The Borrowers* is both a child and a manikin no bigger than thumb. She looks for a safe place to live. The assistant pigkeeper in the Prydain books is made to feel powerless indeed, and he longs to find his father. Hobbits are even smaller than dwarves, yet they must save the world. . . . Arthur, Ged, Arietty, Peter

Pan. Small, powerless, the child-cipher on a journey toward (though not always achieving) maturity. (Yolen, p. 66–67)

It is only once David slays Goliath that his father and brothers acknowledge David's emerging maturity. David's battle with Goliath is what Campbell calls the "hero-task." Like St. George's dragon, King Arthur's beast, or Jack's giant, David's slaying of Goliath represents the mastery of relevant adult-life tasks. He must slay the embodiment of his greatest fears in order to pass through the threshold into adulthood, ready to embrace all that lies ahead.

The Youngest Son

> *And the Lord said to Samuel . . . "I am sending you to Jesse the Bethlehemite, for I have decided on one of his sons to be king." . . . Then Samuel asked Jesse, "Are these all the boys you have?"*
>
> *He replied, "There is still the youngest; he is tending the flock." And Samuel said to Jesse, "Send someone to bring him. . . . So they sent and brought him. He was ruddy-cheeked, bright-eyed, and handsome.*
>
> *And the Lord said, "Rise and anoint him, for this is the one."*
>
> (I Samuel 16:1, 11–12)

Before David ever volunteers to defeat Goliath, he has already been singled out by God through the prophet Samuel as the next king of Israel. Although this is often overlooked in retellings of the David story for children, many of which focus solely on the episode with Goliath, he is not just a simple shepherd boy who unexpectedly rises up and kills the giant. It is already known to readers of the biblical text that this boy is in some way special or set apart from others.

It is common in fairy tales for the hero to have a protector who provides special, and often magical, help. Despite the term "fairy godmother," these figures appear in many guises throughout folklore and can be male or female. The story of *Keloglan and the Magic Hairs* is about a young Turkish boy who, like David, is teased and mistreated by his wicked older brothers (Walker, 1986). He is helped to successfully complete three tasks and win the hand of the princess by a fairy godmother figure, in this case an old man who gives Keloglan three magic hairs. In *Yeh-Shen: A Cinderella Story from China,* the fairy godmother appears as a magic fish, a frequent bringer of good luck in Chinese fairy tales (Louie, 1982). Campbell points out that in hero stories it is common for the hero to be a youngest child, and for both helpful and harmful figures to be encountered on the hero journey. He writes, "The child of destiny has to face a long period of obscurity. This is a time of extreme danger, impediment, or disgrace. He is thrown inward to his own depths or outward to the unknown. . . . And this is a zone of unsuspected presences, benign as well as malignant: an angel appears, a helpful animal, a fisherman, a hunter, crone or peasant" (p. 326). God, with mortal help in the form of Samuel, provides David with his call to adventure and, like the fairy godmother of traditional fairy tales, becomes David's protector on his hero-journey.

The prophet Samuel is told by God to go anoint a new king who will one day succeed Saul (I Samuel 16:1–3). Saul, who had been God's first choice (I Samuel 9:15–17), has proved to be less than an ideal leader, often disobedient and unpredictable. God then tells Samuel to go visit the town of Bethlehem. There he will find a man named Jesse and anoint one of his sons, who will one day become king. Auld begins her version of the David and Goliath story by recounting the prophet Samuel's mission to choose a king for Israel. When Samuel comes to Jesse's house, he assumes that the firstborn, Eliab, will be God's choice. But God tells him,

"Don't judge Eliab by his appearance. He is not my first choice. Remember, you can only see what a man looks like. I can see into his heart." So Samuel passed on to Jesse's next son, and the one after that, and then yet another, until he had seen seven of his sons. But still God did not show His choice.

"Haven't you any other sons?" Samuel asks Jesse.

"There is only my youngest, David, who is away looking after the sheep," replied Jesse.

In Auld's retelling, as in the biblical text, it is the "rosy-cheeked and bright-eyed" David who is God's choice. He may be young, but there is something special about him beyond just his looks. At God's instruction, Samuel anoints him with oil, and "from that day onward, the spirit of God filled David and was always with him." By including this introductory material, Auld provides an explanation for the strong faith in God that David will later exhibit. His act of bravado in offering to fight Goliath seems considerably less rash when viewed in the context of this earlier experience. This is no mere shepherd-boy, but a young man who has already been singled out and has formed a relationship with the God who has chosen him.

In *David: A Biography* (1995), Barbara Cohen retells the bulk of the biblical material about David. She too includes the story of David being chosen by God and anointed by Samuel. She describes him as being handsome, in fact the most handsome of all the brothers, but not arrogant or even particularly knowledgeable about strategy or statesmanship. After being anointed, he poses a straightforward, child-like question:

"Sir, what does this mean?" David asked. "Why are you anointing me with oil?" His question was in everyone's mind, but he was the only one with nerve enough to ask it out loud.

All David is told is that the Lord is no longer with Saul, but is now with David. But as Cohen points out, nothing much changes for David on a daily level. He still goes out and shepherds the sheep in the hills.

Although Cohen stresses that life went on as always once David was anointed, she also writes that David did feel a special connection to God:

[David] always listened carefully when talk turned to politics and war. And always, from the time he was a very young boy, he'd felt inside himself the presence of God. Even before Samuel had come, he'd thought perhaps God had chosen him for something.

There is a sense in this retelling that fate plays a large role in the events that take place. In this depiction, David is no ordinary youth, and it had only been a matter of time before God's plan was made known to him.

It is also not entirely surprising that it is David, the younger son, who emerges as the leader. As happens throughout the Hebrew Bible, the story of David is a story of the victory of the younger son over the older. While the eldest son is supposed to be the one who gets the power, money, or land, that expectation is upended time and again in the Hebrew Bible. There is always a sense that it is the younger son who is actually more deserving and better suited to be a leader. Isaac is the younger of Abraham's two sons, Jacob is younger than his twin brother Esau, Joseph is the second youngest next to Benjamin, and Moses himself is younger than his brother Aaron. Cohen notes that God's initial choice of Saul, from the tribe of Benjamin, may have been related to his lineage, writing, "By encouraging the election of a man from the smallest, weakest tribe, Samuel hoped to defuse rivalries between the stronger, more powerful tribes." Saul was from the tribe descended from the youngest of all of Jacob's twelve sons. The choice of David, as the youngest of Jesse's sons, would seem then to be no mere accident but part of a continued deliberate strategy.

The motif of a younger brother, usually teased and mistreated, appears frequently in fairy tales. Campbell discusses the youngest son as a common theme in hero stories, writing that these tales often use the motif of "the despised one, or the handicapped: the abused younger son or daughter, the orphan, stepchild, ugly duckling, or the squire of low degree" (p. 325–26). The story of David, like the stories of Joseph and Moses, is in its own way part of this story-telling tradition. David, as the youngest brother who is considered "simple" because he lives in harmony with nature, talks to the young sheep he tends, and believes unquestioningly in a power higher than man, is typical of this familiar fairy-tale character. Three tasks are usually assigned the youngest brother to prove his hero status and David too succeeds at all three tasks: slaying the lion, the bear, and Goliath.

Fairy tales about the triumph of the younger son are stories about becoming independent, asserting one's own increasing physical and emotional maturity, as well as separating from parents. Similar scenarios are found in stories like the Grimms' "The Three Feathers," "The Three Brothers," and "The Queen Bee." In these stories, as well as in David's story, the younger brother is first encountered as a young boy, not yet an adolescent, who spends most of his time in solitude, as David does while tending his father's flocks. The younger son has long periods of quiet time alone to contemplate the world and his own place in it, just as David is seen out in the bucolic, Edenic meadow, strengthening his belief in God and starting to compose his psalms. His introspective nature is emphasized even though his older brothers interpret this as weakness and respond with cruel and hurtful words.

There are some stories in this genre that are about girls. In the case where the younger sibling is a daughter, as in the story of Molly Whuppie, she usually cares for the father's house and prepares his meals. In this type of story, whereas the younger brothers generally respond with aggressive behavior, most often, girls respond by turning inward. David responds by integrating both these elements of his nature: his belief in God strengthens as he becomes more aware of the natural beauty surrounding him, and he succeeds at the first two of his three physical trials by slaying the lion and the bear with his bare hands.

All these stories involve the successful completion of three tasks that are assumed to be impossible, but are successfully executed due to the compassion and gentleness of the "simple" brother. The elder brothers fail in their efforts because of their thoughtlessness, brutish ways, and lack of compassion for nature and living creatures. They fail to see the goodness of all God's creations, while their "simple" younger brother radiates such emotion. In "The Three Brothers" an old man sends his three sons out into the world to learn a trade. Whoever learns it best shall inherit the family home. They each agree and spend the year mastering a chosen trade, but it is the youngest brother who is

most successful with his sword. His feat of repelling a rainstorm wins
the admiration of his brothers and his father, and they willingly agree
that he should inherit the house, which he shares with them for the
rest of their lives.

Relationships among the three brothers in "The Three Feathers"
and "The Queen Bee" are not so smoothly negotiated or agreeable.
In "The Three Feathers," an old king sends the three sons out into
the world by blowing a feather to point them in the direction they
should go to complete a designated task and determine who shall inherit the kingdom. The two older brothers, like David's brothers, are
certain their younger brother Dumbkin will be unsuccessful and thus
don't apply themselves in earnest. Dumbkin, a dreamer like David, sits
down to ponder his course of action, and, because this is a fairy tale,
is helped to succeed by magical intervention. The brothers are dumbfounded with Dumbkin's success at completing the assigned task and
ask for successive rematches, all of which Dumbkin continues to excel
at. The brothers eventually agree that he should inherit the kingdom,
where he reigns wisely for many years.

A similar motif is apparent in "The Queen Bee." Once again, two
thoughtless, wastrel brothers are rescued by their youngest brother,
whom they call Duncehead. As they are trying to make their way
home, the older brothers are chastised by Duncehead, first for wanting to disturb an anthill, then for chasing ducks in a lake, and finally
for wanting to build a fire and smoking out bees from their nest. Each
time Duncehead tells them to "leave the poor creatures in peace," as
he "can't bear to have them tortured." When they reach an en-
chanted castle, the older brothers are unable to help break the spell
and are turned into stone. The gentle Duncehead is rescued by each
of the creatures he had saved from his brothers' intended torture. He
solves all the riddles put before the brothers, and wins the hand of
the beautiful stone princess, now returned to life with the help of the
Queen Bee.

All of these stories have elements in common with the story of
David. The older brothers live active, adventurous lives, and assume
that their youngest brother is incapable of succeeding at real life prob-

lems. But David, like Dumbkin and Duncehead, has inner resources to draw upon that they don't have. It is the gentle disposition and self-assurance of the so-called simple, ridiculed younger brother that helps him call upon both aspects of his nature: the thoughtful, dreamy, imaginative inner self combined with his outer physical strength which impels Duncehead to call for the cessation of his brother's cruelty to the helpless tiny creatures just as Dumbkin utilizes the help of a toad and his own strength to complete his tasks. David's dreaminess and Psalm-writing lead him to imagine he can defeat Goliath, whereas his determination and strength help him to complete the task to the dumbfounded amazement and disbelief of his older brothers. Bettleheim refers to this behavior as the "symbolic struggle of personality integration against chaotic disintegration" (p. 76). In the process of maturing and growing up, the two aspects of a child's personality are in conflict. The sweet, compliant youth struggles against the enforced obedience imposed by parents and the community. As the process of physical maturation takes place and the child begins to look outwardly more like an adult, the child begins to assert independence, still unsure of which aspect of his or her personality needs to dominate or be harmoniously integrated. The completion of heroic challenges at the narrative level are expressed by the satisfying conclusion of inheriting a kingdom, winning the hand of a beautiful princess, earning the respect of his older brothers and father, and slaying a monster.

David as a Young Boy

> But Saul said to David, "You cannot go to that Philistine and fight him; you are only a boy and he has been a warrior from his youth!"
>
> (I Samuel 17:33)

A story in which a small boy defeats a mean and terrible giant is a story of sweet revenge—the young child's classic fantasy. "Jack and the Beanstalk," in all its variations, is a fairy tale that exemplifies the idea of a boy exacting vengeance on an outsize figure. As the story begins, it is clear to readers that Jack's mother considers him weak and incompetent. Nevertheless, she sends him off to sell the cow. Easily tricked into trading the cow for a handful of seemingly worthless beans, in the end Jack proves himself worthy of rescuing his mother from starvation. At the same time, he exacts revenge for his humiliation by slaying the terrifying giant who has eaten all the other boys who have come to his castle. The story of David and Goliath belongs in this genre of stories.

Shortly after David is introduced into the biblical text in I Samuel 16:13, he volunteers to go up against Goliath of Gath, a Philistine warrior often referred to in stories as a giant. The biblical text implies that they are mismatched in its use of the word *naar*, which can be translated as either "boy" or "youth," to describe David, and the use of the expression *ish-milchamah*, warrior or literally "man of war" to describe Goliath. Goliath, who is "six cubits and a span tall," comparable to roughly fifty centimeters, fights with a sword, spear, and javelin, whereas David has only his slingshot and some stones (I Samuel 17). It can thus be inferred that David is young and inexperienced at warfare, while Goliath is experienced, tough, and very large.

Despite the widespread popularity of the story in Western culture, and despite the large size attributed to Goliath, he is not actually called a giant in the biblical text. However, the motif of a young hero fighting a giant or dragon appears frequently in folklore and mythology, where the large, mythic creature represents the young boy's inner struggle to separate himself from his father and assert his emerging sense of physical, emotional, and sexual independence and maturity. Appearing at the crossroads between the end of childhood and the onset of adolescence, the giant–dragon–behemoth represents the culmination of oedipal and familial conflicts. Just as Jack's mother questions his ability to be a provider and trade the cow for something nutritious with which to sustain them, so David's father and brothers doubt his ability to do a man's job and serve in the army. His brothers are dismayed at the prospect of David going to do battle with Goliath. His father tells him to wait, that he is too small, and Goliath himself echoes their words.

David is portrayed as a very young boy in Hans Wilhelm's cartoon-ish illustrations for *David and the Giant* (1987), written by Emily Little. He is small, barefoot, and wears only a piece of cloth hung from his waist. He is shown happily tending sheep, not afraid of anything because "God looked after David." David, like Joseph, is the young-est son who stays at home while his brothers go off to fight a war. When his father sends him to bring food to his brothers, he goes un-noticed as they focus their attention on the enemy and on the up-coming battle. Then Goliath appears, a huge, wicked-looking giant in armor and a Viking–like hat, armed with a spear, who towers above everyone else, as broad as he is tall. No one wants to fight this impos-ing figure, and when David volunteers he is told that he is too small. He is shown staggering under the weight of the sword the king gives him. Like the archetypal bully in the schoolyard, Goliath taunts and mocks him. But David is able to achieve the wish of every child who has ever been picked on or denied something for being too young, and proves that it isn't necessary to be big or strong to bring down a giant.

The story of David is but one in a long tradition of stories about bullying in children's literature. It is forever intriguing and deeply sat-isfying for children to see the victim succeed and the bully get his comeuppance. Charles Dickens's *Oliver Twist*, though not originally written for children, has long captured the imagination of young read-ers and moviegoers. The idea of having to endure relentless physical and verbal abuse from the adults and children Oliver lives among and then being vindicated ensures the story a place among the list of chil-dren's classic favorites. Though read less frequently but retold in con-temporary abridgements and on television, Thomas Hughes's *Tom Brown's Schooldays*, also from the same era, lives on as the ultimate story of tyrannical boarding-school bullying, with the character of Flashman personifying the consummate, relentless bully.

Bullying is no less a real issue in children's lives today than it was in the nineteenth century. Instances of bullying and hurtful, vicious taunting abound in contemporary children's stories. The serious consequences that can result from classroom teasing are the subject of Eleanor Estes's Newbery Honor Book, *The 100 Dresses* (1944). An immigrant child, Wanda is teased every day by her classmates, Peggy and Maddie, until she can no longer bear to go to school. By the end of the book, Wanda has moved away and Maddie is remorseful, not knowing how to assuage her guilty conscience. The bullying theme appears in the 1970 Caldecott Honor book *Goggles*, in which Ezra Jack Keats creates a character who is picked on and bullied by the other boys until he figures out how to protect himself. Now considered a classic, Robert Cormier's *The Chocolate War*, a 1974 ALA Best Book for Young Adults, created controversy with its discussion of peer pressure, intimidation, and bullying by fellow students and faculty. All are still hotly debated today. In the 1990s, Jerry Spinelli created memorable characters who wrestle with daily bullying in his 1991 Newbery Award–winning *Maniac Magee* and 1998 Newbery Honor Book, *Wringer*.

That this is still a critical issue in children's lives today is further evidenced in recent award-winning books which have won places in children's hearts. J. K. Rowling's Harry Potter is a victim of merciless bullying at the hands of Draco Malfoy and his sidekicks. Carl Hiasson's *Hoot*, a 2003 Newbery Honor title, and Kate DiCamillo's 2004 Newbery Award–winning *The Tale of Despereaux* both revolve around incidents of bullying and illustrate the devastating impact that threatening and intimidation have on individuals and communities. In Louis Sachar's *Holes*, a 1999 Newbery Award title, Stanley Yelnats is so accustomed to being victimized by his peers and his family that throughout much of the story he submissively accepts the court's pronouncement of his guilt and subsequent detention. Not until he finds his own voice is he able to overcome the demoralizing consequences of bullying by the other juvenile detainees and administrators.

The popularity of bullying as a theme in children's books emphasizes the widespread nature of abusive actions among children, the fear of becoming a victim, its impact on whole communities, and the search for effective ways of responding to such behavior.

Notable also are the bullies memorialized in Iona Opie and Maurice Sendak's *I Saw Esau: The Schoolchild's Pocket Book* (1992), a book of rhymes the Opies recorded in schoolyards and playgrounds, that include verses like:

> *Donkey walks on four legs*
> *And I walk on two;*
> *The last one I saw*
> *Was very like you.* (No. 22, p. 33)

and

> *Je suis–*
> *I am a pot of jam;*
> *Tu es–*
> *Thou are a juicy fart.* (No. 131, p.99)

David found that the best way of responding to bullying behavior was to respond directly to the bully. Facing the giant, as David does in Wilhelm's illustrations, readers see David facing his fears and not giving in to Goliath's threats and bullying taunts. With his slingshot and a few well-aimed stones, David is able to kill Goliath. At the end of Emily Little's gentle retelling, "David was a hero." He is shown as a small boy being carried on top of a shield, holding a puppy. This version of the story is not about passing into adulthood, but a story of boyhood and of conquering childhood fears.

Ashley Bryant's woodcut illustration for "David He No Fear" in Lorenz Graham's collection *How God Fix Jonah* depicts David as a very young child, almost a baby. Except for a short garment covering his midsection, he is undressed. He is positioned in the right hand corner of the image, and the lower half of Goliath towers over him. The rest of him is too big to fit into the picture. Graham writes that "He be high past ten men." This Goliath is not merely a tall man, but clearly a giant many times the size of tiny David. The illustration echoes the language of the text, which emphasizes the differences in both size and age between the two fighters:

> *The giant say*
> *"Ho! Small boy done come to say how-do."*
> *David say*
> *"I come for fight!"*
> *Giant say*
> *"Do you mommy know you out?"*
> *David say*
> *"Now I kill you!"*
> *Giant say*
> *"Go from my face less I eat you!"*

The language of the encounter sounds like same kind of typical schoolyard taunting recorded by the Opies. Goliath invokes David's mother as a way to put David in his place, but it only makes him more determined to kill Goliath. He wants to earn his rightful place in the world of men, not stay at home under the care of women.

In Mary Auld's *David and Goliath* (1999), illustrated by Diana Mayo, Goliath is shown to be a large, menacing figure, especially in comparison to David. David's youth is emphasized in the illustrations by both his size and his lack of a beard, which are worn by all the grown men in the book, Philistine or otherwise. The implication is that he lacks a beard not because he chooses to be clean-shaven, but because he is simply too young to grow one. Yet in her attempt to stick closely to the original biblical text, Auld does not overtly refer to Goliath as a giant. Instead, she finesses the point by writing that Goliath was "a giant of a man."

The difference in size between David and Goliath is shown dramatically in Lisbeth Zwerger's *Stories from the Bible*. David is a tiny figure in the foreground of the illustration. He is barefoot and bareheaded, and carries in one bare hand a small, white bag, in the other, a shepherd's staff. Goliath, in contrast, is so large that, as in Bryant's woodcut, not all of him can fit in the frame. He rises up from a valley on the other side of a range of hills from David, his feet hidden from view and the top of his head outside the frame. His substantial bulk towers over the horizon line. In one gloved hand he carries a knife, in front of him is a sword, and in his other hand he carries a sharp spear.

Zwerger depicts Goliath as the exact opposite of David. Every part of Goliath's body except his face is covered up and protected, while David's bare feet, hands, neck, and head project openness and vulnerability. David's unstructured cloak curves gently behind him, whereas Goliath's clothes contain sharp edges and metal studs.

The first part of David's story focuses on his attempt to reach beyond the confines of childhood. Whether Goliath is a real giant, or simply a strong fighter who is much bigger than young David, he is a force to be reckoned with. In volunteering to fight Goliath and defeating him, David learns to stand up for himself and conquer his fears. In spite of his small size and youth, he learns that he can make his voice heard, and that he does not need to be intimated by the preconceived notions of others regarding his abilities. He comes to understand that size and strength are not everything, and that quick-thinking, self-confidence, and self-reliance can take him far.

The Obedient Son

> David would go back and forth from attending on Saul to shepherd his father's flock at Bethlehem.
>
> (I Samuel 17:15)

The motif of obedience to authority figures runs throughout the David narratives and is as relevant to the stories of David's later life as it is to his childhood. As a boy, David is expected to be obedient to his father, brothers, and King Saul. When he becomes a man, obedience is still an issue in his relationships with the prophets and with God. Though David is presented initially as obedient and docile, his attempt to get permission to fight Goliath is the beginning of his struggle against authority that continues throughout the rest of his life.

David wants the approval of those whom he perceives to be in positions of authority, but is at the same time constrained by what it takes to get that approval. David plays his harp while he shepherds his father's flocks in the green hills of Bethlehem against a perfectly blue sky in Leonard Everett Fisher's *David and Goliath* (1993). Fisher writes, "The music of David's harp filled all who heard it with joy." He is a simple young man in this depiction, living in harmony with nature and animals, and able to bring joy to others through his music. In this version, David is not singled out by Samuel as he is in the biblical text, but rather he is sent by his father to give comfort to King Saul who is plagued with "dark spirits." David is the light that can banish the dark from King Saul. In this retelling, when his father tells him to go help Saul, he obediently goes. When Saul tells him to stay, he stays. He is a model of obedience and innocence. But when war looms on the horizon and Saul sends him back home to resume tending sheep, he becomes frustrated. Fisher writes that David is "restless." He wants to fight, but his father, telling him he is too young, sends him to bring food to his brothers on the battlefield. Fisher stresses this point so much so that it actually contradicts the biblical text, which notes no conflict between David and his father. In fact it is David's father who sends him to the battlefield to bring food to his brothers and check on them (I Samuel 17:17–18).

Fisher's obedient boy hero begins to make his transition into more complicated young adulthood as he starts making choices for himself. As David begins his internal transition from obedient boy to independent young man, the sky in the illustrations also changes. Gone is the pastoral blue and in its place are bold, angry shades of orange, red, and pink. Meanwhile, David finds no support for his suggestion that he fight Goliath. King Saul tells him to go home, just as he had told him earlier. But this time he stands up to Saul, his brothers, and the other soldiers. He identifies God as the source of his strength and courage, and King Saul accepts this argument, sending him into battle. Despite not being properly armed or armored, David quickly wins with the use of his slingshot and his faith in God's protection. Fisher does not shy away from the inherent gore in the story, showing a triumphant David holding up Goliath's severed head and a bloody sword. David is now mature enough to face up to the consequences of his actions. In holding up Goliath's head, he is announcing not only the communal victory of having vanquished a threat to his people, but also his personal victory in overcoming his youth and innocence. The last page shows

David back in his original peaceful setting, tending sheep and playing the harp against a bright blue sky with small puffy clouds. The book ends here, but the last words remind readers that this is only the beginning of David's story and that someday he will become king of his people. The sky is clear once again, but this is no longer the same naive boy introduced at the beginning. The symbolism is evident—just as he leads the sheep, someday he will lead the people.

Beatrice Schenk De Regniers's *David and Goliath* (1996) also skips over David's being chosen by Saul and emphasizes David's heroic victory over Goliath. The contrast depicted between David and his brothers in Scott Cameron's rich oil paintings is as obvious as the differences between the good guys and the bad guys in Hollywood Westerns. The brothers are swarthy, bearded men in dark tunics, whereas David is not only young but "small for his age," clean-shaven, blond, and dressed in white to signify purity and innocence. All the brothers appear to be part of Saul's army, while only David is left out. This division between David and his brothers that both De Regniers and Cameron create is stressed to a much greater extent in this version of the story than in the biblical version, in which only the three eldest brothers join Saul's army. In this retelling, similar to that of Fisher's, David is described as being closely connected to the natural world and to have the gift of bringing happiness to others. De Regniers writes:

> While he watched his father's sheep, David sat under a fig tree and played his harp so sweetly and so gaily that the lambs danced and skipped in the meadow. Even the ewes and the old rams skipped and danced in their grave fashion.

At the same time, De Regniers imagines that these skills of David are considered irrelevant and of little consequence by his brothers, and she writes of the brothers' refusal to let him join them whether to hunt, work, or play. Like Joseph's brothers, they treat him with scorn and tease him. David is able to forget his brothers' bad behavior toward him by being out in the hills with the animals, and making up songs of praise to God, a reference to the Psalms attributed to David.

Late childhood is a time of co-regulation of behavior, when children gradually take responsibility for their behavior in concert with their parents. At this stage, children identify strongly with the parents and family and, in most instances, still readily defer to the parents' judgment. When Samuel appears at Jesse's house and chooses his youngest son to be anointed, Jesse offers no objections and, thereby, encourages David to be cooperative. As children enter adolescence, this practice of co-regulation begins to be eroded. According to Piaget and Erikson, adolescence is a time when the effort to search for and establish one's own identity and independence is central. It is a time to try new ideas and self-concepts, build up self-esteem, and develop relationships with peer groups, while becoming less reliant on parental authority and judgments. It is also a time when they become acutely aware of their own place within the family, seen here in David's newly formed desire to be considered an adult among his brothers. Out of this growth, a sense of self-identity emerges. But even while the adolescent is attempting to self-direct, the parents, like Jesse, are often ambivalent about surrendering control and encouraging their adolescent's emerging independence.

When David's brothers go off to fight in the king's army, David wants to go too. Recalling the episode in which Jacob refuses at first to let Benjamin go down to Egypt with his brothers, De Regniers's Jesse doesn't want to let his beloved and youngest son go. She presents a classic scene of the conflict between children and parents over the formation of an independent identity. David wants to go and be part of something exciting and meaningful. But his father isn't ready to let go. In De Regniers's retelling, David's father claims that he needs his help at home and his emotional support, saying, " 'Little David, if you leave me, who will sing to me? Who will play on the harp to comfort me in my loneliness?' and the old man wept." David's father repeatedly refuses to let David join his brothers. David is thus desperately torn between conflicting needs: that of being the obedient son or pleasing himself. Though this conflict between Jesse and David is not overtly present in the biblical text, it appears in many retellings of the story, manifested in Jesse's attempts to protect his youngest son from the dangers of battle when he wants to join his brothers at the battlefront. In the biblical story, Jesse simply sends David to the battlefront, perhaps implicit recognition on the part of the biblical text of David's urgent need to join his brothers even if he is not quite their equal. Jesse's compromise is to permit David to go to the battlefront as an observer and to bring his brothers the much-needed supplies, but warns him not to linger there. David is told to report back to his father about what he sees.

When David finally does leave home and find his brothers, in De Regniers's version as in the biblical text itself, David's brothers are angry to see him. They mistrust his motives, claiming that he has come to the battlefield simply so that he can boast about it afterward (I Samuel 17:28–29). When he volunteers to fight Goliath, they are even more incensed and don't take him seriously. As Auld faithfully includes in her retelling, David responds to their criticism like a petulant, whiny child, saying, "What have I done now? I was only asking!" (I Samuel 17:28 29). But of course he is not only asking, and he goes on to question more people about Goliath until word of his questioning reaches the king. King Saul listens as David states his case that God has been with him before and will continue to be with him when he fights Goliath, and agrees to let David go fight (I Samuel 17:31–37). Although David has defied the authority of his father and brothers, he goes up against Goliath with the overt assent of a higher authority, that of King Saul, and the implied assent of the greatest authority of all, God. This extreme act of disobedience toward a parent is thus in actuality obedience to an even more powerful, higher authority. In her retelling, De Regniers has built much more conflict into the story than that which exists in the biblical text. She uses the original biblical story to create a tale of a child's struggle for independence in both thought and action.

In Patricia and Fredrick McKissack's *Let My People Go* (1998), the giant represents oppression in the form of the slave master and slavery itself. When Charlotte, the fictionalized daughter of a free-black abolitionist, agrees to help her friend Peter Willy, a slave, escape to the

North, he tells her, "Charlotte, you have helped slay the giant." Later, she asks her father to explain what Peter meant, and he tells her:

> I 'spect he was talking 'bout his massa. To a slave, his mas' seems like an undefeatable giant, a Goliath of sorts. As you done come to know, to slay a giant you got to have faith in God and confidence in yo'self— just like David.

For Charlotte's father, David is a role model of faith and self-confidence. It is these two qualities that enable David to overcome oppression and enslavement. In this collection, the story of David relates to the very real suffering of the African American slave experience. In framing the story in this way, they show how it can serve as a model of release from the bonds of metaphoric lack of empowerment as well, a lesson that Charlotte's father surely wants her to understand.

David is the universal underdog who manages to gain power by slaying the symbolic giant who stands in his way. David thus serves as a role model for the agonizing process of growth and eventual separation that every child must make from the parent in order to have control over his or her own life. Though the separation is difficult and painful, and no less so for the parent than for the child, it is a necessary part of healthy growth and individuation that every child must go through.

David's Trials

> David replied to Saul, "Your servant has been tending his father's sheep, and if a lion or a bear came and carried off an animal from the flock, I would go after it and fight it and rescue it from its mouth. And if it attacked me, I would seize it by the beard and strike it down and kill it. Your servant has killed both lion and bear, and that uncircumcised Philistine shall end up like one of them, for he has defied the ranks of the living God."
>
> (I Samuel 17:34–36)

In the biblical text, David's encounters with the lion and the bear are told only in retrospect, as David tries to persuade Saul to let him fight

Goliath. That they are told only in this context calls into question how to understand these encounters. Are they meant to be understood as retellings of actual events, or simply a boy's imaginative attempts to sound brave and experienced? Are they a literary device meant to foreshadow the way in which David will later protect his "flock" from predators? Though these questions have no clear answers, these episodes play an important role in David's ongoing development and are significant forerunners of David's interaction with Goliath.

David's encounters with the lion and bear figure significantly in some of the retellings for children. Fisher's *David* mentions those battles when he tries to convince his father that he can go fight like his brothers. In De Regniers's version, these events take on a much bigger role. She fills in the details missing in the biblical source, setting these encounters in the period before David leaves home to find his brothers. David first meets up with a lion, while out shepherding one day. The lion snatches David's favorite lamb, and David tries to kill him with his slingshot. She writes:

> The lion was wounded, but still he did not let go of the lamb.
> Though the lion was so big and David so little, David ran up to the lion and struck him with his staff, and snatched the lamb out of the lion's mouth.
> Then the lion turned on David and would have killed him, surely, but David struck a mighty blow with his staff and killed the lion.

This meeting serves as a kind of rehearsal for his engagement with Goliath. Though he nearly loses his life, he manages in the end to triumph, learning something of his own will and strength and gaining a taste for and knowledge of battle. The lion serves as the catalyst to move David on the path toward determining his own fate. Having defeated the lion, he feels ready to go fight in the king's army, but even when presented with the lion skin as proof of his victory, his father is still not convinced that he is ready.

After introducing the arrival of Goliath and the threat he represented to Saul's army, De Regniers goes on to create the encounter between David and the bear. Like the lion, the bear tries to prey on David's flock. This time David is better prepared, and kills the bear right away with his slingshot. David's skill and self-confidence have improved, but his father will still not let David join the king's army, though he does allow David to go to the army for the sole purpose of bringing back news of his brothers.

David's encounters with the lion and the bear are similar to the rite-of-passage encounters with beasts that occur in stories such as "Seven at One Blow," "The Dragon and His Grandmother," and "The Earth Gnome," all from Grimm. His fight with Goliath is also similar to other mythological battles, in which the hero uses his wits and strategy to outwit the bigger, stronger enemy, for example that of Theseus and the Minotaur. As in those stories, his battles are the turning point for David in his relationships with his father and King Saul, a father figure. He has proven that he can do a man's job and must now be taken seriously. He has earned their respect and in so doing has successfully made the transition to manhood.

The trials that are part of the David story are reminiscent of the stories concerning Hercules as well. Like David, Hercules was said to have played the lyre. Because of his great strength, he is sent to be a shepherd so that he can protect the sheep. But what he really wanted to do was fight. Many stories are told of Hercules' battles, which include his success at ridding the countryside of Thebes from predatory lions and wolves. He is later sent to perform twelve impossible tasks, which include killing the monstrous Nemean Lion and the nine-headed hydra, and capturing the three-headed watchdog of Hades. As Hercules performs these tasks, he is constantly proving himself, over and over, to his father Zeus.

Joseph Campbell writes about the hero having to "survive a succession of trials" as a common phase of the transformative hero's journey (p. 97). These trials are milestones on the road from childhood to maturity. Passing through these trials successfully, culminating in the defeat of Goliath, is David's rite of passage into manhood. Along the way, the hero comes to know both his own internal strength and the exterior powers he can call on for help. Campbell writes, "it may be that he here discovers for the first time that there is a benign power everywhere supporting him in his superhuman passage." For David, this power is God. Though David had an early connection to God, it is only at this stage that God's support is being overtly manifested for David, as he struggles to simultaneously find within himself the skills he needs to pass through these trials successfully.

At the same time that David comes to better understand God's role in his life, David also learns that part of the power that has helped him get through his trials can be found in himself. As Campbell observes:

> it appears that the perilous journey was a labor not of attainment but of reattainment, not discovery but rediscovery. The godly powers sought and dangerously won are revealed to have been within the heart of the hero all the time. . . . From this point of view the hero is symbolical of that divine creative and redemptive image which is hidden within us all, only waiting to be known and rendered into life. (p. 39)

As he passes through these trials, David will learn that he has within him the skills he needs to take care of himself, succeed at adulthood, and become a respected leader. What a critically important message this is for children, that hidden within each one of us is an all-powerful heart of a hero that can help us get through the toughest of trials.

The Hero's Garb

> Saul clothed David in his own garment; he placed a bronze helmet on his head and fastened a breastplate on him.
> David girded his sword over his garment. Then he tried to walk but he was not used to it. And David said to Saul, "I cannot walk in these, for I am not used to them."
> So David took them off. He took his stick, picked a few smooth stones from the riverbed, put them in the pocket of his shepherd's bag and, sling in hand, he went toward the Philistine.
>
> (I Samuel 17:38–40)

When Saul agrees to let David fight Goliath, he offers him clothing appropriate for battle. David, however, chooses to forego the battle dress and instead faces Goliath with only a slingshot and stones. This choice could be either the height of hubris or an expression of absolute faith. It is also the introduction of another theme of the David story, the dichotomy between nature and culture. Many of the retellings of the David and Goliath story, including those of Fisher and De Regniers, make a strong connection between David and the world of nature. He is at one with himself in the hills, where he knows how to care for the animals, and celebrates the joy and beauty of the natural world. He appears in the illustrations of many of the retellings for children as a down-to-earth boy, dressed in simple, unadorned clothing. He lacks many of the accoutrements of civilization, even as imagined in the ancient world.

The garments and weaponry offered to him by Saul are made of metal. Crafted for the sole purpose of war and violence, these are the usual items worn by those who regularly engage in the business of battle. They are made of man-made materials, as opposed to the cotton that grows from the land and the leather from animals, and represent a more sophisticated use of technology. David's stones, on the other hand, are purely of the natural world, found objects that are gifts from nature. David's use of these materials is a reflection of his close connection to God's natural world and his inherent lack of artifice. A natural fighter and leader, he needs only the tools of nature and God's support to win his battles.

Several of the retellings cite the size of these items as reasons why David chooses not to use them. They are too big on him, and not comfortable. In Hans Wilhelm's humorous illustrations for *David and the Giant,* David is shown barely able to hold the oversize sword cradled in his arms. In his *David and Goliath,* Fisher writes, "Saul offered David armor for protection, but David refused to wear it. The armor was too heavy." De Regniers goes into even more detail in her version of *David and Goliath,* writing:

> But when little David was clothed in all his heavy armor, he could not walk. So heavily did the armor weigh upon him, he could scarcely move. "I am only a shepherd boy," he said. "I cannot wear this armor.

I cannot carry this sword." And David took them off—the helmet and the coat of mail and the sword.

The language used and the explanation given for his refusal reinforces the image of David as a child, naturally smaller than the soldiers, and thus emphasizes the magnificence of his victory all the more. But beyond the issue of size, in rejecting Saul's items, David is rejecting taking on the role of a full adult. He wants to fight like a man, but isn't fully ready to exit the world of youth, of simpler technology and softer, gentler materials.

In the biblical account, David's life is never the same afterward. Saul does not allow him to return home, and he immediately goes into service for Saul as a soldier, now properly equipped with a sword. He fights one battle after another and soon becomes commander of all of Saul's troops (I Samuel 18:2–5). But in most of the retellings for children, David's ongoing role as a warrior is not emphasized. The last images in both Fisher and De Regniers's versions depict David back with his sheep. That David will someday become king himself is alluded to in the endings of books by Auld, Fisher, De Regniers, and Little. Yet in all these retellings, there is a strong sense that when David fights and kills Goliath, just as when he fought and killed the lion and then the bear, he does so impulsively and defensively, only because of an impending threat. It is as if David may have been willing the one time to defeat Goliath for the good of the people, but he is not yet ready to take on the role of soldier or warrior on a regular basis, in other words, he is not ready to grow up and take on adult responsibilities or be involved in the world of violence. Embedded in these retellings are the eternal questions about when and how to wage wars, and when, if ever, is it right to fight back if attacked. David's extensive military history is only dealt with in Barbara Cohen's *David* (1995), which is intended to cover the whole of David's life. There seems to be a reluctance on the part of those telling this story for children to portray David as the warrior he is in the Bible. In their reluctance, these retellings allude to a contemporary discomfort with a warrior hero-figure, despite the emotionally symbolic significance of David as a fighter.

Winning the Hand of the Princess

> *The man who kills him will be rewarded by the king with great riches; he will also give him his daughter in marriage . . .*

(I Samuel 17:25)

There are many reasons that can be imagined for David's astounding show of bravery in offering to fight Goliath. It could be that, in the typical manner of young children, he was trying to show off in front of his brothers. It could be that he was truly motivated by his connection to God, and that his act of bravado was an act of faith. In retellings for children, David's battles are generally portrayed as defensive battles rather than battles involving strategy and material benefits to the winner. However, it cannot be ignored that there was a reward in the offing for the person who managed to defeat Goliath, a promise of both wealth and marriage to one of Saul's daughters.

It is not uncommon in hero-stories for the hero to be rewarded for accomplishing his great deed. Jack of beanstalk fame slays the giant and gets the goose who lays golden eggs, a permanent solution to his family's poverty. More commonly, the warrior who slays the dragon or giant is also given the princess as a prize. As Campbell writes, "The motif of the difficult task as prerequisite to the bridal bed has spun the hero-deeds of all time and all the world" (p. 344). St. George slays the dragon and wins the hand of the princess. King Arthur slays the giant Caulang and wins the hand of Guenivere. Jack the Giant Killer slays the giant Galligantua, breaking the enchantment over the kingdom, and thus is rewarded with the king's daughter as his bride. Similarly, in the British folktale "Red Ettin" the younger brother manages to slay the three-headed beast and kill him, freeing the king's daughter who had been imprisoned within Red Ettin's castle, and in gratitude the king gives him his daughter in marriage. The King of Thebes was so grateful to Hercules for ridding the countryside of dangerous animals that he gave him his daughter's hand. Whether or not the possibility of a reward was part of David's motivation, it is clear that after his victory, David's life becomes inextricably bound with Saul and Saul's family.

That David might have been motivated by a reward seems inconsistent with the image of David as a naive, sincere young boy. Yet there are other ways to read David's early character. Given the amount of material within the Bible about David, it is no surprise that there are contradictions about David within the biblical account itself. Toward the beginning of the material related to David, in I Samuel 16:18, before he ever encounters Goliath, he is called a warrior by Saul and seems to already be in Saul's service. This provides a very different dimension to the story than if he was an innocent child who suddenly emerged out of the meadow to fight Goliath.

Taken as a whole, there are discrepancies within the combined biblical accounts of David. He is described as young (I Samuel 16:11, 17:14) and as a boy who, according to Saul, cannot possibly fight the outsize Goliath, who has "been a warrior from his youth" (I Samuel 17:33). Saul and David had already had a conversation, during which David volunteered his services and Saul offered to provide the appropriate garb and weapon, but when David approaches Saul and presents Goliath's severed head, Saul has to ask who David is (I Samuel 17:55–56). At the same time, one chapter earlier, the biblical text reports that David was already regarded as a warrior (I Samuel 16:18) and was an arms-bearer in Saul's service (I Samuel 16:21).

Some scholars suggest that the Bible is a composite of material from different sources that passed through the hand of different editors, which would help explain inconsistencies in the text. Whatever the reason for these seeming contradictions, the authors of retellings for children have had to contend with them, and make choices about how to weave them into their version of the story. The idea of David taking on Goliath because of money or the promise of the king's daughter paints David in a much less heroic and selfless light than showing him to be motivated by faith or even simply by youthful passion and the search for justice. In addition, the idea of David marrying can seem inconsistent with a version that emphasizes David's youthfulness, making the story harder for children to relate to.

In Little's version of the story, *David and the Giant,* David is shown to be galvanized into action by his faith in God. He is not afraid of Goliath, because he knows that God will take care of him. Fisher's David is also motivated by his connection to God as well as by the conviction that Goliath's threat is simply wrong and that someone needs to stand up to him. In neither of these versions is there mention of David receiving a material reward, or the hand of one of Saul's daughters. In contrast, De Regniers includes in her retelling that David is told of the reward, but does not stress that this is the factor stirring him to take up Goliath's challenge. Instead, he confronts Goliath "in the name of the Lord, the God of the armies of Israel." De Regniers does return to the idea of David's material reward, writing that David received gold and silver from Saul, married one of his daughters, and became a soldier for the king. However, in keeping with the emphasis on David as a child, all of this lies in his distant future. De Regniers includes these details in such a way that David comes off as the righteous recipient of Saul's gratitude, rather than as a mercenary.

Whatever David's motivation in pursuing his goal of defeating Goliath, it is an act that propels David into a new stage of development. In taking on the challenge to fight the enemy whom no one else is prepared to stand up against and conquer, he creates a new sense of himself and begins to compose the rest of his own life story. Marrying the princess is one piece of his passing into a new stage of his life. Bettelheim discusses the motif of winning the princess as a symbolic way for the hero to achieve his own personal realm of maturity, writing:

> In many fairy stories a king gives his daughter in marriage to the hero and either shares his kingdom with him or installs him as the eventual successor. This is, of course, a wishful fantasy of the child. . . . Gaining his kingdom through being united in love and marriage with the most appropriate and desirable partner—a union which the parents thoroughly approve and which leads to happiness for everybody but the villains—symbolizes the perfect resolution of oedipal difficulties, as well

as the gaining of true independence and complete personality integration. Is it really all that unrealistic to speak of such high achievement as coming into one's own kingdom? (p. 129–30)

In fighting and slaying Goliath, David has passed through the threshold between childhood and young adulthood. Winning the hand of the king's daughter indicates that just as David has reached a new stage of emotional development, he has also arrived at the awakening of his mature sexuality. Though he has many trials ahead of him before he becomes the actual king, he has become an official part of the king's family by marrying the king's daughter, and has gained the respect of his brothers, his father, the king, and everyone around him. Never again will David be seen as a simple shepherd, a disregarded youngest son, or just a boy.

David the Psalmist

> *Whenever the evil spirit of God came upon Saul, David would take the lyre and play it; Saul would find relief and feel better, and the evil spirit would leave him.*

(I Samuel 16:23)

David is a hero who is also an artist, a creator in his own right. The image of David as a musician whose art could soothe and heal is at odds with the image of David the warrior. Yet part of what is so compelling about David as a hero is that there are many sides to his personality. He is not only a brave boy, a good son, and a skilled warrior, but he is a talented psalmist and musician. His personality is over-sized and multifaceted. The biblical book of Psalms has long been popularly attributed to David, though scholars are not in agreement as to whether there is any historical basis to this claim.

Although most authors of David stories for children have chosen to focus solely on his encounter with Goliath, others have tried to weave in his musical side. De Regniers imagines David composing Psalms of praise to God while he shepherds the sheep, and Fisher portrays David with a harp that "filled all who heard it with joy." In *David's Songs: His Psalms and Their Story* by Colin Eisler and elegantly illustrated in watercolors by Jerry Pinkney (1992), the focus is on David the Psalmist. In Eisler's own words, the Psalms highlighted in the book provide a "self-portrait" of David and his relationship to God.

Eisler imagines David's motivation as well as the setting for the composition of the Psalms:

> In the long, cold evenings, before a camp fire, the shepherd boy would take out his harp and sing. David made up the words and the music for these songs to God. Singing them made him feel safe and gave him courage. He often praised the Lord, thanking him for all his wonderful works, for making golden sunsets, silvery stars, strong mountains, gentle valleys, flowing waters, rich harvests, and healthy children. Seeing the beauty of all God had made, David made joyous sounds with his voice and harp.

In this retelling, the Psalms are David's childlike expression of thankfulness at being alive, and his attempt at expressing the wonder he saw in the world around him. They are both a joyous expression of his awe at the wonder of God's creation, and a naive expression of his place within that creation.

Where this side of David is explored in children's books, it allows children to recognize that they too are made up of disparate parts. They may be a great soccer player, but also enjoy ballet. Being good at writing poetry doesn't preclude being a black belt at karate, and being an avid player of Dungeons and Dragons doesn't preclude playing with dolls. Introducing children to this side of David encourages children to develop the different sides of themselves.

Eisler points out though that as David matured and had other kinds of experiences in the world, he created Psalms that reflected his new experiences. Alongside the Psalms of praise and wonder are Psalms that ask for forgiveness, Psalms that deal with pain, war, sorrow, and loneliness. Just as the earlier Psalms helped him feel less lonely and scared, perhaps the later Psalms helped him deal with the pain he experienced at seeing his own shortcomings. By allowing this collection of

Psalms to represent more than just David's young self, Eisler has allowed a full picture of David to emerge. He first appears in Pinkney's illustrations as a young shepherd tending his sheep, but by the end of the book he is an old, gray, bearded man, a man who has seen and experienced a lot in his life, a man full of both wisdom and pain.

David's life is long and complicated. Though many of the episodes that come later in his life make captivating tales, they are rife with questionable ethics, violence, and complicated sexual themes. They make for wonderfully rich adult study and reflection, but are not necessarily well suited as stories for children. It is understandable therefore that most of the retellings for children focus on David's childhood and, in particular, the story of his victory over Goliath that are the core of the hero journey segment of David's story. It is the stories of his youth that depict the transformation he undergoes in order to become the king and leader of the later stories.

Campbell writes, "When the hero-quest has been accomplished . . . the adventurer still must return with his life-transmuting trophy" (p. 193). When David cuts off Goliath's head, he is doing exactly that, returning with a trophy of his mission successfully accomplished. That physical act is an important part of David's maturation as it visually signals his success and shows him to have effectively transformed himself. For the slaying of Goliath is more than a mere physical triumph for the young David, it is an emotional and developmental triumph as well. In so doing, David manages to prove his own self-worth, gain the respect of those around him, and conquer his own fears. Defeating Goliath is life changing for David; nothing will ever be the same for him after that. Not only will others always look at him differently, he will look at himself differently after that as well.

The story of David is full of universal elements found in hero literature from around the world. It shares many motifs with fairy tales, legends, and myths, and speaks to classic themes for children. Framed as a story about a younger son who becomes a brave warrior, marries the king's daughter, and becomes the king himself, this is a universal story of a child's emotional development and journey into adulthood.

Campbell argues that every child can relate to these themes and to the hero's journey: "The mighty hero of extraordinary powers . . . is each of us: not the physical self visibly in the mirror, but the king within" (p. 365). More than a story about one particular boy's adventures, this is a familiar story about growing up and realizing one's own potential. Bettelheim similarly focuses on the role of the metaphor of royalty in stories for children. The hero struggles against the forces of evil, in David's case symbolized by Goliath, as a way to overcome the negative sides of himself. Once children win this battle, they gain sovereignty over their own lives, the right to self-rule, and can live happily ever after as mature adults.

> No child believes that one day he will become ruler over a kingdom other than the realm of his own life. The fairy story assures him that someday this kingdom can be his, but not without struggle. How the child specifically imagines the "kingdom" depends on his age and state of development, but he never takes it literally. To the younger child, it may simply mean that then nobody will order him around, and that all his wishes will be fulfilled. To the older child, it will also include the obligation to rule—that is, to live and act wisely. But at any age a child interprets becoming king or queen as having gained mature adulthood. (p. 127 28)

Royalty is a metaphor that allows children to come to terms with their present state of subjection to the rules and needs of others, and to imagine that one day they will be able to assume their rightful place as rulers over their own lives and choices.

David is thus a role model for children of growth and self-realization. Unlike retellings of the story of Noah, which tend to emphasize the importance of obedience and the dangers of disobedience, the stories of David generally acknowledge that there comes a point when children must assert their own needs in order to make the proper transition into adulthood. David's journey into maturity mirrors children's real-life journeys, from the expectation of obedience and the experience of powerlessness to the attainment of self-determination and self-rule. In getting to know David and his struggle to grow up and become a warrior and king, children are able to glimpse the king or queen they have waiting within themselves, struggling to grow up, become free, and live relatively happily ever after through the act of "ruling" their own lives wisely and well.

6
JONAH

The image most associated with Jonah is surely that of a whale. Often referred to as "the reluctant prophet," Jonah is best known for winding up in the belly of what is often called a whale but in fact is simply identified in the Biblical text as "a huge fish." The details of what happens before and after that pivotal event, however, are less well known.

The Book of Jonah is a short book of four chapters, located in the Prophets section of the Hebrew Bible. In this brief but action-packed book, Jonah is called by God to go the city of Nineveh and, on account of the wickedness of the people there, "proclaim judgment upon it" (Jonah 1:2). Jonah tries to run away from God and from what he is being asked to do. He boards a ship, only to learn that he cannot escape God. God causes a great storm at sea that threatens to destroy the ship. In order to save themselves, the sailors wind up throwing Jonah overboard into the sea where he gets swallowed up by a huge sea creature. After praying to God and vowing to do what God asks, Jonah is spit out onto dry land, and told again to go to Nineveh, where he now does as he has been commanded. However, because the people repent from their evil ways, God decides not to destroy them after all. Jonah is distraught that God has had a change of heart and asks to die. Using a plant, God teaches Jonah a lesson about compassion.

Like the story of Noah, this cautionary tale was long seen as a suitable story to tell children, in part because of the role of the fish and possibly also because the drama makes for good storytelling. Yet there are deep theological and psychological issues in this story that could just as well terrify children as entertain them. It could well be that generations of parents and educators felt that there was a critical message for children inherent in this story about behaving and listening to parents—if you don't, you might, figuratively, get thrown overboard and wind up in the belly of the beast.

Jonah is a different kind of hero than the obedient Noah. Unlike Noah, who unquestioningly goes about building the Ark according to God's exact instructions, Jonah at first tries to shirk his responsibility. He doesn't want to do as he has been told to do by God. Even when Jonah finally does as he has been told, he sulks, angry and annoyed about his role in God's plan. In the end though, through some difficult lessons, he comes to see the importance of doing as he is told. While Jonah proceeds on his physical journey to Nineveh, he undergoes a developmental journey from the self-centered irresponsibility of youth to a more mature, compassionate adulthood. Many of the motifs in this story are similar to those of classic tales like "Little Red Riding Hood" or "Pinocchio," in which the child protagonist acts irresponsibly and gets swallowed up by a beast, in the former case a wolf, or in the latter a whale, before learning to act in the manner considered acceptable by the adult authority figure.[9] This theme is also echoed in modern stories like *Pierre* by Maurice Sendak (1962), in which Pierre, a boy who only says, "I don't care" and doesn't do anything that is asked of him by his parents, is eaten by a lion. After Pierre comes to realize that he does in fact care, he is removed, unharmed, from the lion.

Jonah is a hero who is able to learn and grow. Central themes in this story are thus about accepting responsibility and about learning to care for the fate of others. In learning to do so, Jonah also learns that second chances are possible. Something done wrong the first time can be attempted again, with a more positive outcome once the appropriate emotional growth has occurred.

Why Jonah?

The word of the Lord came to Jonah, Son of Ammitai . . .

(Jonah 1:1)

The Bible provides some rationale, albeit sketchy, for why certain protagonists are given their central role. We are told, for example, that

---

[9] Most contemporary versions of "Little Red Riding Hood" have been sanitized and recount only the grandmother being swallowed by the wolf. However, in earlier versions of the story, such as those recorded by Perrault (*Perrault's Fairy Tales* by Charles Perrault and illustrated by Gustav Doré, 1969) and by Grimm, as seen in *Little Red Riding Hood by The Brothers Grimm*, retold and illustrated by Trina Schart Hyman (NY: Holiday House, 1983) the girl is swallowed as well.

Noah was righteous and that Joseph was his father's beloved son. In the case of Jonah, almost no information whatsoever is given, other than that Jonah was the son of Ammitai. No further clues are provided about his age, his profession, his history, or his character. The reason that he was hand-picked by God for his particular mission is left unexplained in the biblical text. Jonah is therefore a stand-in for Everyman in this cautionary tale. He is a blank slate, ready to be written on by the reader's imagination or fleshed out by the reteller or illustrator. In some retellings he is young, in some he is old. Some authors have chosen to provide reasons for him having been God's choice, and other versions leave the question unanswered. The idea of Everyman, or Everychild, resonates with children because they too can fill in the blanks and thereby easily identify with him.

Jonah cares primarily about himself and how events will impact on him, not on others. He has not yet developed a sense of empathy. These are elements of the story that make it one that children can easily relate to. According to Piaget's stages of development, children are naturally egocentric until about age eight. When children read this story, they see themselves, like Jonah, as the center of the universe. Campbell identifies the moment when a figure, in Jonah's case God, appears to guide the hero and lead him into a new stage or period as the hero's "call to adventure" (p. 55–56). At first Jonah refuses the call from God because he doesn't see why he should bother to obey. As Campbell writes, "the refusal is essentially a refusal to give up what one takes to be one's own interest" (p. 60). This call from God is going to be Jonah's defining moment that delineates between Jonah's "before" and his "after," his transition from egocentric youth to a more empathetic adulthood.

The Jonah depicted in Marcia Williams's *Jonah and the Whale* is a grown man, as evidenced by his beard. Even so, the cartoon-style illustrations show Jonah to be a childlike figure with whom children can identify. Despite the beards, in Williams's art all the adults look like young children. When the word of God comes to Jonah in this volume, he is asleep in his bed. Like the ostrich sticking his head in the sand, Jonah runs away because he does not believe that God would really destroy Nineveh.

In the illustrations in *The Book of Jonah* by Peter Spier (1985), Jonah is depicted as a man of middle age, whose hair and beard are still dark. In the endpapers he is shown to be hard working, as evidenced by his labors threshing in the fields. While he works, a ray of light shines down upon him from above, implying that he was chosen by God because he was hard working and responsible. The sense of Jonah as Everyman is evidenced in Spier's language as well: "One day, as Jonah the prophet was going about his everyday work, the Lord God spoke to him." In this retelling, there is, therefore, nothing special about Jonah. He was picked specifically because he was just a man going about his everyday work. Another detail that Spier provides is that Jonah is a family man. He is a man with a wife and children, to whom he says good-bye before he sets out. His decision to flee from God's command is seen then not as the impetuous, impulsive decision of a young man, but rather a thoughtful choice by a mature adult.

In contrast to Spier's Jonah, the Jonah in Geoffrey Patterson's 1991 *Jonah and the Whale* is "a lazy man, who spent most of the day lying in the sun doing nothing while his neighbors worked hard." In fact, in this version he is so lazy that his neighbors want nothing to do with him, which makes Jonah unhappy and causes him to question himself, wondering "why he found it so difficult to be like them." Far from Everyman, this is Jonah as a wretched, pitiable outcast. Then Jonah hears the voice of God telling him to go to Nineveh. Whereas in the original biblical text Jonah simply ups and flees to Tarshish, Patterson's Jonah engages in self-doubt and mortal fear, saying, "I can't possibly do that. I am just an ordinary man. Perhaps the people of Nineveh will kill me. I won't go!" God answers, telling Jonah that he has been chosen by God and must go. Instead of feeling good about having been singled out, Jonah chooses to run away.

The figure of Jonah in Rosemary Lanning's *Jonah and the Whale*, illustrated by Bernadette Watts (2001), is shown to be a man taken by surprise by God's command. In the folkloric illustrations, Jonah is depicted as a simple man, going about his business, who is suddenly surprised by contact with the divine. The text states:

> Long, long ago there lived a man named Jonah. One day Jonah heard the voice of God, saying, "Go to the city of Nineveh . . ."

Jonah looks up at the sky, his hands full of the fruit he has been in the middle of picking from a tree, his eyes big and open in wonder. He asks, "Why me?" and runs away, feeling that what happens in Nineveh is no business of his. Although the Book of Jonah is in Prophets, he is never actually referred to as a prophet in the biblical text. Most of the retellings of the Jonah story for children don't deal with the concept of prophecy. Mordicai Gerstein's *Jonah and the Two Great Fish* (1997) is an exception. Like Patterson's Jonah, Gerstein's Jonah also claims that he is not the right man for the job. However, in this version his reluctance comes across as humility rather than lack of self-confidence. In an echo of Moses' response when God tells him to tell Pharoah to let the Israelites go, this Jonah tries to demur, claiming, "God has made a mistake. I am not ready to be a prophet. I will forget what to say. I will stutter and the people will laugh at me." These ideas are expressed only in Jonah's head. He does not actually speak his thoughts and concerns to God, rather, his only actual response is to run away.

Jonah may be a prophet but he is also a hard headed man who needs to be repaired by God in *How God Fix Jonah,* Graham Lorenz's collection of bible stories from the African oral tradition. Lorenz writes: *"Jonah was a prophet. / God put Him hand on Jonah / But Jonah head be hard. / Jonah head be hard too much. / Lord God Almighty can fix the thing. / Can fix hard heard / Can fix weak back / Can fix crooked leg. / God can fix anything."* Though Jonah is identified here as a prophet, he does not act like one when God tells him to go to Nineveh and "preach My word." God must thus "fix" Jonah that he will act in an appropriate manner and do as God commands.

Jonah is acknowledged as a prophet in "Change of Heart: The Story of Jonah" in Patricia and Fredrick McKissack's *Let My People Go: Bible Stories Told by a Freeman of Color.* Yet here his status as prophet is not in and of itself a positive quality. He is presented as a kind of false or foolish prophet. They write:

> Some folk *say* one thing at the front door, then run 'round to the back door and *do* just the opposite. See, Jonah *said* he was a prophet of God. But when it came time for Jonah to actually *do* something God wanted him to do, po' Jonah fell 'way short of the mark.

Just saying he was a prophet was not enough. He needed to also act like a prophet, and this he didn't do. Jonah is set up right at the beginning of this retelling as someone who needs to learn a lesson. Throughout the first part of this version, Jonah is referred to with negative attributes, such as "Jonah, oh foolish Jonah," "Jonah, oh pitiful Jonah," and "Jonah, oh disobedient Jonah." As in Graham's version of Jonah, this is a man who needs fixing. But as the story continues, the change in Jonah is reflected by changes in the language. Jonah is "frightened" when he is thrown overboard. Once he is in the belly of the fish he becomes "prayerful," then "sorrowful," and "repentant." Yet Jonah still isn't quite there. When God decides not to kill the Ninevites, the text reads, "Jonah, oh unforgiving Jonah." It is only through God's direct example of caring and compassion that Jonah can learn in the end to behave like a real prophet.

The Story of Jonah as retold by Mary Auld and illustrated by Diana Mayo (1999) is another example of a retelling that does not shy away from the idea of Jonah as a prophet. This version tries to answer the question of why Jonah was chosen by imagining a relationship with God that exists before the beginning of the written story. Auld writes: "Long ago in the land of Canaan there lived a man called Jonah. He was a prophet and God often spoke to him. One day God told Jonah to go to the great city of Nineveh." According to this retelling, this is not the first time that Jonah and God have been in touch. He has been chosen because he and God already have an established connection. God already knows that Jonah is the right man for the job, though it is not clear for what reasons. In providing answers to some questions, Auld has raised additional questions. For example, does God know that Jonah can be trusted with such a mission? Or does God know that Jonah needs to learn something from the experience?

A prior relationship between God and Jonah is also assumed in Chaikin's "Jonah and the Whale," in her collection *Children's Bible Stories from Genesis to Daniel.* When God talks to Jonah in this retelling, there is no element of surprise, only a sense of predictability of the outcome. Chaikin writes: "Jonah did not want to go. He knew God, and knew just what would happen. The people of Nineveh would say they were sorry. They would ask God to forgive them. So why go to Nineveh. What was the point?" Chaikin has created a Jonah who does not want to go not because he is lazy or scared, but because he does not see the point in exerting himself when the result of his efforts is, for him, easily foreseeable and not worth it. Instead of being scared because he doesn't truly know or understand God, Jonah thinks that he knows God so well that he can predict God's actions. Being obedient to God seems to this Jonah to be pointless.

Jonah himself asks, "Why must I go there?" in Clyde Robert Bulla's *Jonah and the Great Fish* (1970). Jonah is depicted as a simple farmer, plowing his field in the land of Israel. The story uses the language of traditional fairy tale and folk literature, starting with the very first words: "Long ago in the land of Israel there lived a man named Jonah." It is immediately set apart from the familiar realistic stories children are used to and invokes a magisterial, third-person voice. The illustrations, by Helga Aichinger, portray a simple farmer with his plow, pulled by a donkey, working under the palm trees in his furrowed field. His head is bowed as he concentrates on his work, an altogether ordinary, humble man as confirmed by his activity and the illustrator's earth-toned palette.

Bulla maintains the sense of Jonah as Everyman by writing nothing about Jonah's character or whether he had any previous relationship with God. One day after Jonah has worked in his field he lays down to rest. God awakens Jonah with a commanding voice "like wind and rain and thunder." He tells Jonah to rise and go to Nineveh to "preach" to the inhabitants to repent their wicked ways. Like the kind of specific command, phrased in absolute and precise language, that an adult might use with a child, God's command leaves no room for negotiation. A youthful, unbearded Jonah is shown lying on a small plot of unplowed brown land and dressed in a drab cloak. All around where God has spoken, the page is shown in flaming red-golds with blue-green tipped flames, making it clear why Nineveh is in need of help. Like an obedient child, Jonah responds to God's command by saying "The Lord has spoken, and I must obey," but at the same time he wrestles with himself, asking why he must save them, since the people of Nineveh are the enemies of Israel. He questions whether their wickedness is his responsibility. Even as he decides not to obey God's command, Jonah acknowledges that God will pursue his command to Jonah and will punish him if he does not obey. Jonah's decision to flee from God's command, or be punished for his refusal to obey, is carried out under the cover of darkness. Jonah's belief that God cannot see in the dark is similar to the belief of a young child who thinks that adults cannot see in the dark and thus by extension cannot see into the heart and mind of a child.

The Sailors

> In their fright, the sailors cried out,
> each to his own god, and they flung
> the ship's cargo overboard to make
> it lighter for them.
>
> (Jonah 1:5)

The sailors play an important role in the story of Jonah. In the biblical text, they are worshipers of various gods, pagans in other words. This is a sharp contrast to Jonah and his, albeit resistant, relationship with the invisible, all-powerful God of the monotheistic Judeo–Christian tradition. Yet the sailors come to attest to the power, authority, and omnipotence of Jonah's God over theirs. They understand something that Jonah must still learn. There is a lesson embedded here for Jonah—if these pagan sailors can recognize God's greatness, Jonah's attempt at running away from God is that much more ridiculous.

Despite their pagan practices, the sailors are actually portrayed in the biblical text as people with an ethical sense. Once it becomes clear to the sailors that the answer to their problem can only be found in throwing Jonah overboard, they hesitate, still trying to find other solutions (Jonah 1:13). Miriam Chaikin stresses the idea of the essential goodness of the sailors in the chapter "Jonah and the Whale" from her 1993 collection *Children's Bible Stories from Genesis to Daniel*. She notes: "The sailors had nothing against Jonah. They wished they didn't have to take such a drastic step, but they had no choice. They tossed Jonah overboard, and at once the sea became calm." In this evenhanded retelling, the sailors are presented as decent people who simply had no other options.

The idea of throwing Jonah overboard as a solution to the sailors' problem, knowing he will surely not survive the ferocious storm, is one of the unsettling aspects of this story. Children are asked to consider the point of view of the sailors, who tried to find better solutions but eventually were compelled to act in a harmful manner toward Jonah, while also understanding the story from Jonah's standpoint and to empathize with his plight. Similarly, the story asks children to understand God's actions in requiring Jonah to potentially suffer before being redeemed. Young children are not usually able to see events from different points of view at once. They are also not able to understand two different and potentially conflicting views of one event, to see that there is no absolutely right or wrong answer. It is generally between the ages of six and eight that a sense of social conscience, the ability to understand that others may have a different, and equally valid, point of view, begins to emerge. An additional challenge in this story is the idea that while the sailors did not initially have a relationship with Jonah's commanding and powerful God, they are still good people who try to behave well. This story pushes children to consider the possibility that there can be more than one way to view a situation, and that right and wrong behavior can be relative concepts.

In the story of Jonah, children are asked to see events simultaneously from both the sailors' perspective and from Jonah's. At the next developmental stage, from approximately the end of young childhood at around age seven to the start of adolescence at around age twelve, children can understand that others may have a different viewpoint based on their own needs and reasons regardless of whether that viewpoint differs from their own. It is at this age that parents remind children to behave and make good choices, regardless of what their friends choose. Telling the story of the storm, the fear it inspires from the sailors' point of view and from Jonah's, and their respective reactions to the storm requires a new expanding focus for children.

Many of the various retellings of this story for children leave out different details of this part of the tale, reflecting an ambivalence about how to deal with the issues of paganism, the relationship to God, and even the issue of the sailors' ethics. Spier's text is spare and to the point. He does not provide elaborations or explanations, writing only: "Jonah was running away from God." When Jonah is confronted later by the sailors and blamed for the great storm that had come upon the ship, he says simply: "I am a Hebrew . . . I worship the Lord the God of Heaven, who made land and sea. He has given me a job to do that is too hard for me. I am running away from him." One of the important elements in the biblical story of Jonah is that the sailors are transformed from people who want someone to blame for their troubles and who accept the existence of gods who have control over things like weather into people who come to know that Jonah's God is stronger and mightier than any of their gods. In the biblical narrative, they offer sacrifices and make vows to Jonah's God in thanks for their deliverance. This sense of God's greatness is absent from Spier's retelling, though the illustration of the sailors rejoicing and lifting up a lamb might allude to those actions. But the sailor's acknowledgment of Jonah's God is clearly not a central issue in Spier's retelling.

This element is even less important in Patterson's version of Jonah's story. Here the sailors, albeit reluctantly, throw Jonah overboard when he tells them to. Other than writing, "Everyone on the boat was afraid and prayed to their gods to save them from the storm," there are no theological musings on the part of the sailors in this version.

Mordecai Gerstein's version, which interweaves elements of Midrash to fill in some of the gaps in the biblical story, adds several elements missing from the other retellings of Jonah. The art depicts a boat being rained upon while the rest of the sky is blue. The finger is pointed clearly at this ship—it is there that the problem lies. Jonah is sleeping down below in the hold, in a bed nicely covered in blankets and with a pillow under his head, while up above the sailors are afraid, calling out to their various gods and goddesses. Gerstein uses another piece of Midrash and writes, "People of all nations were on the ship . . ." No matter who they were, they were being affected by the God of this sleeping man. Lest there be concern that this story is xenophobic and merely a polemic about one group of people (Jonah's) being better than other people (the sailors), in this version the sailors are shown to be essentially good people, in that they don't want to throw Jonah overboard. But Jonah convinces them that they have no choice, telling them to put his toes into the sea and take them out again. When they dip him in the roiling sea, the storm stops, and when they pull him back out it starts again. They throw him in only for lack of a better alternative.

Jonah and the Great Fish, retold and illustrated by Warwick Hutton (1983), does not deal with the issue of different gods. It does, however, stand out among the retellings of the Jonah story for children in that it uses an element from the biblical narrative that is rarely used in these retellings, that of the lots drawn by Jonah and the sailors. In language close to that of the biblical text, he writes: "The sailors believed that someone on board had brought bad luck to the ship. 'Come and draw lots, so we may know who is causing this evil,' they said. Jonah drew the black stick. Then they knew that he was the cause of their trouble." The logic behind the idea of drawing lots relies either on random chance or on fate as decided by God. The idea that Jonah's fate could be decided by something as random as the luck of the draw could be a terrifying concept in a children's book. In fairy tales and adventure/ quest stories such as "Cinderella," "Rapunzel," and "King Arthur," the hero's fate is often determined or altered by a magical character such as a fairy godmother or magician who has access to knowledge about the future that the hero does not possess. In these stories, there is a reason, unknown to the hero, that he must take a certain road, open a certain door, or chose a certain stick. That God is determining Jonah's fate here, rather than it being the result of random chance, is in keeping with this type of story.

In Hutton's picture book, the accompanying illustration does not do much to allay these fears, depicting the sailors as piratelike figures with gold earrings and daggers behind their backs. Yet Hutton does allow the sailors to be redeemed as they try to solve their problem with solutions other than throwing Jonah into the water. But when all their hard work accomplishes nothing and they are left without even oars or a sail, there is no further choice for them. "In despair, they begged Jonah to forgive them. Then they lifted him up and threw him into the ocean."

Auld's version of the Jonah story is a bland retelling that tries to be objective, complete and noncontroversial. With its maps, glossary, and discussion questions at the back, this is the Bible as social studies. She leaves out entirely the issue of the sailors calling upon other gods, perhaps because this might lead to a discussion about the existence of people who are not monotheists. However, like Patterson's version, this retelling remains faithful to the biblical original in that it includes the drawing of lots. As in Hutton's version, the sailors try to do all they can before resorting to throwing Jonah overboard, calling out to God, "Oh Lord, please don't punish us for killing this innocent man. We are only doing as you wanted." Still sticking closely to the biblical text, the sailors offer sacrifices and thanks to Jonah's God once the sea has become calm.

Jonah's attempt to flee to Tarshish is told in *A Ship in a Storm on the Way to Tarshish,* a dramatic narrative poem presented as a full-length picture book written by Norma Farber and illustrated by Victoria Chess (1977). The era is indeterminate but feels more contemporary than Biblical as Jonah peers out from the whale using a periscope. The sailors are aghast as a whale keeps butting the ship during a raging storm. Chess uses black-and-white cross hatch drawings to show the frothing, white-capped upheaval and portrays only three sailors on board with Jonah. In contrast to the dramatic narrative, the sailors are reminiscent of the three sailors in a tub from the childhood nursery rhyme "Rub-a-Dub-Dub," diminishing the sense of fear implied in Farber's text. When they appear at the side of the ship, peeking into to the sea looking for a sign to explain the event to them, they bring to mind The Three Stooges. But their frightful plight is real as they tremble at the havoc caused by the lost whale.

The Huge Fish

The Lord provided a huge fish to swallow Jonah, and Jonah remained in the fish's belly three days and three nights. Jonah prayed to the Lord his God from the belly of the fish.

(Jonah 2:1–2)

Places that serve as sites of important transformation are often mysterious or supernatural in folktales and mythology. Campbell writes, "The regions of the unknown . . . are free fields for the projection of unconscious content" (p. 79). Like the whale in "Pinocchio" or the wolf in "Little Red Riding Hood," here the "fish" that swallows Jonah lends a magical or supernatural element to the story and raises many questions. The kind of fish is not identified by the biblical text, but because it is a called a "huge fish" many have chosen to translate it as whale. The Bible is spare in its description of this fish. Is it a friend or a foe? A safe refuge or a jail cell? Is this Jonah's reward for coming clean with the sailors and accepting his fate, or is this his punishment for trying to run away from God? Because these questions are not answered by the text, retellers of the story are provided with fertile ground to fill in details.

In Spier's *Jonah,* the fish breaks the surface of the water to swallow "the helpless Jonah." This terrifying scenario is fleshed out in the illustrations, in which Jonah is shown being chased by an enormous fish. But he is described as being able to breathe inside the fish, supplying a detail to help alleviate possible fears of young readers. After three days in the fish, Jonah is spit out onto dry land, covered in seaweed and looking dazed and disheveled. Then a divine light shines down upon him, and he is told again to go to Nineveh. This time he listens to God.

Lanning and Patterson both use the word "whale," emphasizing the enormity of the creature in contrast to Jonah. In contrast to Spier's predatory fish, Lanning's whale is a smiling, friendly, toothless animal. The interior of this animal is filled with treasure chests, old boats, and fish. It is alight with the warm yellow glow of candles, in which Jonah piously kneels, hands together in prayer. Inside this whale, Jonah looks like a child who has been sent to the safe, cozy confines of his room for bad behavior. After being properly penitent, and promising to do whatever God asks of him, Jonah is spit out onto dry land. Similarly, Patterson's whale also signifies safety and redemption. In this retelling, emphasis is placed on Jonah's experience between being thrown from the ship and being swallowed by the whale. Patterson writes: "But Jonah sank slowly down and down, into the darkness. Surely he would drown. Then out of the blue-black depths appeared an enormous whale many times the size of the ship. With one gulp, it swallowed up little Jonah." In fact, the whale is so central to Patterson's retelling of the story that he ends the book after Jonah's encounter with the animal. As soon as Jonah is released onto dry land, the story is over, with no mention of what happens next. Hutton's retelling also ends right after Jonah is back on dry land, though it does mention that he went to Nineveh as God had commanded and that the people turned back from their bad ways. There is a sense in both Patterson and Hutton's versions that Jonah has been rebirthed, now willing to do God's bidding and be properly obedient. It is as if God and the whale are one, and once Jonah makes his peace with God from within the whale, the story is effectively over. Ashley Bryan's black and white woodcut illustration for Graham Lorenz's *How God Fix Jonah* visually plays off the idea of Jonah's experience in the whale as a gestation period prior to a rebirthing experience. Jonah is shown in a near-fetal position, enclosed in a white amniotic sac-like cavity within the fish, surrounded by the seawater.

In most of the Jonah retellings, he is swallowed by the fish without knowing why, other than that he had to be thrown into the sea in order to calm the storm. In trying to make sense out of these events, it is tempting to ascribe a motive to God. Despite her attempt at sticking closely to the biblical text, Auld does so, writing, "Jonah sank deep beneath the waves. But God did not mean for Jonah to die. He sent a great fish which swallowed the prophet whole." There are to be no loose ends left hanging in this retelling, no question that there is a guiding hand behind the action. Just as God has a prior relationship with Jonah that causes God to give Jonah this task, there are reasons for all that God does. The interior of this fish is shown in the illustration to be an unpleasant place. There is no whimsy used in this version. Rather, Jonah is shown to be sitting, miserably hunched up, in an anatomically correct interior of a fish, what Auld calls "his strange, dark prison."

Gerstein also adds an explanation for the events that are taking place, though a different one than Auld. In Gerstein's retelling, God tells Jonah that he must live in the fish until he changes his mind and does as God has told him to do. Gerstein adds some other dramatic Midrashic embellishments as well, giving the fish and Jonah a long history: ". . . A great fish had been waiting since the creation of the world to swallow him up." Jonah's meeting with the fish was therefore fate, implying that when God first commanded Jonah to go to Nineveh, God already knew that Jonah wasn't going to obey. Jonah's disobedience was part of God's master plan, making it more acceptable and even perhaps an important part of his developmental process. Although the fish is not particularly scary-looking, Gerstein has put teeth on this fish, adding a fear-provoking visual element while at the same time reassuring Jonah and the readers that the fish will not eat Jonah but allow him, at God's will, to live inside until Jonah is ready to do what God has asked and then move on.

Inside Gerstein's fish, there are even more surprises. The interior of the fish is large, comfortable, and well furnished. Jonah dines like a king under a diamond chandelier and has a four-poster bed at his disposal, and can look out at the underwater world through the eyes of the fish. But then God decides that Jonah is too comfortable and will never come to change his mind. So God sends a second, even bigger fish, who makes the first fish give Jonah up. Gerstein bases the existence of this second fish on a Midrash which tries to explain why two different Hebrew words for fish are used in the biblical text. The Midrash imagines that there were indeed two different fish, one a male and one a female. Gerstein picks up on this Midrash, and envisions Jonah being transferred from one fish to the other. The inside of this second fish, unlike the first, is not nice or comfortable. Gerstein writes, "The second fish was a mother fish. Inside, it was dark and crowded with thirty six thousand, five hundred baby fish of all kinds." Like a child being forced to come to terms with the reality of a new sibling in the family, in this second fish Jonah will no longer be the one and only, the king for whom all the creature comforts exist. Now Jonah has to vie for space with all the other baby fish. Jonah must, in other words, grow up and stop seeing himself as the center of the universe. Jonah then cries out to God to save him from this unpleasant experience, promising to do whatever God asks.

Farber's fish is clearly identified as a whale and is altogether a friendly, helpful creature who is depicted as having gotten separated from its mother. It is not intentionally looking to cause havoc, merely bumping around the ocean during a storm looking for its mother and the rest of the whale pod. It is not clear who is more helpless, Jonah or the whale. After Jonah is selected to help the whale, Farber writes:

> Somebody help him find his group!
> Who, me?
> I see. . .

And Jonah travels "down the hatch," proclaiming in childlike language about the whale's belly, "This cabin's great!"

Jonah calmly accepts responsibility for helping the whale find his lost pod but no mention is made of Jonah's culpability for the impending catastrophe. Jonah matter-of-factly accepts his fate, dons a wet suit, and sails off "Down the Hatch!" into the whale's belly, where he is quite comfortable. Just as there is no mention of why Jonah is fleeing to Tarshish, there is no mention of God or retribution in this retelling. Jonah uses the stars, the heavens, and Polaris to help the whale follow his abandoned ship toward Tarshish and avoid danger from sharks and swordfishes. It is dramatic high adventure as they head toward Tarshish, while the whale searches for his mother and lost whale pod. Jonah reassures the whale, "Your mother is bound to be calling to you." Finally, "The happy reunion of whales is sung," and mother and child are shown reaching their flippers out toward each other. As they are about to embrace Jonah cautions:

> Wait! Don't rock! Don't roll me about!
> Don't nuzzle your mother yet!
> Safe in her flippers
> at last—Hey, wait! Just let
> a fellow disembark.

The whale has found safety but Jonah wants to make sure that he too will be safe. Jonah disembarks on what appears to be a deserted beach, saying he'll stay on land awhile. Here at the end Jonah reveals his name for the first time, and in keeping with the breezy tone of the book, says that he's "Joe, for short" and that he never reached Tarshish. The reader is left not knowing whether or not Jonah managed to reach Nineveh to deliver God's message. The implication could be understood that Jonah cannot go home again, having failed to deliver God's message. Farber's book reminds child readers of the necessity to be obedient and responsible, lest they, too, be stranded all alone, unable to go home and receive comfort from a loving but all-powerful parent. The contrast between the whale, happily reunited with his mother, and Jonah all alone on the island reinforces this lesson. The whale's separation from his mother was not a result of disobedience, and therefore he merits being reunited with her. Jonah, on the other hand, having willfully disobeyed God, ends the book in solitude.

The great fish presents for Jonah what Campbell would call a "threshold of transformation." It is not a physical challenge for Jonah, but a psychological one. He enters the fish in the process of trying to flee from God and the world of responsibilities, but he emerges from the fish transformed and ready to do God's bidding. His time in the fish is the critical piece of his hero's journey, as Campbell writes, "the adventure of the hero normally follows the pattern of . . . a separation from the world, a penetration to some source of power, and a life-enhancing return" (p. 35). Having had the experience of being cast out and made to suffer, he is now ready to turn his attention outward toward others.

God as a Protagonist

> *I sank to the base of the mountains;*
> *The bars of the earth closed upon me forever.*
> *Yet you brought my life up from the pit,*
> *O Lord, my God!*
> *When my life was ebbing away,*
> *I called the Lord to mind . . .*
>
> (Jonah 2:7–8)

Unlike other biblical stories in which God stays mainly in the background or off-stage, in the story of Jonah God is a central character. Jonah and God speak, God overtly directs the action, and everyone on stage, from the sailors to the Ninevites, acts in relationship to God. In order for Jonah to truly learn his lesson and for the story to reach its natural conclusion, God must act as a role model for Jonah. In retellings of the Jonah story created for the secular market, this presents a challenge, for the story cannot easily proceed by conveniently writing God out of the story.

Most of Chapter 2 of the Book of Jonah consists of Jonah's prayer to God, thanking God for having saved him and vowing to do as God asks in the future. Prayers in biblical texts are part poetry, part theology. But they are not part of the running narrative thread of a story. Most of the versions of Jonah's tale for children leave out his prayer entirely.

Patterson turns it into regular speech, writing "Jonah spoke to God from the whale's stomach and said, 'I trust you to look after me, and I will do what you ask.'" It is these words that cause a light to glow inside the whale's stomach so that Jonah can see. Spier takes another tack, writing, "He prayed to God, asking to be forgiven for his disobedience." Lanning's Jonah prays to God and offers thanks for having been saved. She writes, "You were angry with me, O Lord, but you rescued me. I will do whatever you ask now."

In Spier's *The Book of Jonah,* God is depicted visually as a ray of light shining down on Jonah from the heavens. Spier's use of this light is carefully considered. It only shines on Jonah at several crucial moments, when Jonah is working in the fields, when God first speaks to him, when he is back again on dry land and God speaks to Jonah again, and when God speaks to Jonah at the end about the fate of Ninevah.

Spier's version of the Jonah story allows for a God who can have a change of mind. This is a rational, caring God, who gives people a chance, who is not spiteful or stern, who can admit that there are other ways of looking at a situation, and who seeks good for the world rather than bad. Spier writes, "Nineveh is a great and beautiful city, holding thousands of innocent people and animals. I take no delight in destruction. I long for the people to leave their wrongdoing and turn to me." There is also another important lesson here: just as God can reconsider and change course, so can we. This is a teaching God, who, like a good parent, uses experiential learning to impart life lessons. He shows Jonah the meaning of loss, and teaches him to appreciate life by first providing the vine and then destroying it as an act of guidance, not vindictiveness.

The idea of God as a teacher and role model is stressed in Patricia and Fredrick McKissack's retelling in their 1998 collection *Let My People Go: Bible Stories Told by Freeman of Color.* Jonah slowly makes his transition from foolish self-centeredness to caring empathy. It is only God's final lesson with the vine that enables Jonah to change his outlook. They write:

> Even today, there're folk who think like Jonah did, who are sometimes stubborn, without passion, and unforgiving. But God is just the opposite. No matter who we are or what we've done, if we turn from wicked-

ness God is quick to show mercy. God's love aine [sic] fickle like ours can sometimes be. It is an eternal spring, overflowing with the sweet water of forgiveness.

God's behavior presents us with the ultimate model of mercy and forgiveness. As a human, Jonah may not be expected to always live up to God's example, but he has been presented with a model to emulate. How reassuring this idea can be for children, that while people may not always act as they should, God is always there as an endless source of forgiveness.

Despite the prohibition against depicting an image of God, Gerstein cleverly uses elements from nature to insert an image of God into the illustrations. When Jonah is spewed out of the mouth of the fish and released onto dry land, Gerstein uses clouds, sky, and a flying bird to depict God in the firmament, helping and guiding Jonah with an outstretched arm. When Jonah begins his trek to Nineveh, God is depicted as a cloud formation in the shape of a huge hand with a finger pointing directly to the town. And again when the Ninevites "wept and asked God to forgive them" an image of a smiling God with an outstretched arm is shown in the cloud formation, with the sun as God's eye. The God of *Jonah and the Two Great Fish* is an integral part of this story, directing Jonah's actions from the beginning and making sure that events unfold according to divine desire.

Nineveh and Beyond

> God saw what they did, how they were turning back from their evil ways. And God renounced the punishment He had planned to bring upon them, and did not carry it out.
>
> (Jonah 3:10)

As noted above, many of the retellings of the story of Jonah for children simply end with Jonah being released from captivity in the fish. It is as if, having learned his lesson about trying to escape responsibility and God's authority, what happens next is simply redundant. Yet

Jonah's reaction to God's actions vis-à-vis the Ninevites is a critical part of the story. God plants a vine to protect Jonah from the sun, and Jonah enjoys the shade enormously. Then God sends a worm to destroy the plant. Jonah is despondent over the destruction of the plant and begs to die. God responds by creating an analogy to the people of Nineveh, reminding Jonah that he did nothing to create or nurture the plant, and yet he is in despair over it. How much more so would God be despondent over the destruction of the people of Nineveh, whom he created (Jonah 4).

Lanning's version takes Jonah all the way to Nineveh, where he does exactly as God has commanded. As in the biblical text, the people listen to Jonah and repent, and God spares them punishment. Though Lanning's version goes this far, it stops before the biblical story of Jonah comes to a complete end, leaving out the last lesson that God teaches Jonah using the vine. The important message in this version is that Jonah has learned to do as God commands. In so doing, he also learns that those who ask for forgiveness and mend their ways will be granted forgiveness.

Auld's Jonah is a changed man after his experience in the fish. Though Nineveh is a "huge city," Jonah "did not hesitate." Now that he has learned to do as God commands, he marches right in and brings the people his message, which they take to heart. In this simplified version, the Ninevites repent, and are spared. In keeping with Jonah's lack of hesitation beforehand, he does not indulge in any soul searching afterward either.

After the divine light shines down upon Spier's Jonah, he does as he is told and goes to Nineveh. Much to his surprise, the people of the city listen to his message. All the people pray to God and repent, even the king. They cover themselves and their animals in sackcloth. God then has a change of heart and decides to forgive them. Yet like a bad-tempered child, Jonah is angry at God's changed attitude. Spier writes, "Jonah stormed out of the city. High on a hilltop, overlooking the city walls, Jonah threw himself down under a rough shelter. He felt so bitter and confused, he wanted to die." High above the city, Jonah is alone, separated from everyone down below like a child who has stomped off to her room in anger. Spier takes the story all the way to its end, in which the purpose of Jonah's whole experience seems to have been to ultimately learn and grow.

The Book of Jonah ends with a direct lesson. Jonah storms out of Nineveh, angry that God has forgiven the people even though they will continue to sin. God then provides a plant to supply Jonah with shade. Jonah is delighted, but becomes despondent when God provides a worm to eat the plant and it dies. God uses this incident to teach Jonah a lesson about empathy, saying, "You cared about the plant, which you did not work for and which you did not grow, which appeared overnight and perished overnight. And should I not care about Nineveh, that great city, in which there are more than a hundred and twenty thousand persons . . . ?" (Jonah 4:10–11). Chaikin's retelling of the story is one version that includes this very final section of the biblical text. She underscores the idea that Jonah is being asked to consider God's feelings, and to use God as a model for his own behavior. In her version, God's lesson to Jonah is reworded in more contemporary colloquial language in which God says, "How must I feel? . . . Shouldn't I give those people another chance? Shouldn't I feel sorry for such a city?" While the biblical text ends the story of Jonah with God's words, Chaikin adds a final sentence to frame the story and make its message unambiguous. She writes, "And Jonah finally understood the meaning of compassion and forgiveness." Jonah has grown and developed emotionally. Despite his feeling at the beginning of the story that he already knew God and knew what God wanted, he has learned something new and important.

It is a different, though related, lesson that Jonah must learn in *Let My People Go*. The chapter on Jonah, entitled "A Change of Heart: The Story of Jonah," is framed by a more contemporary story told to a young girl by her father, a former slave. In this introductory story, the girl, Charlotte, asks her father if God should forgive someone who seems to have changed his behavior. The father replies, "It aine [sic] for me to say what God should and shouldn't do. God sees inside our hearts and knows when we have truly repented. That's what Jonah had to learn." This version of the story teaches a lesson about not being judgmental. Jonah needed to learn not only forgiveness, but also that it is not up to him to judge whether someone has truly repented from their evil ways or not. As all people are inherently flawed, no person has the right to sit in judgment of another. All people should be allowed to do better and try again.

Gerstein's interpretation also takes the story of Jonah all the way to its conclusion. Although the people of Nineveh are quick to ask God for forgiveness, in Gerstein's book they are not quick to forgive Jonah. Having been saved from destruction by God, they angrily accuse Jonah of being a false prophet and laugh at him. Gerstein writes, "Jonah hated being laughed at." He runs into the desert and accuses God of making a fool out of him. By adding this exchange, Gerstein has turned the story of Jonah into a story about pride. The story ends with Jonah being humbled by God. Gerstein writes, "'Dear Lord,' said Jonah, bowing his head. 'I *have* been a fool. Forgive me for my selfish anger. I rejoice at being your messenger. May the world be guided always by your goodness.'" Jonah learns not only that it is important to do as God tells him, but also that he shouldn't think only about himself. By warning the people of Nineveh, he was able to save a whole town of people as well as all their innocent animals who would have also been killed. He learns that actions have consequences, and that helping other people can require putting oneself on the line, even if it means looking like a fool. Gerstein's *Jonah and the Two Great Fish* is a story about maturity and coming to care for others. Even in Farber's retelling of Jonah's story, Jonah is shown as greatly concerned about the whale being reunited with its mother. Jonah rejoices when they are reunited and is depicted smiling from inside the whale's mouth as mother whale embraces her child, a reference to the classic religious image of Madonna and child.

By the end of the story, Jonah has grown and matured. He has come to accept God's authority, as he has learned to shape his behavior in such a way that will help others. He has learned to take into account the needs and norms of the larger community and to care about the fate of others beyond himself. Jonah's journey from Tarshish to Nineveh has been a journey of maturity and self-knowledge that mirrors typical emotional development from early childhood to young adulthood.

According to the psychologist Erik Erikson, by about the age of six, children become aware of the authority of other adults in the community besides their parents. A sense of the significance of "others" in the larger society beyond their immediate family becomes apparent as they interact more frequently with children and adults. It is at this point that a sense of what is right and what is wrong, along with a sense of guilt, emerges and is usually reflected in the rules they develop for play. This sense of what's fair and following the rules of the game is an attempt by young children to maintain a sense of consistency, the rule of "law and order." They become easily upset and frustrated when confronting inconsistency, and when adults change their minds in what often appears as last-minute, arbitrary decision-making, especially when it is directed at them. At this age children are highly moral, and attempting to maintain consistency in their own playtime rule-making is an example of trying to impose a consistent sense of fair play on their world.

Most children, until they are about kindergarten age, will play alongside other children, grabbing a pail, truck, or ball without a lot of interaction. By five or six their play becomes more focused, their games more sophisticated. There is a high degree of cooperation as two or more children work together to construct a block tower. At the same time they are aware of being able to hurt another child's feelings through the words they speak. Again, according to Erikson, as children move toward middle childhood the realization emerges that their behavior may be in opposition to the expectations of their parents, teacher, or other adult authority. This, Erikson writes, produces the earliest sense of conflict and guilt. When their behavior is in opposition to what the adults around them expect, a sense of conflict and confusion about their own behavior and its consequence is likely to arise. It is worsened when adults change their minds or are inconsistent in their expectations and behaviors. By the age of six children are expected to gradually take increasing responsibility for their actions; clear, consistent expectations from the adults around them help children to understand their individual relationships with others and to the larger community.

In late childhood children are able to work determinedly to complete the tasks that are expected of them, to work toward goals that fulfill the needs and objectives of the larger society beyond the immediate family cluster. They are able to work cooperatively with others toward achieving cultural objectives as well as meeting the goals and expectations of their own families. If they are unable or unwilling to develop such competency, Erikson posits, a sense of inferiority and failure emerges, especially when they measure themselves against the behavior of others in their peer group. As children enter adolescence a sense of cultural identity, of membership in an identifiable group, becomes dominant. This sometimes leads to a crisis between the child's emerging identity as an individual versus identity as a member of a specific group. The question of who controls the early adolescent—self, parent, or the community—becomes an all-consuming issue at this point, as is seen in the behavior of Jonah. It is an issue that can lead to diffusion and instability that causes havoc, as is seen in Jonah's response. Though Jonah's response to God's lesson is not recorded in the Biblical text, the implication is that Jonah finally understands the importance of acting as a member of a larger group, and has learned how to balance his needs against the needs of others.

The story of Jonah is a story about redemption, rebirth, and second chances. Part of what makes the story of Jonah such a fitting story for children is that Jonah is given the chance to grow and mature, to reconsider the path he has chosen and start all over. What child does not want a loving, benevolent parent to accede to a "second chance" the way that God does with Jonah? Rather than being presented as a perfect and faultless hero, Jonah's flawed character is allowed to develop and change. He is able, like children, to make mistakes and learn from them.

Jonah says no to God, but the story doesn't end there. God is compassionate and gives Jonah another chance to do right. Having learned and grown, Jonah is allowed a second chance. This is reinforced later in the story when God, in an act of divine compassion, forgives the whole city of Nineveh and its inhabitants, and does not destroy them as previously threatened. They acknowledge the error of their ways and are given a second chance to do better. This is a powerful message for children: there are opportunities for change and growth, and it is possible to learn from one's mistakes.

Parallels between the Jonah story and modern stories for children can be seen in such books as Maurice Sendak's classic *Where the Wild Things Are* (1963). In this story, when Max's mother warns him to behave, Max defiantly responds with his own threat; he resists his mother's admonition and is punished. Banished to his bedroom, he sets off on an imaginary journey across the sea, just as Jonah seeks to escape God's injunction by escaping across the sea. As Jonah lands in the belly of an enormous fish, Max arrives in the land "where the wild things are." Just as the belly of the fish is initially warm and comforting in many of the versions of the Jonah story for children, so too does Max find comfort in his new land. He has escaped into a realm that is beyond the pursuit of his all-powerful mother, just as Jonah thinks he can escape God's command by fleeing to Tarshish. In the end, Max is calmer, wiser, and contrite, able to accept his mother's authority as Jonah is ultimately able to accept the command of God, do as he is told, and not be concerned with retribution. These stories are not exact parallels, in that Jonah initially does nothing to incur God's anger whereas Max provokes his mother. However, in both of these stories there are strong similarities between the main characters and the powerful authority figures against whom they try to rebel. God and Max's mother are caring, loving, benevolent, forgiving, and compassionate figures, not given to indiscriminately inflicting relentless punishment. The strength of both of these stories is that they are analogous to the real-life emotional development of children.

One of the striking aspects of this Bible story is that it features a hero who interacts with God in a back-and-forth dialogue. This model is strikingly different from the straight path of immediate obedience seen in the story of Noah. Jonah is a different kind of hero even than Moses, despite Moses' initial reluctance to do as God has commanded him, in that Moses protests but is then quickly convinced to go along with God's wish. These elements of the story of Jonah also raise questions for children who are, in any case, at the developmental stage of grappling with the concept of who is God, what is God, the nature of God, and what it means to be obedient to God and thus, by extension, adult authority.

The question of adult authority continues to be a central theme in contemporary stories for children. In *Where the Wild Things Are,* Max is sent to his room without dinner after he continues to misbehave, seeing the situation from his own egocentric point of view and not anticipating the consequences of his actions. In Dr. Suess's *The Cat in the Hat,* the behavior of the children is an example of typical childhood impulsivity. They permit a stranger—the cat—into the house and have a wild time. It is only after the fact that they understand that they have not behaved appropriately and have not done as asked by their mother. Afterward, realizing that they have done wrong, they clean up, and tell their mother that nothing out of the ordinary has happened, that they have done as she instructed.

At about the age of seven or eight, children learn that their choices and behaviors have consequences, and that there are causes and effects for all behaviors. Both Jonah and Sendak's Max begin their stories at the early Piagetian stage, where there is only one morality in which everything is seen in black and white, and they don't yet have the inner control necessary to restrain their own behaviors. Stories that show the struggle to arrive at the next developmental stage are important for children, because these stories validate children's own internal effort toward changing their behaviors and understanding what is right and wrong. As an example of this struggle to arrive at the next milepost on the journey of emotional growth, the story of Jonah resonates powerfully.

7

ESTHER

It is only in recent times that there has been serious interest expressed in the stories of biblical women. Historically, biblical stories have been read as tales about men, in which women are present, but play largely secondary roles. While this has begun to change dramatically in recent decades, there are still far more stories written for children about male biblical characters than female. Many of the biblical stories involving women are not filled out and detailed the same way as those of the men. Yet heroic, dramatic, important stories about women do exist in the biblical canon, and in recent years some authors have taken upon themselves the task of reacquainting us with stories that have been too often overlooked or ignored.

There are many fascinating women of the Bible whose stories deserve to be told and more widely known. The stories of the biblical matriarchs Sarah, Rebecca, Rachel, and Leah are filled with pathos, love, heartbreak, jealousy, longing for children, rivalry, trickery, and tragedy. Dina, Jacob's one daughter, is the central protagonist in a tragic episode, in which she is raped and violently avenged (Genesis 34). Tamar, Judah's twice-widowed daughter-in-law, seduces her father-in-law, gets her long-awaited children, and makes him take responsibility for his mistreatment of her (Genesis 38). Zipporah, Moses' wife, figures prominently in several scenes but ultimately fades out of the picture. There is Deborah the Judge who acts as a military strategist, and Yael, who bravely seduces, nourishes, and then murders Sisera with a tent peg, securing a victory for Israel (Judges 4–5). Michal, one of David's wives, is a curious figure, the only woman in biblical text said to be in love with a man,[10] who saves David's life by helping him escape through her window (1 Samuel 19:12). Abigail is another full-blown personality, a shrewd strategist who goes behind the back of her then-husband Nabal to align herself with David and become his wife (1 Samuel 25). There is the young widow Ruth, about whom a whole biblical book is written, who faithfully follows and cares for her bereaved mother-in-law, accepting both her mother-in-law's fate and

---

[10] Rebecca is said to love her son Jacob (Genesis 25:28), but Michal is the only woman in the biblical text to be said to "fall in love with" a man (I Samuel 18:20).

faith, ultimately remarrying and bearing a child who will become a progenitor of the Messiah. And there are many, many more, some named, like the temptress Delilah who aids in the downfall of Samson, or the harlot Rahab who helps Joshua, and many, like Noah's wife, Lot's wife, or Jephthah's daughter, who remain unnamed other than by their relationship to a man.

Out of all of this two women in particular stand out. The first is Miriam, the sister of Moses and Aaron, and a prophet in her own right. The second is Esther, the main protagonist of the dramatic story that bears her name. The stories of both of these women are multidimensional, evolve over long periods of time within the text, and, like those of their male counterparts, involve journeys of transition and transformation.

The Book of Esther is a biblical jewel box, a short but complete tale containing a rich and dramatic beginning, middle, and end, all within ten chapters. There are many elements that differentiate the book of Esther from other biblical books, not the least of which is its unusual setting in Persia. It has much in common with classic fairy tales, including a befuddled king, good guys and bad guys, a beautiful queen, and a happy ending. The Book of Esther tells an important story about overcoming subjugation and about standing up for oneself and one's people. Because of its fairy-tale nature and the important lessons embedded within, the story of Esther is a biblical story that has always been a popular one for children. For Jews, the Book of Esther is the basis for the holiday of Purim, during which generation after generation of Jewish children have dressed up as the revered heroes Esther and Mordecai. Like many of the biblical stories that have served as the basis of retellings for children, the story of Esther is often distilled into a tale of obedience to authority figures. An additional central theme in versions meant for children is that of courage. Yet despite its apparent appeal and appropriateness for children, a closer look reveals it to be quite a complex story. It is one of the most colorful and racy of all the biblical books, involving raucous drinking parties, a harem, a eunuch, hidden identity, revenge, jealousy, sexuality, and violence. In addition to its lush descriptive passages, one of the most extraordinary aspects of the story contained within the Book of Esther is that the main character is a woman.

Esther is an orphaned young woman being reared by a relative, Mordecai. Their exact relationship is unclear. Though he is generally referred to as Esther's "foster-father," he is also identified as her father's nephew, making him her cousin, or, as in some of the retellings, her uncle. After Ahasuerus, the king of Shushan, has his queen Vashti banished for disobeying him, he instructs his advisers to search his kingdom and find the most beautiful virgins in the land. Those women would be brought into his harem, and the woman who most pleased the king would become his new queen. Esther is chosen to join the king's harem, and then eventually to be the new queen. Mordecai warns her not to reveal her identity to the king and Esther obediently complies. Meanwhile, the king appoints a man by the name of Haman to be the highest official next to the king. Haman becomes very angry when Mordecai will not kneel or bow to him, and in retaliation, arranges to have all the Jews in the kingdom killed by order of the king. Upon learning of this plan, Mordecai asks Esther to reveal her identity to the king and beg for his intervention. At first Esther demurs, saying that no one is allowed to approach the king without first being summoned, and anyone who does so risks death. But Mordecai tells Esther that since she is a Jew, her life is now at risk anyway, and finally Esther agrees to act. She is allowed to approach the king, and invites him and Haman to a feast, during which she invites them to join her for another feast the next day. Meanwhile, the king cannot sleep that night and asks to have his record book read to him. There it is written that Mordecai had reported a plot he had overheard against the king's life. Wishing to honor Mordecai appropriately for his loyalty, the king has Haman lead Mordecai around on a horse, dressed in fine clothes, and announce to all that this is a man whom the king wishes to honor. Haman is both completely humiliated and infuriated.

At the second feast, the king again asks Esther what she would like. At that point she asks him to save her life and the lives of her people against the decree instigated by Haman. Haman is then impaled on the stake he had built for Mordecai, and though the decree to kill the Jews cannot be revoked since it was made by the king, the Jews are allowed to fight back and save themselves. Esther is thus the heroine of this dramatic story, a woman who risked her life to stand up for an entire people that would have been destroyed.

Like David, Esther is a young person who does as she is told by the authority figures around her. Yet unlike David, her story is not one of rebellion, rather it is more similar to Moses or Joseph's process of gradually growing into the person she is expected to become. It is a story of loyalty to family and to a people, a story of courage, and a story about learning how and when to take risks. Esther's transformative hero's journey moves her from a Noah–like state of unquestioning obedience to a Moses–like state of taking on a leadership role in order to manipulate authority and save her people. Along the way, she spends time in the king's household, an experience analogous to that of Jonah in the great fish, from which she emerges ready to take on new experiences and challenges. However, one element that differentiates it from other biblical stories about obedience is that God is never overtly mentioned in the story. In the story of Esther, the authority figures are all human. Mordecai, not God, is Esther's guide on this journey, prodding her along and telling her what to do, but leaving it up to her to make her own decisions at the crucial turning point in the journey.

Esther's Obedience

> . . . for Esther obeyed Mordecai's bidding,
> as she had done when she was under his tutelage.

(Esther 2:20)

The story of Esther begins with an example of the danger of disobedience. Though Queen Vashti has become a popular feminist heroine in recent times for standing up to the king, her brief appearance in the biblical text serves as a warning of what can happen to those who don't obey, particularly women. Vashti is giving a banquet for the women when the king calls her to appear at his banquet wearing a royal diadem to show off her beauty. Vashti refuses and the king, incensed, consults with his advisers. Concerned that her rebuff will lead to women across the land refusing to listen to their husbands, the advisers recommend that Vashti be banished from the king's presence and that another be chosen in her place (Esther 1).

Vashti is the anti–Esther, the woman who won't do as bidden. Though she is only mentioned at the very beginning of the biblical story, her absence looms large throughout the rest of Esther's tale. The details of Vashti's refusal are unclear, but her subsequent plight serves as a warning for Esther. Some of the retellers of this story have felt a need to provide an explanation for Vashti's refusal to heed the king, perhaps out of a belief that children need to know whether or not her punishment is justified. Children are taught to obey the adult authority figures in their lives, like parents and teachers, and at the same time to use good judgment when told what to do by peers. Is Vashti, like a child who won't obey her parents, stubbornly trying to assert her autonomy? Or is she using good judgment by refusing, because there is something about the king's request that is not appropriate? Providing reasons for Vashti's refusal deals with the question of who is in the wrong. Is Vashti's punishment warranted, or is she in the right and punished unjustly?

Why Vashti won't go in front of the king's guests is filled out in further detail in *Miriam's Well: Stories about Women in the Bible* by Alice Bach and J. Cheryl Exum (1991), in which Vashti declares: "Tell the king that Queen Vashti does not appear before drunken courtiers. The Queen refuses his invitation." This Vashti is a queen who knows her mind, knows what is appropriate, and doesn't mind saying what she thinks. At first the king is not overly concerned that Vashti has not obeyed him, but his advisers stir him up, telling him that Vashti sets a bad example for other women. Bach and Exum echo the original biblical version of the story by characterizing the king as a weak man who is told what to do by his advisers. By adding this motivation for Vashti's action, Bach and Exum present a king who, while technically an authority figure, is not a good role model of appropriate adult behavior and who should not necessarily be obeyed. He is revealed to be a showoff, concerned with his image and easily swayed by the negative influences around him, all of which foreshadow what is to come later in the story. It is not the king, but one of his advisers, who then announces:

> Let the decree state that the king will confer the royal dignity of queen on another, lovelier woman, who will be worthy to be his queen. And let the decree clearly state that all the women of the kingdom, of high rank and of low, will now bow to the authority of their husbands and obey their every word.

Esther is thus meant to be the antidote to Vashti. She will be more obedient and "lovelier," the proper wife for a king, a wife who knows how to act appropriately.

Though obedience to authority figures is a common theme in literature intended for children, the issue of obedience between the king and queen, or a woman to a man, is of a different nature than obedience of a child toward a parent or teacher. Both a king and queen are adults and wield power over others. That the king has authority above the queen and that the queen can be punished for not obeying him may make little sense for contemporary children who are taught that mothers and fathers ought to be of equal authority within the family. Mordicai Gerstein resolves this potential dilemma in his *Queen Esther the Morning Star* (2000) by depicting the king as a kind of fool who abuses his authority. He writes of the king's reaction to Vashti's refusal in the following way: " 'Won't come!' roared the king. 'I'll teach her! Guards! Throw her out! Let her beg in the streets! I will find a new, *more* beautiful queen. One that *obeys* me!' " Gerstein tells the story in broad strokes, emphasizing the cartoon-like elements of the story. This is an impetuous king who sounds like a spoiled young child. When Mordecai consoles a weeping Esther who doesn't want to go and become the new queen, he tells her that the king "can be foolish." Moreover, Mordecai also tells her that the king can be cruel. The implication is that, having been chosen by this capricious king, she had better do as he wants, or her fate will be like that of Vashti. He is to be obeyed not because he deserves to be, but because disobedience comes at a high price.

The king is depicted in a similarly unflattering way in *Queen Esther Saves Her People,* written by Rita Golden Gelman and illustrated by Frané Lessac (1998). Gelman writes:

> Ahasuerus, king of the Persian Empire, was vain, foolish, and hot-tempered. He liked to show off his riches at huge parties where guests drank from golden goblets and ate from silver bowls.
>
> The business of running the empire was left to the king's advisers. Ahasuerus was too busy drinking and eating to bother with thinking.

These negative qualities are a way to explain to children why the king may have acted as he did with respect to Vashti, and lay the groundwork as well for explaining why Haman comes to wield so much power. This king is not evil as much as he is a buffoon. The role of true evil is left solely to Haman. However, not all the authors of retellings of this story let the king off the hook so easily. In *Daughters of Fire: Heroines of the Bible* (2001), Fran Manushkin describes the king as "a cruel and impulsive man" who "loved to flaunt his power and wealth." Manushkin's king is not an incompetent fool controlled by those around him, but an abusive monarch.

The biblical text is not forthcoming in details about Esther herself. She is depicted as an obedient young woman who does as she is told by her foster-father, Mordecai. Everyone who encounters her, from Hegai, the guardian of the women in the harem, to the king himself, seems to react favorably to her. She appears to know what to do in order to please the men around her. But her side of the story is not revealed. Whether or not she sees the king as someone to take seriously is not known, nor is her reaction to being first rounded up by the king's courtiers and then chosen by the king himself. She simply does as she is told by those in authority around her, be it Mordecai, Hegai, or Ahasuerus. She is, at this stage of her story, a cipher. The authors who retell Esther's story must therefore use the clues provided by the biblical text to imagine her motivations, her inner thoughts, and her emotional responses to what happens around her.

The illustrations in Lisl Weil's 1980 retelling, *Esther*, show an Esther who is submissive and, in clear contrast to the previous queen, willing to do as the king commands. In one illustration all the women in the harem, with the exception of Esther, look out directly at the reader, their eyes fully open. Only Esther is drawn looking demurely downward. In the next illustration, she is shown in an even more submissive position, kneeling down, presumably before the king, with her head bowed.

Tomie dePaola begins his 1986 retelling after Vashti's banishment and does not mention this first queen at all. Rather than contrasting Esther with Vashti, he reinforces the idea of Esther's acquiescent nature through his illustrations for *Queen Esther*. In the very first illustration, she is shown seated on the ground at Mordecai's feet, a reference to her lower status. When the king admires her and chooses her for his queen, her head is bowed in submission.

The importance of obedience comes across strongly in *Daughters of Eve: Strong Women of the Bible*, written by Lillian Hammer Ross and illustrated by Kyra Teis (2000). In this retelling, the young Hadassah (Esther) discusses Vashti's disobedience with her aunt and uncle. She asks, "The queen has refused the king?" and then wants to know what will happen to the queen. It is clear to Hadassah that Vashti has done something unacceptable. Several days later, when Hadassah learns that Vashti's fate is to be hanged, an embellishment the author has added to the biblical text, she exclaims, "Death for disobeying the king!" followed by, "How terrible!" Her aunt brings the point home, saying, "It is a lesson for all the women of Shushan and the entire kingdom of Persia." There can be no doubt in this retelling: for a woman, to obey is right and proper and is the safe course of action—to disobey is to lose one's life.

The version of the tale retold in *Esther's Story*, written by Diane Wolkstein and illustrated by Juan Wijngaard (1996), is much more nuanced. Both the writing and the rich, dense, Persian–influenced illustrations attempt to tell a detailed version of the story as seen through

Esther's eyes. In this rendition, Mordecai tells Esther what has happened to the queen. "Will the new queen be beautiful?" Esther asks. Mordecai replies:

> *"As beautiful as you are."*
> *"Will she be kind?"*
> *"As kind as you are."*
> *"And brave?"*
> *"As brave as you are. . . ."*

Wolkstein uses Vashti's banishment as a way not to focus on the issue of obedience, but rather as a way to foreshadow the qualities that will be required later by Esther.

When Esther is chosen to be part of the king's harem, and then again when she is chosen to be the new queen, Mordecai tells her not to reveal her identity. This point is made and then repeated for emphasis. It is not clear in the biblical text why Esther must not do so, but she obeys Mordecai's instructions. Gerstein adds an explanation based on what is to come in the text, writing, "There are those at court who hate our people." Esther is thus presented in this retelling as a reverse of the stubborn, strong-willed Vashti, compliant and unquestioningly doing as she is told.

Not all authors of retellings of the Esther story choose to show Esther as docile and compliant. Instead, some emphasize her inner strength and determination, or her sense of adventure and readiness for new experiences. In Rita Golden Gelman's *Queen Esther Saves the Day* (1998), obedience is not stressed to the extent that it is in other versions. Once the king begins to search for a new queen, Mordecai tries to hide Esther, lest she become another victim of the king's capriciousness. When that plan is not successful, she does as is required of her and goes with the king's soldiers to the palace. In this version, the king's advisers are not looking for a new queen who is more obedient, but rather one who is "even more beautiful than Vashti." Having no choice, Esther goes with the soldiers, and also obeys Mordecai when he tells her upon leaving not to let anyone know that she is Jewish.

But she never comes across as subservient or submissive in this version; rather, she is merely doing what is expedient. The illustrations depict her with her head held high. Despite missing Mordecai, she enjoys the opportunity to meet different kinds of women while she is in the harem, here more politely called the "special house," for the women inside the palace. And when she meets the king, she does not look decorously down but looks him directly in the eye. In Manushkin's *Daughters of Fire,* Hadassah, as she is still referred to at this point in the story, actually hides herself away so as not to be found by the king's courtiers. She is galvanized by her great fear of being chosen by the king. She only appears before the king so as not to risk being killed. In this version, it is not Mordecai who tells her she must, but her fear for her own life that motivates her. Once she is chosen queen, Manushkin underscores Esther's unwillingness to play the part in which she is cast, writing, "Never was there a more reluctant queen!"

The Esther depicted in James Ransome's art for the McKissacks' *Let My People Go* is a strong, confident young woman. The king is raised on a platform above her, yet she does not seem to be in the least docile or subservient. She stands straight and tall, looking up at the king. His arm is raised out to her, and her arm is similarly raised up at him. This young woman, about to be chosen as the new queen, is an active player in determining her destiny. It is clear in this painting that this Esther is going to become a hero.

In Wolkstein's portrayal of Esther there is also a hint of the brave woman who will later emerge. When it is finally her turn to meet the king, she engages in friendly, flirtatious banter with him. Their exchange is not typical of that of a king and a subservient. Wolkstein writes:

> The king was standing by the window. He looked a little lonely. His arms were folded. I folded mine in the same way. He scratched his head. I scratched mine, and a tiny pink rose fell to the floor. As I bent down to pick it up, the king said, "How beautiful you are."
>
> I put the rose in his curly hair and said, "How beautiful *you* are!"
>
> He laughed. I liked his laugh. It was deep and growly and unexpected.

"Laugh again!" I said, and I tickled him.

A big happy laugh came bursting out of him, like water from a fountain.

Their encounter in this version has nothing to do with obedience. Esther shows herself to be capable of engaging the king in dialogue, and of finding something likable in him. This Esther is no shrinking violet. She takes the initiative with the king, and goes so far as to even touch him. Their interaction here alludes to their sexual relationship that is to come.

The theme of obedience appears again in the encounter between Mordecai and Haman. It was the king's orders that all courtiers kneel and bow low to Haman, but Mordecai would not do so. His explanation in the biblical text is merely that he is a Jew (Esther 2:3–4). The idea that a Jew would not kneel or bow is traditionally understood by some Jewish commentators as a reference to Jews not bowing or kneeling to anyone other than God. Gerstein makes this point explicit for children:

> "Who are you that will not bow down to me?" snarled Haman.
> "I am Mordecai, a Jew. I bow only to God."
> "I'll have you *hung!*" raged Haman. "And *all* your people, too!"

So while Mordecai defies the human authority of Haman and by extension the king, he does so because he is being obedient to a higher authority. Despite Haman's decree, meant to punish all Jews throughout the kingdom for Mordecai's disobedience, in the end their obedience to God wins out and the Jews are saved while Haman is killed. Mordecai's lack of submission is presented as a model of selective obedience. In his *Queen Esther,* Tomie dePaolo makes this selectivity an unambiguous matter of choosing the appropriate kind of obedience:

> *Several years pass,*
> *and then King Ahaseurus made an evil and jealous man*
> *named Haman his chief official.*
> *The king commanded all the other officials*
> *to bow down before Haman.*
> *Mordecai would not bow!*

The reason for Mordecai's refusal is given, that ". . . Mordecai was a Jew and obeyed the Jewish law. . . ." The message is clear: it is not enough to simply be obedient, but it must be the right kind of obedience, to the right authority figure.

The motif of obedience that runs throughout this story is intrinsically connected to the issues of gender and power, for the story of Esther is also a story about a woman in a man's world. Other than Esther herself, the story is essentially bereft of women. Vashti is removed from the story right at the beginning. There are other women in the harem with Esther, but they are a nameless, faceless, generic group. The only other named woman is Zeresh, Haman's wife, who plays only a brief supporting role. Esther has no mother, no aunt, or other female family member. She is a young, initially powerless girl being reared by a man, her foster-father Mordecai. It is not accidental that Mordecai can choose to obey or not, while Esther at first seems to be powerless to choose at all. The Book of Esther sets down in written form approved gender roles and delineates socially acceptable behaviors for women. Esther and Vashti represent the classic dichotomy of female sexuality. Esther is the "good" to Vashti's "bad." Vashti is the sultry seductress, invited to titillate her husband's courtiers. Esther is the pure, virtuous, modest maiden who does as she is told. In her chasteness and purity, she is like a Joan of Arc figure, able to rescue her people and serve as an eternal model of proper behavior for girls. It is the men who have the power to choose their style of obedience and to exert their authority over others. Each in his own way, Mordecai, Ahasuerus, and Haman all hold sway over Esther and have the power to determine her fate.

Mordecai guides, protects, advises, and instructs Esther. When she leaves his household, his direct authority over her is replaced by that of the king. She has, for all intents and purposes, exchanged one father for another. Yet the king is such an inept character that he lacks the ability to be a real authority figure for Esther. Though she is afraid of the king's power over her when it is time to approach him unbidden, it is really Haman, through his ability to control the king's actions and affect Esther's future, who fills the role of Esther's replacement father.

Where the good father, Mordecai, wants to take care of her and keep her safe, the bad father, Haman, wants her destroyed. Either way, she lacks the power to determine her future for herself.

When the story begins, Esther is young, powerless, and untried. Until she becomes part of the king's harem, her world is small and confined, consisting primarily of herself and Mordecai. In joining the king's household, she trades Mordecai's authority and protection for that of the king's and Haman's. Enclosed in a safe, ordered, rule-bound environment, she has not yet been challenged to think or act on her own. As the story unfolds, however, Esther's sense of herself and her own power will be greatly tested. In making the transition from the good, safe father to the bad, dangerous father, Esther must manage along the way to take care of herself. As she learns to do so, she begins to make her own decisions and to grow up. Without having been pushed to assert her own authority and work against Haman, she might never have been able to find within herself the adult skills she needs to succeed, and in so doing get her first taste of power. Like Jonah, she will move from self-centeredness to a deep understanding of others. After this experience, obedience will no longer be a motivational factor for Esther, for she will have become a powerful authority figure in her own right.

Esther's Identity

> In the fortress Shushan lived a Jew by the name of Mordecai . . . He was foster father to Hadassah—that is, Esther—his uncle's daughter, for she had neither father nor mother. . . . Esther did not reveal her people or her kindred, for Mordecai had told her not to reveal it.
>
> (Esther 2:5, 7, 10)

Identity is an ongoing motif in the story of Esther, just as it is in many fairy tales and legends. Hidden identity plays an important role in the story of Cinderella, as well as in the stories of Rapunzel and King Arthur. Snow White and Sleeping Beauty are princesses in disguise, and both the beast in "Beauty and the Beast" and the frog in "The Frog Prince" are really handsome princes underneath repulsive exteriors. Part of the healthy process of growth and separation that children go through involves discovering their true identities as they transition from child to mature adult. Stories of hidden or dual identity thus have great resonance for children, as they engage in discarding the identities placed upon them by their parents, and struggle to reveal their true inner selves to the world.

Like Moses, who grew up in Pharaoh's household and later became leader of the people into which he was born, Esther also has two identities, one of which must be hidden for a time. Through the use of two separate names, the text of the Book of Esther emphasizes her dual identity. She is the Jewish woman Hadassah, and in the king's court she is Esther, the queen. She purposely keeps her Jewish identity a secret when she becomes part of King Ahasuerus's household, revealing her true self only in order to save her people. In both these biblical stories, identity plays an important role in the hero's struggle to understand what it means to be part of, and ultimately lead, a people.

The biblical text provides different names for Esther's two identities, but it does not explain the significance of the names. Many of the retellings of the Esther story for children do not even deal with the complication raised by the fact of Esther's two names. Some, though, use this detail as a way to underscore the complications of Esther's dual identity and as a way to provide insights into Esther herself.

Gerstein uses the name Esther to highlight one of her qualities, writing, "Out of all the beautiful young women of his kingdom, one seemed to shine and leave the others in darkness. Her name was Esther, which means morning star." Esther, he writes in the introductory author's note, means Venus, which is the last star to fade upon the arrival of a new day, hence the morning-star imagery. There is no lack of explanations about the meaning of the two names though, and other retellings offer different possibilities. Wolkstein looks to the Hebrew meanings behind the two names, giving explanations that are in keeping with the way the two names have been understood in Jewish tradition. She writes, "Your mother named you Hadassah for the sweet-smelling myrtle. But tonight I shall give you the new name of Esther, which means secret or concealed." Hadassah is the name her family gave her at birth, the name of her grandmother from Jerusalem, but Esther is to be the name she uses when trying to conceal her identity. Wolkstein goes on to connect Esther to the goddess Ishtar, who is also the first planet to appear every night in the sky. Whereas Gerstein uses the idea of the morning star as a metaphor for Esther's great beauty, Wolkstein uses the concept of the first-star-to-appear as a metaphor for Esther's great courage in appearing alone before the king.

Both of Esther's names reveal aspects of her identity and her character. Hadassah identifies her as Jewish, and Esther intimates the notion of hiddenness. There is an important message in the Esther story for children about knowing who you are no matter how other people may see you. The corollary to this is the importance of staying true to yourself. Though Esther is told by Mordecai to hide her identity, she is never told to change it. And when the time is right, she is instructed to reveal her true, inner self.

Mordecai is Esther's link to her Jewish identity. It is Mordecai who has a relationship with the broader Jewish community, whereas Esther's direct connection is not mentioned in the biblical text. When Mordecai visits Esther in *Esther's Story,* he brings her favorite foods, and tells her stories about her ancestors. Through both the food and the stories, he tries to keep her connected to her identity while she is living in the king's household. Like Moses living in Pharaoh's household, she is supposed to remember her minority identity while living as a member of the privileged majority. Yet whereas Moses' story abounds with details about the hardships of life in Egypt for Jews, the story of Esther is silent about the life of Jews in Persia. The text reveals little about their situation before the ascendancy of Haman. The details of their lives are unclear—how much were they accepted or oppressed? When Esther is taken to be part of the king's harem, Mordecai tells her right away to keep her identity a secret, a hint of the potential danger in being a Jew. Yet at the same time, Mordecai, who does not keep his Judaism a secret, has been allowed to rise to a position of relative power.

These questions are addressed in a multiplicity of ways by the authors of various retellings. The difference between Esther's minority identity and that of the mainstream comes across strongly in Rita Golden Gelman's *Queen Esther Saves Her People* (1998). She writes unequivocally, "Esther and Mordecai lived in Persia, but they were not Persian; they were Jewish." Esther and Mordecai are described as being descendants of Jews taken prisoner by the king of Persia and brought to Persia against their will. She goes on to describe what it means to be a Jew in Persia:

> By the time Ahasuerus became king, the Jews were no longer prisoners. They spoke Persian and dressed like their Persian neighbors. They lived by the laws of their new land. They bought and sold in the market. They even served in the king's army. But in their homes, they practiced the Jewish religion.

Gelman describes a status of being accepted, but not completely. Even though they were born in Persia, they are not Persians, but "other." Echoing the reality of nineteenth and early twentieth century Jewish life in Europe, they may look and dress and work like everyone else, but there is a significant difference that separates the Jews from those of the majority culture and religion in Persia.

The reason that Esther must hide her identity is made explicit in Lillian Hammer Ross's *Daughters of Eve: Strong Women of the Bible* (2000). Though Haman's antipathy for Mordecai in particular, and Jews in general, is not known until later in the biblical text, in this retelling it is already assumed as fact. Mordecai changes the name of his charge to Esther, telling her that *Hadassah* is a Hebrew name, and that "Haman, the leader of the King's Council, hates Jews. He would willingly have you murdered." He gives her the name Esther, telling her that it means "to conceal." It will thus serve as a constant reminder for her of the need to conceal her true identity. Esther understands what is at stake, and agrees to the name change and the concealment. " 'Very well, Uncle,' Esther said sadly. 'My true name, my true religion and my true self will all be hidden.' " Ross's Esther is not happy about allowing herself to be chosen as the new queen, but she does so in order keep her aunt and uncle from getting in trouble for hiding her. She reassures both them and herself that despite whatever she may have to go through if she is chosen as the queen, and despite whatever she may have to declare about her identity, her God will watch over her, a strong statement of faith. And even while concealing her true identity, Ross imagines Esther maintaining her identity by keeping kosher in the king's harem. She refuses to eat meat, chicken, or fish, presumably because they would not have been kosher, and agrees to eat only vegetables.

The theme of bigotry and anti-Semitism embedded in the story of Esther, which by extension is about all forms of intolerance and discrimination against "others," is difficult and complicated for children. Why must Esther hide her identity? Why didn't people like the Jews? Why do people hate groups of other people, even if they do not know them? Why docs hatred even exist? All of these questions are raised by the story of Esther and must be addressed in some way in retellings for children.

In *Queen Esther*, Tomie dePaola tries to answer. The Jews were simply different from the Persians, and it was the fact of this difference that made people not like them. He writes:

> *The Jewish people followed the laws God gave to Moses.*
> *Some of these laws were different*
> *from the laws and customs of Persia.*
> *Because of this difference,*
> *some people in Persia hated the Jews.*

This is a very careful, measured explanation that makes sure not to blame all the Persians, only "some." Its explanation of prejudice also sounds quite contemporary, similar to the explanations of racism based on mistrust bred by differences.

The Hebrews, as they are called in Lisl Weil's *Esther*, are "lawbreakers." Haman is angry that Mordecai won't bow down to him, and he tells the king:

They do not keep your royal laws, but follow their own ways. It is not good that they should be allowed to live. I will pay into your royal treasury ten thousand silver coins if you will allow me to kill these lawbreakers.

The explanation that Weil offers follows the biblical text closely. As his offer of payment makes clear, Haman's problem with the Jews is both personal and urgent. He has been defied, and humiliated, and he needs to destroy all those who, like Mordecai, would refuse to bow down to him. He is willing to sacrifice his own wealth to achieve his goal. By adding this detail, Weil shows how Haman used his money to gain power, and how he was able to easily manipulate the king into putting the power of the throne behind Haman's schemes.

Pharaoh wanted to get rid of the Hebrews because he feared that they might rise up against him. Haman uses this same argument to convince King Ahasuerus to get rid of the Jews in Gerstein's *Queen Esther the Morning Star*. Haman tells the king, "Your majesty, there is a people who have strange customs and obey only their own laws. They scorn you and your rule. They are dangerous and you must rid your kingdom of them." The Jews are different, and difference is threatening. Being the same is being safe. And yet in all the stories of Esther the pervasive message is that of being true to who one really is, since in the end it is Haman the bigot who is killed, while Esther, Mordecai, and all the Jews, having stood steadfast in their faith, survive.

Wolkstein's Esther does not understand why she must hide her identity. Her question about Mordecai's purpose in telling her to keep it a secret, and her concerns about having to live in fear, echo those of a child hearing this story: "I don't know why he worries so much about this. The king allows everyone in the kingdom to worship whichever gods they wish. I don't want to grow up being afraid because I'm Jewish." In this version there is no sense that there is a pervasive anti-Jewish sentiment in the kingdom. Esther is shown to be relatively happy in the king's harem, making friends with the other young women. She is presented in the early pages of this retelling as a typical self-centered child, annoyed that the adult in her life is making such a big deal over something that does not seem to touch on her existence. Having not yet developed the ability to see from the point of view of others, she can only judge through her own experiences. For her, despite the adjustment to living in the king's palace and away from Mordecai, life is an adventure. She is being treated well, and does not sense any discrimination.

Queen Esther is a model of courage in the face of prejudice in *Let My People Go: Bible Stories by a Freeman of Color.* In this version of the story, Haman is guilty of, among other things, abuse of power. The McKissacks write:

> Everybody feared Haman and with good reason—he wore his wickedness like a robe of honor and forced folks to bow down when they greeted him. They all did so, not out of respect, but absolute fear. But Mordecai the gatekeeper wouldn't do so. Say, "I bow only to the one true God, the Almighty."
>
> This didn't set well with Haman, and a terrible hatred rose up in his heart 'gainst Mordecai. On that account Haman turned his hand 'gainst all Jews, promising to destroy every one that was livin' in the kingdom! Oh, what woes befall good people when wrong is in power. (p. 106)

Here, the situation is an allegory for the mistreatment of African Americans at the hands of whites in America. Esther is identified right at the beginning of the story as someone who "was a captive, living in a foreign land." This detail, not found in the biblical text but based on the theory that the Book of Esther may be a result of Jews having been exiled to Persia after the fall of Jerusalem, connects Esther to a personal history of oppression and slavery. Implied in this connection is that she has experienced the loss of autonomy and has suffered at the hand of others. Yet by creating this connection to American slavery, this retelling inspires hope and optimism. In the end, righteousness triumphs. The evil Haman gets his comeuppance and the good guys win. Doing good and staying faithful to one's values and identity is rewarded. This is an encouraging message for children of all backgrounds.

The Problem of Beauty

The maiden was shapely and beautiful . . .

(Esther 2:7)

Beauty plays an important role in the story of Esther. The biblical text itself comments on both Esther's beauty and her body. Esther has been held up as an example of great beauty for girls to aspire to. Historically, youth and beauty have always been considered important attributes for women, as is attested to in fairy tales as well. Like Cinderella at the prince's ball, Esther's great beauty marks her and makes her stand out so that the king notices her and chooses her as his new queen. And yet Esther is not simply just pretty. Her beauty is in service to a greater cause, as it enables her to be in the right place at the right time to save her people. Just as in fairy tales such as "Cinderella," "Beauty and the Beast," and "Sleeping Beauty," where the heroine's beauty is not merely on the surface but is a manifestation of inner goodness, the same holds true for Esther. Yet beauty is not without its downsides, as is seen in the Book of Esther as well as in the many fairy tales, folk tales, and myths in which female characters often undergo grave danger because of the reactions of others to their physical attributes.

Esther's beauty is the first thing that readers learn about her in Lisl Weil's *Esther* (1980). The story begins, "This is the true story of a beautiful girl. . . ." When Vashti is banished and the king needs a new queen, his concern is how to find one as beautiful as Vashti. His advisers come up with a plan to have all the beautiful girls in the land sent to him, so that he can choose from among them. In this version, her beauty is what defines her. Though being beautiful might have been an acceptable goal for girls in times past, beauty is a more problematic concept today. That beauty is still an ideal to aspire to is attested to by the ongoing popularity of beauty pageants, Barbie Dolls, and makeup sets for girls; modern girls are also expected, like boys, to be brave, smart, and successful. Contemporary retellings of the story of Esther must navigate carefully between the emphasis the biblical story places on beauty, and more current, balanced views regarding women.

The concept of beauty in this story is even more complicated, since the beauty alluded to in the biblical text is not simply that of a pretty face but of a clearly sexual nature. In the Hebrew of the biblical text, the young women are called *naarot betulot,* a combination of the word meaning *young women,* and a word that can connote either generic *young women* or specifically *virgins.* Just as violence is inherently problematic in any story for children, so is overt sexuality. Most of the fairy tales familiar to contemporary children are sanitized versions of earlier sexually charged stories, more acceptable to today's parents and teachers. Many fairy tales, before being sanitized by publishers for mass market consumption, inclusion in basal readers, and animated children's movies, were originally intended for adult listening and contained frequent instances of overt sexuality. "Little Red Riding Hood," for example, has been traced back hundreds of years by scholars to its roots in the oral storytelling tradition. Early versions of the story include graphic descriptions of Red's ripeness and lusciousness. The use of red to describe her cloak signifies to listeners that this is a pubescent young girl, delicious and ready to be "eaten" by a "wolf." The term *wolf* survives to this day as a popular image of men who prey on naive young women for their own pleasure, sometimes calling to them with a "wolf whistle." Red is a prominent color in fairy tales that deal with girl's coming of age, from the description of Snow White's very red cheeks to the pricking of her finger and the drawing of blood in the story of Sleeping Beauty. These references to blood contrast their emerging sexuality with that of their mother's fading beauty and the loss of her former youthful appearance.

In some of the surviving early versions, Red strips off her clothes and willingly gets into bed with the wolf. Catherine Orenstein traces the history of "Little Red Riding Hood" from its earliest tellings through to the 1996 Hollywood interpretation of the story in the movie *Freeway.* She notes that Red Riding Hood is one of the few fairy-tale characters who does not marry and get to live "happily ever after" at the end of the story. Orenstein posits that this is because Red has strayed from the path both literally and metaphorically; she has wandered off on her own and is presented as a proactive character, not in any way passive and lacking in initiative like other female fairy-tale characters. In contrast, Rapunzel gives in to the prince's demand to "let down her hair," allowing herself to be controlled by his desire. Snow White, Sleeping Beauty, and the princess in "The Frog Prince" are all young women in conflict with their mothers or mother figures over their developing bodies and budding sexuality. As a result of their passive nonresistance to the wills of their mothers and stepmothers (mother surrogates), these heroines cross the threshold into maturity and are rewarded by marriage to a prince. They are now ready to be obedient wives. But not so for Red, who is an active heroine making her own choices.

So too, the story of Esther is similarly "cleaned up" in order to make it more acceptable for children. In the biblical text, the women are held in a *beit nashim*, literally the *house of women* but generally translated in English as "harem."[11] They were to spend a year there preparing themselves for the king, "six months with oil of myrrh and six months with perfumes and women's cosmetics" (Esther 2:12), after which they would go before the king. The text reads, "She would go in the evening and leave in the morning for a second harem. . . . She would not go again to the king unless the king wanted her, when she would be summoned by name" (Esther 2:14). Like the early versions of many fairy tales, this is not a G-rated children's story about a chaste beauty contest. The sense conveyed by these lines is that the women were virgins, preparing themselves to be sampled sexually by the king. Only those who performed to his liking would be invited back. When it was Esther's turn to go to the king, "the king loved Esther more than all the other women, and she won his grace and favor more than all the other virgins [*betulot*]" (Esther 2:17).

The nexus of beauty and sexuality is all too clear in this story. That the two were inseparable was as clear to the rabbis of the Talmud 1,500 years ago as it is to us today. In their commentary on the story, the reason they provide for Vashti's refusal to appear before the king was

---

[11] Jewish Publication Society, American Bible Society and Revised Standard Version all use "harem."

that he asked her to appear nude, clad only in her royal diadem.[12] Along similar lines, Esther's touching the tip of the king's royal scepter provides for some none-too-subtle interpretations (Esther 5:2).

Later in the story, when the king hears that Haman has planned to kill the Jews, the people to which Esther belongs, he goes out to the garden. He is distraught but as yet undecided about what to do. One reads, "When the king returned from the palace garden to the banquet room, Haman was lying prostrate on the couch on which Esther reclined. 'Does he mean,' cried the king, 'to ravish the queen in my own palace?' "(Esther 7:8). It is only then, in his fury, that he orders Haman to be impaled on the stake he built for Mordecai. Until then, Haman's plan was perhaps disturbing, but not yet insulting to the king's own manhood. It is not enough that Haman is trying to lay claim on Esther's life, but Haman has tried to claim Esther's sexuality as well. When the king finds Haman in the act of ultimate betrayal, trying to take sexual advantage of his queen, he cannot tolerate Haman's existence any longer. The Hebrew in this line is not circumspect—Haman is accused of trying "to ravish" or "conquer" the queen. However, what is ambiguous is what exactly Haman really was doing, and why. Is this truly a scene involving sexuality, or can there be other ways to read Haman's actions? As Adele Berlin (2001) writes, conquering the queen "has all the political connotations always associated with an attempt to take someone else's (especially a king's) wife or concubine: it signals an attempt to supplant the husband's authority and replace it with the usurper's" (p. 70). Haman's real crime here could therefore be interpreted as either attempted treason or attempted rape.

Most retellings omit this challenging scene entirely. In *Esther*, Weil presents a more simplistic version, in which Haman "stayed behind to plead with Esther for his life." The accompanying illustration shows Haman genuflecting next to a kneeling Esther, a far different picture than the biblical description. Wolkstein, telling the story from Esther's perspective, also imagines Haman appealing to Esther to spare his life,

---

[12] Babylonian Talmud, Megillah 12b

and provides a sensible explanation for the reason that Haman winds up on top of her. "Just then the king returned, and Haman, in terror, tripped and fell on top of me. As I cried out, the king shouted in fury, 'Does this man dare attack the queen when I am in the room?'" Here Haman is revealed to be, instead of a lech, a scared, even pathetic, man whose dirty tricks have been revealed. He is no longer to be feared but simply to be pitied.

The authors who re-create the Esther story for children must therefore find a way to downplay the inherent sexual undertones. Just as in contemporary versions of fairy tales, the importance of beauty in the story tends to be emphasized in compensation for omitting references to sexuality. But at the same time, retellers must find a comfortable zone in which beauty can be referenced without going against contemporary attitudes toward girls and physical appearances. Some resolve this dilemma by showing the price that must sometimes be paid for great beauty. In *Daughters of Fire* (2001), Manushkin's Esther tries to hide herself away "in the darkest corner of the house" so as not to be noticed by the king's courtiers. Similarly, in Gelman's *Queen Esther Saves Her People*, Esther's beauty is her potential downfall. Aware of the king's treatment of his former queen, Mordecai tries to hide Esther from the king's men who are on the lookout for a new queen: "But Esther's beauty was known throughout the city. One day, soldiers came to the door, and Esther was taken to the palace." Far from trying to win the king's approval and use her beauty for material or political advantage, Gelman's Esther would rather be left alone at home with Mordecai. Here her beauty is a curse that takes her away from her home and family against her will.

Beauty is a cause for trouble in Mordicai Gerstein's *Queen Esther the Morning Star* as well. In this retelling, when the king boasts that he is the richest king, the men at his banquet agree. But when he boasts that his queen, Vashti, is the most beautiful of all queens, the men ask to see her. The king summons her to come and "display her beauty." She refuses, and is banished. Esther, whose beauty "seemed to shine and leave the others in the darkness" is unhappy at being chosen in her place. Esther's unhappiness at being chosen comes across even more strongly in Diane Wolkstein's *Esther's Story*. In this retelling Esther says, after being brought to the palace, "I don't want to be queen. I miss Uncle Mordecai. I want to go home." And yet in this retelling, once Esther is chosen to be the new queen, she is not initially unhappy. She even enjoys herself in the palace, saying, "We eat a lot, we laugh a lot, and everyone in the palace is happy."

Lillian Hammer Ross resolves the dilemma of Esther's good looks by describing her beauty as being more than a physical attribute in her *Daughters of Eve: Strong Women of the Bible*. When the orphaned, grieving Hadassah is taken in by Mordecai and his wife, she learns to be happy once again.

> In this warm and loving family, she found happiness, and she grew to be a beautiful young woman—beautiful not only in her face, but in her manner and her speech. She studied with her uncle and aunt, and learned the mitzvot, or holy commandments, that all Jewish women must perform.

This was a beauty that came from being a good young Jewish woman who behaved in all the expected, proper ways. When Esther goes before the king to be examined by him, she refuses to put on the "glittering gowns, costly cosmetics and perfumes." Instead she chooses to go unembellished, simply as herself.

> When Esther approached, simply dressed in the clothes of an ordinary Persian woman, her face scrubbed clean and her long hair hanging straight down her back, he gasped. He had never seen unadorned, natural beauty before. She was splendid in her purity.

Esther refuses to look like all the heavily made-up women trying to sell their wares to the king. So too in *Daughters of Fire*, Manushkin's Esther forgoes the opportunity for opulence and glamour.

> Soon the 127 most beautiful women in Persia were assembled inside the palace. Vain and proud, they were attired in glorious silken gowns of every color of the rainbow, and in pearls and diamonds.

One alone wore a plain, modest dress, befitting her guileless spirit. Ah, but Esther's beauty could not be denied.

In both of these versions of the story, Esther refuses to be objectified and made to look different from how she would naturally appear. Having seen Esther in her pure state, the king chooses her to be his new queen. In these retellings it is both her natural beauty and her purity of character that seem to attract him. And it is that combination, along with what he perceives as her wisdom, that will later enable Esther to get what she wants from the king in order to help her people. In this retelling, Esther's beauty is thus both a reflection of her character, her purity of soul, and a powerful tool that later enables her to approach the king.

Esther's beauty is only one of her remarkable attributes in *Let My People Go*. The authors describe Esther as "natural-born pretty, and as smart as she was beautiful." Her intelligence and her beauty go hand in hand in this retelling. The implication, then, is that when Ahasuerus sees her and is immediately sure that this is the woman for him, it is not just because of her beauty but also because he senses the intelligence that goes along with it.

Beauty is Esther's best weapon in Alice Bach and J. Cheryl Exum's *Miriam's Well* (1991). She is able to use the power of her looks to get the king's attention when she disturbs him unbidden. At first the king reacts in anger, but his attitude quickly changes once he sees her, saying, "You are the loveliest woman in my empire. Your face, brilliant like the shining stars, sparkles more than all the jewels in the royal treasury." He is pleased to accede to her request to come to her banquet with Haman the following night.

Some contemporary retellings of the Esther story downplay her beauty and emphasize her other qualities, such as courage, loyalty, and kindness. Though Yona Zeldis McDonough calls her "Beautiful Queen Esther" in her collection *Eve and her Sisters: Women of the Old Testament* (1994), she writes that it was Esther's courage and loyalty that impress the king and persuade him to grant her wish.

In the biblical text, when Esther prepares herself to approach the king she puts on her royal garments (Esther 5:1). Gerstein adds more details to Esther's preparation, writing that she puts on her "most beautiful robes, jewels, and perfumes." Similarly, Wolkstein's Esther puts on her crown and "the dress the king likes best." She wants to make the best possible impression. Having been chosen to be the queen because her beauty appealed to the king, Esther wants to use her ability to be singled out by him once again. In the chapter "Esther Saves her People," in *Tomie dePaola's Book of the Old Testament*, de-Paola connects Esther's beauty to her success in saving her people, writing that the king allowed Esther to approach and speak to him because he saw her and "was pleased with her."

For every child who has ever wished to be more beautiful, this story comes as a cautionary tale about the terrible price that is sometimes paid for being the most beautiful or most popular. Beauty can be a burden as well as a gift, a message conveyed in fairy tales like "Snow White," "Cinderella," and "Beauty and the Beast," in which the young women are hated, resented, or risk being taken away from their homes or even killed because of their beauty. But their beauty, as noted, is also a reflection of their inner righteousness and purity, in contrast to the internal and external ugliness of their antagonist, whether witch, stepmother, or beast. As in these fairy tales, in the end Esther overcomes the hardships that she encounters and comes out on top, as good conquers evil. As Esther grows into herself, she learns to use her beauty for her own ends, putting it in service of the values that matter to her. As she grows from child to adult, she takes control of her beauty rather than allowing it to control, define, or victimize her.

Taking Risks

> Do not imagine that you, of all the Jews, will escape with your life by being in the king's palace.
>
> (Esther 4:13)

When Mordecai tells Esther that she must go to the king and try to save her people, she is at first averse to the idea. Like Moses when told to speak to Pharaoh, and Jonah when told to speak to the Ninevites, she anticipates failure. She sees herself as young and powerless in a world ruled by others. She sends a message to Mordecai that the king has not sent for her in thirty days, and that anyone who approaches the king without having been summoned faces the penalty of death (Esther 4:11). It is personal failure she is thinking about at this point, not what her success or her failure will mean for others. Mordecai admonishes her, saying, "Do not imagine that you, of all the Jews, will escape with your life by being in the king's palace. On the contrary, if you keep silent in this crisis, relief and deliverance will come to the Jews from another quarter, while you and your father's house will perish. And who knows, perhaps you have attained to royal position for just such a crisis" (Esther 4:13–14).

In asking Esther to take this risk, Mordecai is acting in the role that Campbell has termed the "herald," providing Esther with the call to adventure that will propel her on a journey of personal transformation. It is only after Mordecai's words that Esther is convinced to take action, saying in reply, "If I am to perish, I shall perish" (Esther 4:16). With these words, a dramatic transformation has begun to take place in Esther. No longer concerned only with her own welfare, she realizes that she is just one of many and must do her part to help her people. Her own life, while precious, is worth risking to help save the lives of many others. This new awareness of her role as part of a community is further emphasized by her request to Mordecai that the Jews of Shushan fast on her behalf for three days and nights (Esther 4:15–16). Three is often a magical or powerful number in fairy tales and mythology. Three is a central number in many of the stories from the Grimms, including "The Three Feathers" and "The Three Languages." Many stories employ three challenges that the hero must face, or three-headed animals like Cerberus of Greek mythology, the three-headed dog charmed to sleep by Orpheus. In Norse mythology, the world has three levels, in Hindu mythology there are the three deities of Shiva, Vishnu, and Brahma, and, of course, Christianity has the Holy Trinity. Bettleheim writes that the number three in fairy tales is a representation of the aspects of developmental stages along the way toward achieving a mature, integrated adult personality (p. 103). Here, three is the number that will enable Esther to gather the strength she needs to go through the threshold that lies between her passive childlike state and her new sense of powerful adulthood.

If she is going to take this risk, she must take it as part of a community, with the community standing symbolically alongside her. Joseph Campbell writes, "The agony of breaking through personal limitations is the agony of spiritual growth" (p. 190). This period of fasting and praying enables Esther to get in touch with her true self as well as her spiritual source, from which she is able to draw strength for the task ahead. These three days are not unlike Moses' time alone on Sinai with God, before coming down to the people with the Law.

In *Daughters of Fire*, Manushkin elaborates on the biblical text by having Esther pass through six of the king's courtyards until she reaches him in the seventh. She is stopped along the way by guards who doubt the success of her mission. But as she continues to get nearer to her goal, she prays to God. When she finally reaches the king, her face is radiant. The number seven has its own significance. In the Bible and in Jewish tradition, seven, representing the seven days of creation, is the number of wholeness and completeness. Seven, in fairy tales, often represents the seven days of the week and seven planets that were believed at one time to circle the sun. This connection to the planets is consistent with the idea of Esther's hidden name corresponding to the goddess Ishtar, the first planet to appear in the night sky. In going through seven courtyards, she has gone through the complete set of tests, moved toward maturity, and is now prepared to meet the king. These seven courtyards that Manushkin has added to the tale are also appropriate symbols of the progress of Esther's hero-journey. As Campbell writes,

> The adventure is always and everywhere a passage beyond the veil of the known into the unknown; the powers that watch at the boundary are dangerous; to deal with them is risky; yet for anyone with competence and courage the danger fades. (p. 82)

There is danger inherent in Esther's approach to the king. Just as in fairy tales and mythology there are dragons, gargoyles, or dwarfs who guard the entrance to the sacred center, here there are royal guards at the entrance to each courtyard. Getting to the king and being allowed to approach is Esther's trial in Manushkin's retelling, in the same way that killing the giant is David's.

Like Psyche's journey to the underworld, there is also a physical dimension to Esther's particular trial. This is Esther's journey both to the heart of darkness and to the source of mortal power. But her success at both approaching and then entering the king's sacred precinct is critical to her self-transformation. It is as if she sloughs off another layer of her old self the deeper she gets into the king's realm. And once inside, she is reborn. Campbell writes, "Allegorically, then, the passage into a temple and the hero-dive through the jaws of the whale are identical adventures, both denoting, in picture-language, the life-centering, life-renewing act" (p. 92). The radiance that the king sees on Esther's face is her new-found confidence and sense of purpose. With the addition of these elements, Manushkin has placed Esther's story firmly in the realm of mythic hero-journey tales.

The prophetic or preordained is stressed in Gerstein's *Queen Esther the Morning Star* through details gleaned from classical Midrash. Mordecai has a strange dream one night, in which two dragons battle each other, similar to Arthur's portentous dreams of fighting dragons.[13] It was only with the appearance of the morning star that the sun rose, the innocent were saved, and the wicked destroyed. Once Mordecai learns of Haman's evil plan, he understands the meaning of his dream and determines to get a message to Esther to go plead before the king for the lives of her people. The message is carried in this retelling by a servant of the queen, who Gerstein intimates may be none other than the angel Michael. Esther stubbornly refuses to go to the king, but Mordecai sends another message that she must take the risk in order to save lives. Upon hearing this, Esther dresses, bejewels and perfumes herself, and sets right off to the king, who is "overcome with love" and allows her to make her request. This Esther had not needed any time to prepare herself emotionally to grow into her new

---

[13] Esther Rabbah 8:5

role, but is ready immediately once Mordecai insists she do so. The impetus from Mordecai was all she needed to galvanize her into action and out of her complacency.

The Esther presented in Gelman's *Queen Esther Saves Her People* is at first a woman disconnected from her people and her purpose. Her only connection is filtered and managed by Mordecai. She lives in the king's household, oblivious to what is going on in the land. Gelman writes, "Queen Esther, sheltered inside the palace walls, never even heard about the decree until Mordecai sent her a message." When she receives Mordecai's exhortation to save her people, she reacts with trembling and fear for her life. But Mordecai tells her that she cannot think about herself, and exhorts her that it might be for this very purpose that she became queen. Gelman draws on the details of the biblical text, writing that Esther fasted and prayed, and that her people did the same. In doing so, Esther is able to remember who she truly is, to reconnect with her people, and to approach the king with the confidence gained from a new-found sense of herself and her connection to a larger community and a purpose in her life.

Wolkstein's Esther is strongly connected to her people. As in the biblical text, she asks the Jews to fast and pray for her, while she too fasts and prays. By doing so, she weaves herself back into the fabric of the community, as she fasts herself back into a state of greater purity. But Wolkstein imagines an even greater connection between Esther and the Jewish community, writing:

> Then today, as I was lying on the floor of my room, I heard a gigantic cry—it seemed to rise up from the bottom of the earth, loud enough to pierce the heavens. It was the sound of thousands of rams' horns! Uncle Mordecai must have had each of the priests in the city blow his shofar to give me strength.

There is a dialogue between this Esther and her people. She is not simply benevolent royalty, but one of their own, a young, frightened woman who needs to hear their message of strength and support before she prepares to risk her life. As she bathes and readies herself to appear before the king, she thinks about her ancestor Sarah, praying that she will be able to summon those of Sarah's qualities that helped her get through difficult challenges. Wolkstein adds these details to describe a scared young woman who draws strength and inspiration from her history and her people as she prepares to transform herself into a hero and take the greatest risk she has ever had to take.

Not every author of a retelling chooses to depict Esther with a re-newed connection to her community. Some emphasize the courage of her actions by downplaying Mordecai's role and portraying Esther as acting on her own. In Weil's *Esther*, Mordecai is worried that Haman's plan to kill the Jews and take their property is his fault for not obeying Haman. After Mordecai sends word of Haman's plan to Esther, she says to herself, "Perhaps it is for a time like this that I have been made the queen." In this version, it is not Mordecai who delivers this mes-sage to Esther. Rather, here it comes from within herself, as she begins to grasp more fully the significance of her role and her potential to wield power.

In Ross's *Daughters of Eve*, Esther chooses to risk going before the king without the added encouragement of Mordecai. It is only the recognition that she wants to save her people that convinces her to risk her life. She does not involve the Jewish community in her actions, but focuses on her personal relationship with God, asking God to be near her. This is an independent Esther, who is enough a part of her people to want to save them, but hasn't truly aligned herself with them.

In Graham's *How God Fix Jonah*, it is again Esther who takes it upon herself to find a solution. This retelling emphasizes Esther's courage and inspires those who feel powerless to be proactive and take matters into their own hands, an important message for children. When Esther sees Mordecai moaning over the fate of the Jews, she takes action. Graham writes:

> *When she savvy how the palaver lay*
> *She grieve.*
> *She pray.*

> *She call she uncle and she say*
> *"For this*
> *God raise me up.*
> *For this*
> *God set me up in mansion house.*
> *For this*
> *I going go and stand up fore the king*
> *To beg him for my people.*
> *And if I die for this,*
> *I die."*

She has found her purpose in life and is ready to die, if necessary, for something bigger than her own personal fate.

Esther's transformation coincides with Lawrence Kohlberg's theory of the six stages of moral development, starting in early childhood and lasting through late adolescence. At the last, highest stage of moral development, young adults acknowledge the rights of the individual even as they recognize the necessity of acting for the good and welfare of society. The conflict between wanting to act on her own and acting for the good of the community contributes to Esther's need to both fast for three days and to ask her people to make the fasting a communal effort.

In *Queen Esther* and *Queen Esther Saves Her People*, the texts are unequivocally explicit. When Esther is told that she must respond to the king's command and participate in his search for the most beautiful woman in the kingdom, she listens to Mordecai. At that point she is still an obedient young woman, responding to the father figure in her life. Her thoughts are still centered on what is best for herself and so she hides her identity as instructed.

When her obedience and allegiance are transferred from the wise, loving father figure of Mordecai to the ogre/beast figure of King Ahasuerus, Esther responds seductively, just like Beauty in the fairy tale "Beauty and the Beast" or the princess in "The Frog Prince." Whereas they kissed their beasts and were richly rewarded, Esther invites her "ogre" to a lavish feast she orders be prepared for him and his evil henchman, Haman. Beauty, the princess, and Esther each triumphs because she has stepped out from her customary obedient posture and used her wits to secure her own happiness. Esther moves her story beyond the realm of "they lived happily ever after" by acting in the best interests not just of herself but of her entire community. She has put the good of the community ahead of her personal happiness and her fear of the consequences. DePaola, Gelman, and other authors place the moral dilemma Esther faces in words easily understood by children, and stress the importance of acting morally when facing difficult choices, even when we don't know the consequences of our actions. DePaola writes:

> You must not keep quiet at a time like this.
> Perhaps it was for this reason you were made queen.

Using one brief sentence per line, dePaola lifts Esther's story beyond standard fairy tale fare and introduces a level of choice and consequence beyond anything usually offered in fairy tales.

Gelman is even less oblique in her retelling, stating Esther's dilemma as a universal ethical dilemma. She brings the problem into focus as a real-life situation that children can relate to their own lives when she has Mordecai trying to calm Esther's fear of approaching the king unbidden:

> "You cannot think about yourself," he responded. "It is possible that you have been put on the throne for this very moment. You must go."

Esther and all the Jews of Shushan fast and pray for three days as Esther considers her choices, real-life and ethical. On the third day, her mind made up, she approaches the king: "If I die, I die, she thought." What a stunning decision! Children are focused on the wonder of her awesome decision and are led by Gelman's text and Frané Lessac's powerful illustrations. Lessac first shows a nervous Esther being prepared to go before the king, and then follows this image with a full-page illustration of a self-assured Esther with her head held high and arms raised in fearless supplication, approaching the foot of the king's throne. Esther proudly stands alone while the king, on his raised throne, surrounded by armed soldiers and a benign lion wagging his tail, has his arms folded meekly across his lap.

Having taken the risk of approaching the king and revealing her true self, Esther has passed over Campbell's "threshold." She is no longer a child who will be told what to do by the authority figures around her. Not unlike Belle of "Beauty and the Beast," who acts to save her town, Esther has moved beyond her youthful narcissism and has learned the importance of caring about others. Bettelheim writes:

> . . . narcissism, the fairy tale teaches us, despite its seeming attractiveness, is not a life of satisfactions, but no life at all. Beauty comes to life when she learns that her father needs her. In some versions of the tale he has fallen seriously ill; in others he pines away for her, or in some other way is in great distress. This knowledge shatters Beauty's narcissistic non-existence; she begins to act and then she—and the story—comes to life again. (p. 307)

It is only in learning to care about others that Esther can come fully into her own and truly matter in the story. Once she makes the choice to risk her own life for her people, she becomes a full player, no longer simply the obedient, docile young girl who is told what to do by the men around her. As Campbell writes, "The conclusion of the childhood cycle is the return or recognition of the hero, when, after the long period of obscurity, [her] true character is revealed" (p. 329). Esther has reached down deep into herself and found that she can be a brave and compassionate leader, and a true hero.

Violence

> So the Jews struck at their enemies with
> the sword, slaying and destroying;
> they wreaked their will upon their enemies.
>
> (Esther 9:5)

Violence plays an important role in the story of Esther. Haman's decree to kill all the Jews is terrible, but in the end it is only an empty threat. Instead, the biblical text reports that Haman and his sons were impaled upon the stake (Esther 9:25) and that the Jews killed thousands of others while defending themselves (Esther 9). This is hardly a simple "they-all-lived-happily-ever-after" ending. Instead, it is an ending similar to that of fairy tales, in which wicked characters are not saved but rather their fate is to have the evil they would inflict on others inflicted instead on them—as the witch in "Hansel and Gretel" or the stepmother in "Snow White." To the ancient reader, there was surely something satisfying about the violence embedded in the story. The Jews, having been victimized by Haman, are finally able to defend themselves, kill those who would kill them, and triumph in the end. It is sweet revenge for the unprotected underdog and a fulfilling fantasy for anyone who has felt victimized and powerless.

In contemporary retellings of the story of Esther for children, the violence of the biblical story becomes more problematic. We live in a society that is at once rife with examples of violence on television, in the newspapers, in movies, and in video games. And at the same time our society is prone to attempts to whitewash other intimations of violence for children, as seen in the "Disneyfication" of so many traditional fairy tales. While we allow children to witness horrible violence on television, we don't want them to be too scared by the witch in "Sleeping Beauty." We are, as a society, deeply ambivalent about children and violence—how much can they handle, in what form, and using what kinds of metaphors?

The violence in this story is in part also representative of the birth pangs of Esther's new sense of self, a manifestation of her pain and struggle to break free and become herself. Esther must battle that which will keep her from growing up and into herself, that which will keep her from her destiny. It is not uncommon in fairy tales and legends that the violence of inner transformation is manifested in outer physical violence. In discussing stories that deal with the hero having to kill the father figure in order to emerge whole out of childhood, Campbell writes, "Hence, too, the irresistible compulsion to make war: the impulse to destroy the father is continually transforming itself into public violence" (p. 155). In order for Esther to truly kill the bad father figure, Haman, she must destroy not only him, but also his sons and all those who would continue to threaten her survival and that of her people on his behalf.

Journeys of self-discovery often involve violence. Just as David must slay his giant, and Moses' transformation involves both the killing of the slavemaster and the killing of the firstborn of the Egyptians, Esther and her kinspeople slay those who have threatened their future. As Iona and Peter Opie put forward in their landmark *The Classic Fairy Tales* (1974), children need to see the transformation from unhappiness, fear, and life-threatening predicaments to a happy, satisfying resolution in their stories/literature. The Opies note that it is especially significant when this transformation to a happy state does not come about by magic or the intervention of another person, even a fairy godmother, but by the action of the story's main character. Children learn from these stories that action can bring about a positive change. The Opies write about characters who, like Esther, were always noble but were initially unable to exhibit or act on that nobility until qualifying circumstances present themselves. Esther was frightened, but choosing a noble response to danger allowed her to overcome her great fear and respond proactively and heroically (p. 17). It is Esther's actions that make a difference in the story. The threat of violence against herself and her people is the catalyst that propels her to act. The violence that ensues on her behalf is not an end in and of itself, but a way to achieve an ultimately better time of peace and justice in the future.

When Esther is transformed from a shy, passive young woman into a woman of action and power, it is as if a spell has been broken. Now she is truly beautiful and noble. Haman, on the other hand, is so wicked that he, like the ogres, monsters, and beasts in fairy tales, is beyond redemption. He is thematically related to the witch in "Hansel and Gretel," the stepmother in "Sleeping Beauty," and the giant in "Jack and the Beanstalk"; he and his followers are set up to deserve their final painful fate. For each of these fairy-tale characters, their ultimate punishment is what they would have inflicted on the fairy tale's main character. In the case of the evil Haman it is perfectly clear: the horrifying fate he would have subjected Esther and the Jewish people to is now inflicted on him, he is hung from the gallows he had constructed as an instrument of death for the Jewish people.

Being scared and dealing with fear is frequently addressed in children's books. Children are given an opportunity to try different roles and responses, and see what feels comfortable to them. Without having to face frightening situations in real life, children can see what solutions might work for them and how others have dealt with fear. These scenarios suggest positive ways to confront their fears, from sports to school to parents and friends, and effectively deal with them. The 2004 Newbery Award–winning book, *The Tale of Despereaux* by Kate DiCamillo, uses a traditional fairy tale setting and an undersized mouse as its unlikely hero. The book affirms, first of all, that it is all right to be different, just as Esther is different from the other young women brought to Ahasuerus's palace. Despereaux is unlike the other mice in the king's castle; he is dreamy and removed from traditional mouse activities, just as Esther is removed from the concerns of the other young women over appearance and makeup. When Despereaux is confronted by a large rat, Roscuro, a Haman–like evil character who hates all mice and is anxious to kill him, he, like Esther, devises a strategy and goes about rescuing princess Pea and saving his own life. In the process he grows in inner strength and confidence because he is so convinced of the rightness of his cause. Children applaud Despereaux's resourcefulness and bravery just as they do Harry Potter's.

Most of the retellings for children skip the biblical story's violent ending, and instead frame Esther's tale in other ways. In *Let My People Go,* the McKissacks note that the king allowed the Jews to defend themselves and save themselves from death, but they don't provide any details. Instead they use the end of the story as an opportunity to drive home the lesson of Esther's bravery and risk-taking. They write, "Queen Esther could have remained silent and let thousands of people die. Instead, she risked her own life to save others. There is nothing braver a person can do." Rather than focusing on the violence that accompanied the victory of the Jews over Haman, and the fact that while many lives were saved, many others were lost in the process, they leave readers with a moral about the imperative of speaking up and using whatever tools are available to right wrongs.

In keeping with the farcical approach used throughout his retelling, Gerstein allows for limited violence so that the bad guy, Haman, can have his comeuppance in *Queen Esther the Morning Star*.

> *Haman was hung on his*
> *own gallows the very*
> *next day.*

This is a clear-cut case of the bad guy getting what he deserves. But Gerstein fashions his retelling with a sense of humor and no connection to real-world violence. The illustration accompanying the text merely shows a tall pole extending out beyond the borders of the frame, with only Haman's feet hanging at the very top of the illustration, his shield falling down from above, and a dog scratching itself on the ground. Ignoring the rest of the violence in the biblical story, the good guys then celebrate the holiday of Purim with great rejoicing and the eating of Hamantaschen, triangular pastries shaped like Haman's hat.

Haman is led away with a noose already around his neck in Frané Lessac's illustrations for Gelman's *Queen Esther Saves Her People*. The text speaks of Haman hanging on the gallows that he had built for Mordecai, and mentions that in place of the Jews dying, it was their enemies who died. There is no further mention though of the violence that takes place. Instead, the story ends with the king right back where he began, busy with drinking and eating rather than running his kingdom: "But now, instead of Hamen's [sic] evil, it was the wisdom of Mordecai and his cousin Queen Esther that ruled the Persian Empire." The king has not been transformed in the least. He simply has better advisers to make decisions for him. The innate goodness and wisdom of Mordecai and Esther has triumphed over the evil and destruction represented by Haman. The outsiders are now the ultimate insiders.

The violence is more palpable in Wolkstein's *Esther's Story*. Mention is made of the hundreds that have been killed by the Jews as they try to defend themselves. This violence, the direct result of Haman's evil plan, is presented not as a desired outcome, but as a necessity that will ensure safety and peace for the Jews. Once the fighting has ended, they are able to enjoy themselves and relax, no longer afraid for their lives. "Haman tried to destroy the Jews. Instead, he destroyed himself," Wolkstein writes. The implication is that violence is not the answer, and that in trying to hurt someone else you are just as likely to get hurt yourself. It is up to Esther and Mordecai to try to be better leaders than Haman and not be corrupted by power. Wolkstein's story ends not with violence, but with a projection into the future, when Esther is a woman of seventy. As she reflects on her story, which she is about to tell as part of the annual Purim festivities, she thinks, "Once it was my story. Now it belongs to each of us." Toward the end of her life, Esther recognizes that her story is a bigger story, one that belongs to her people as much as to herself. Having conquered evil, her story will live on and become part of the ongoing story of her people, while Haman's story comes to an end.

In *Daughters of Eve*, Lillian Ross makes a point about the evil and turbulence spread by Haman by contrasting it with the peace that comes after he is gone. Yet she does so by actually changing an impor tant element of the story from the original. In her retelling, the king is able to revoke Haman's decree to kill the Jews. Whereas the biblical version goes to pains to explain that the decree cannot be rescinded because it was made by the king, here the responsibility is put on Haman. The king says, ". . . Let it be known that King Ahashverosh [sic] wishes his people and the Jews to live together in peace. With my seal, this decree cannot be broken." The king comes out looking like a "good guy" who has been taken advantage of by the evil Haman. It is not the evil decree to kill the Jews that cannot be broken, but the king's decree reversing it. This change, while it serves to paint the king in a better light, reverses a significant element of the story. In this way, the Jews have no need to defend themselves and a much happier ending can be provided in this version:

Joy rang out through Shushan. Mordecai was praised as a hero as he walked through the streets wearing royal robes of purple and white. The Jews gathered on the thirteenth and fourteenth day of Adar, and celebrated. They called their celebration Purim, vowing that these days of joy and peace should be remembered and kept for each generation in every family and in every land.

This version skips right to the good part and bypasses the violence of the biblical text, providing a much more palatable ending for the contemporary reader, but misses the opportunity to allow the Jews their chance for righteous vengeance. The risk Esther took in going to the king becomes somewhat less heroic without the Jews having to fight their way to victory.

In the end, after the violence of breaking through the turmoil of change, she is able to help usher in a period of peace and beneficence for her people. Esther and Mordecai are the counter examples of Haman as a leader. Where Haman tried to use his power and influence for destruction and violence, they are able to choose to lead with wisdom and caring.

At the conclusion of the story, Esther is able to rule wisely. She can take control of her emotions and actions, and in so doing be a good ruler and role model for her people. These images of beneficient rulers are ultimately as important for children as the bad rulers in stories. For whereas the bad rulers provide a way for children to appropriately channel their negative feelings about the wicked authority figures in their lives, good rulers provide children with positive models of the rewards of growing up and taking control of the kingdom of one's own life. Bettelheim writes:

> In fairy tales, unlike myths, victory is not over others but only over oneself and over villainy (mainly one's own, which is projected as the hero's antagonist). If we are told anything about the rule of these kings and queens, it is that they ruled wisely and peacefully, and that they lived happily. This is what maturity ought to consist of: that one rules oneself wisely, as a consequence lives happily. (p. 127–28)

In achieving maturity and coming into her own sense of self, able to use her power and act with confidence, Esther is able to achieve a truly happy ending for herself and by extension, for her people.

The presence of violence in the story teaches children that it is possible to grow from powerlessness to power. Success is more meaningful when it must be fought for. The violence is the means through which success is assured. Seen through the lens of contemporary values, the emphasis for children should be on achieving power and righting wrongs not through violence, but through other means. But because the system portrayed in the biblical text is set up in such a way that once decreed, a king's edict could not be undone, the violence that ensued in this story was inevitable. The important part of the lesson for children though is not the violence itself. Rather, it is that using only the tools at her disposal, her wits, her beauty, her courage, and her brain, Esther was able to do away with the threat to herself and her people and to experience triumph. It is an empowering, encouraging message to children.

When Mordecai tells Esther to go speak to the king, she is afraid and reluctant. It is only when Mordecai urges her on, using strong language and hinting that there may have been a bigger purpose to her attaining the position as queen does she agree (Esther 4). That is the defining moment in Esther's story. From that point on, the remaining choices are up to her. Mordecai has dispatched her to do her duty for their people, but she must decide how to achieve success. This is the ultimate test of Esther's character. This huge responsibility is on her shoulders alone. She makes a plan and embarks upon it, saying, "If I perish, I perish" (Esther 4:16), putting the survival of her people above her own.

Esther is a passive, obedient girl throughout her years at Mordecai's home and during her initial time at the palace as queen. Her two main characteristics are her submissiveness and her extraordinary beauty. In each children's book these qualities are emphasized all through the time Mordecai is grooming her and presenting her at the palace. When Mordecai later tells her to speak to the king on behalf of her people, she reacts by telling him it is improper to approach the king, and that it is not her place to initiate contact, but rather to please the king as he requires. At this point Esther is still the obedient, naive young woman she was at the start of the story, not yet ready to undertake her hero journey. When, at last, Esther realizes that the fate of the Jewish people is in her power, she gathers her strength and courage and asks her people to help her prepare for this test. She is finally ready to confront her destiny, to complete her hero journey, and to relinquish the role of dependent, obedient child and become a self-confident, self-reliant adult. Despite the fasting of her people, and the motivation provided by Mordecai, Esther must, like all heroes, undertake her journey alone.

Esther's journey fits Joseph Campbell's classic mold of the hero's journey as seen throughout fairy tales, quest stories, and other Bible stories. It is a journey from obedient child to self-reliant adult and Esther accomplishes her epic task with monumental success. In both Campbell and Otto Rank's paradigms of the hero's story, the tale begins with the birth and early childhood of the hero in shrouded or indeterminate circumstances (Campbell, p. 326; Rank p. 62–63). Esther's story fits this model, with the mysterious absence of her natural parents and her ambiguous relationship to her relative Mordecai. After an otherwise uneventful childhood, a kind of extended-latency period, Mordecai decides Esther is ready to enter Persian society and vie for the king's hand as the most beautiful woman in the kingdom. This new-found belief in her status as a beautiful woman, eligible for marriage, foreshadows the third and final stage in the hero's journey, that of returning to society as a socially and sexually mature adult. This is a common pattern of fairy tales involving girls, in which the heroine wins the hand of an appropriately royal prince and "lives happily ever after," having fulfilled her quest.

Yet for Esther, the conclusion and resolution of the hero journey is not her royal marriage, but something far more important: the survival of her people. It is this goal that indicates the final stage of Esther's particular heroism. Upon entering the harem and becoming part of the king's household, she experiences a critical stage of her journey consisting of what Campbell characterizes as "a separation from the world, a penetration to some source of power, and life-enhancing return." It is this that enables her to gain the inner strength needed to act to save her people. She is put to a test, and manages to come through it successfully, having been able to both rely on her own skills and to think about the needs of others.

That Esther is a queen is of no small significance in this story. The connections between Esther's story and fairy tales are important. This story matters for children in much the same way that fairy tales matter. As Bettelheim writes:

> Every child at some time wishes that he were a prince or princess—and at times, in his unconscious, the child believes he is one, only temporarily degraded by circumstances. There are so many kings and queens in fairy tales because their rank signifies absolute power, such as the parent seems to hold over his child. So the fairy-tale royalty represent projections of the child's imagination. (p. 205)

Esther's transformation from powerless youth to powerful queen is an important metaphoric journey for children. Through her actions, she is able to point the way, and to reassure children that they too will have a chance to express their true identity.

The story of Esther acknowledges with honesty the pain and violence of growing up and taking charge of one's life. The fear of failure at important tasks is real, whether those tasks are internalized or originating in the outside world. Yet the story challenges children to take charge, to take risks, and to look beyond their own selves to those around them. It tells children that to be truly powerful and brave is to consider the needs of others. Through the language and images of the fairy tale, Esther is evidence that all children will grow up and have an opportunity to reveal themselves as the heroes they already know themselves to be.

Conclusion

AS WE MOVE FORWARD in the twenty-first century, William Godwin's words to Charles Lamb in 1808 regarding the power that adults have over what children read still hold true. So many variables factor into the choices adults make. But remembering that Bible stories serve a dual purpose should help make the choice easier. There is no question that the plentiful abundance of beautifully illustrated editions of these classic stories present a visual delight for children, from Jerry Pinkney's lush illustration in *Noah's Ark* to Ashley Bryan's dramatic woodcuts in *How God Fix Jonah*. For countless children, these books represent an introduction to stunning museum-quality art. The details in the artwork extend and explain the accompanying text. The language of many of these stories introduces children to another kind of beauty, that of a well-told tale that manages to connect in some way with the child's life. Visually, aurally, emotionally, and psychologically, not to mention in some cases spiritually, well-chosen books for children can have a powerful impact upon their readers.

The authors of *Stories of Heaven and Earth* hope that this book serves its intended purpose of being a resource for parents, educators, librarians, clergy, and all those who work with children. Each of the Bible stories discussed stands alone as an exciting adventure. What child would not like an opportunity to save her family, her friends, and her community? What child doesn't dream of slaying giants and becoming a famous warrior? These stories allow children to imagine themselves in different roles and experiment with different identities and outcomes. The Bible stories give children the ability to imagine themselves as heroes of their own life journeys; these stories provide models for children of how to pattern their own lives and enable them to envision what choices they will need to make along the way.

Stories of Heaven and Earth examines these works critically within the context of children's literature. Their importance in passing on religious values and traditions is apparent as well. As such, they are read within certain belief systems and imbued with specific importance. But we believe that part of the power of these stories lies in their ability to also be read as a significant source of world literature and archetypes; that they speak to the basic universal experience of human development. Ultimately, these stories are about making choices when there is not always a clear or easy choice to make. Each Bible hero is a real human being with faults as well as virtues, a character who changes, grows, learns from experience, and in due course makes good decisions. Adam and Eve start their journey as children living in paradise until they face the supreme decision of whether or not to obey the command of their parent–God and eat from the Tree of Knowledge. As children mature they have to make similar decisions in their own lives. At what point can they see the effects of their decisions? Will their parents still love and accept them even if they have made a poor decision? When children hear the story of Adam and Eve, they can internalize it in preparation for learning to make their own decisions independently while knowing they can never lose their parents' love, even when their parents are unhappy with the decisions they make. Each retelling of Moses' story, despite the emphasis on differing aspects of his personality and journey, shows him, notwithstanding his handicap, as a wise leader who sometimes lets his anger get the better of him. Joseph is a universal story of sibling rivalry and perceived parental favoritism, something children often believe is their own plight. Yet, Joseph overcomes his arrogance and matures to the point at which he is able to initiate reconciliation with his brothers. What wonderful role models these complex Bible characters are for children just starting out on their own hero journeys through life!

Each story, in whichever version is chosen, is brimming with issues to be discussed in great detail with children. Each provides an example for passing on family and community models of ethical behavior. At the same time, they also emphasize that decision-making is not an easy process but rather often involves difficult choices and great emotional courage. By encouraging children, their families, and the institutions responsible for the education of children to connect with these important stories from the biblical tradition, we hope that *Stories of Heaven and Earth* supports the emotional development of children and families. These ancient Bible stories offer a treasure chest of literary models that provide reassurance for children, showing them that it is possible to get through the tremendous trials of growing up. These stories are critical for children's emotional development for they provide models of heroes who gain wisdom, internal strength, and necessary life skills in the process of meeting the challenges ahead of them and ultimately attaining adulthood. In doing so, they allow children to imagine the possibility of becoming the heroes of their own lives.

Bibliography

Arbuthnot, May Hill, comp. *Arbuthnot Anthology of Children's Literature*. 4th ed. Zena Sutherland, ed. New York: Lothrop, Lee & Shepard, 1976.

Auld, Mary, illustrated by Diana Mayo. *David and Goliath*. Danbury, CT: Franklin Watts, 1999.

———. *Exodus from Egypt*. Danbury, CT: Franklin Watts, 2000.

———. *Joseph and His Brothers*. Danbury, CT: Franklin Watts, 1990.

———. *The Story of Jonah*. Danbury, CT: Franklin Watts, 1999.

———. *Moses in the Bulrushes*. Danbury, CT: Franklin Watts, 1999.

Bach, Alice and J. Cheryl Exum. *Miriam's Well: Stories about Women in the Bible*. New York: Delacorte Press, 1991.

Barrie, J. M., illustrated by Arthur Rackham. *Peter Pan in Kensington Gardens*. New York: Scribner, 1906.

Berlin, Adele. *The JPS Bible Commentary: Esther*. Philadelphia, PA: The Jewish Publication Society, 2001.

Bettelheim, Bruno. *The Uses of Enchantment: The Meaning and Importance of Fairy Tales*. New York: Knopf, 1976.

Bialik, Hayyim Nachman and Yehoshua Hana Ravnitzky. *The Book of Legends Sefer Ha-Aggadah: Legends from the Talmud and Midrash*. Translated by William G. Braude. New York: Schocken Books, 1992.

Bottigheimer, Ruth. *The Bible for Children: From the Age of Gutenberg to the Present*. New Haven, CT: Yale University, 1996.

Brett, Jan. *On Noah's Ark*. New York: G. P. Putnam's Sons, 2003.

Bulla, Clyde Robert. *Jonah and the Great Fish*. New York: Crowell, 1970.

Campbell, Joseph. *The Hero With A Thousand Faces*. Princeton, NJ: Bollingen, 1968.

———. *The Hero's Journey*. San Francisco: HarperCollins, 1990.

Carpenter, Humphrey and Mari Pritchard, *Oxford Companion to Children's Literature*, New York: Oxford University Press, 1984.

Chaikin, Miriam, illustrated by Charles Mikolaycak. *Exodus*. New York: Holiday House, 1987.

————, illustrated by Yvonne Gilbert. *Children's Bible Stories from Genesis to Daniel*. New York: Dial Books, 1993.

Cohen, Barbara. *David: A Biography*. New York: Clarion Books, 1995.

Cook, Elizabeth. *The Ordinary and the Fabulous: An Introduction to Myths, Legends and Fairy Tales*. 2nd ed. New York: Cambridge University Press, 1976.

Cormier, Robert. *The Chocolate War*. New York: Pantheon, 1974.

Courlander, Harold and George Herzog, illustrated by Madye Lee Chastain. *The Cow-Tail Switch and Other West African Stories*. New York: Henry Holt, 1947, re-issued in 1986.

Cousins, Lucy. *Noah's Ark*. Cambridge, MA: Candlewick Press, 1993.

De Regniers, Beatrice Schenk, illustrated by Scott Cameron. *David and Goliath*. New York: Orchard Books, 1996.

dePaola, Tomie. *Queen Esther: A Bible Story Book*. New York: HarperCollins, 1986.

————. *Tomie dePaola's Book of Bible Stories*. New York: Putnam/Zondervan, 1990.

————. *Tomie dePaola's Book of the Old Testament*. New York: G. P. Putnam's Sons, 1990.

DiCamillo, Kate. *The Tale of Despereaux*. New York: Candlewick Press, 2003.

Dickens, Charles, illustrated by George Cruikshank. *Oliver Twist*. London: R. Bentley, 1836.

Dickinson, John. *The Liberty Song*. First published in *Boston Gazette* in July 1768. Cited in *Songs of Dickinson*. Carlisle, PA: Dickinson College, 1937.

Dickinson, Peter, illustrated by Michael Foreman. *City of Gold and Other Stories from the Old Testament*. Boston: Otter Books, 1992.

Douglas, Kirk, illustrated by Dom Lee. *Young Heroes of the Bible: A Book for Family Sharing*. New York: Simon and Schuster, 1999.

Eisler, Colin, illustrated by Jerry Pinkney. *David's Songs: The Psalms and Their Story*. New York: Dial Books, 1992.

Emberley, Barbara, adaptor, illustrated by Ed Emberley. *One Wide River to Cross*. Englewood Cliffs, NJ: Prentice-Hall, 1966.

Erikson, Erik. *Childhood and Society*. 2nd Edition. New York: Norton, 1950, 1964.

————. *Insight and Responsibility*. New York: Norton, 1964.

————. *Identity, Youth and Crisis*. New York: Norton, 1968.

————. "Identity and the Life Cycle," in *Psychological Issues,* vol. 1, 1959, International Universities Press.

Estes, Eleanor, illustrated by Louis Slobodkin. *The 100 Dresses*. New York: Harcourt Brace, 1944.

Farber, Norma, illustrated by Victoria Chess. *A Ship in a Storm on the Way to Tarshish*. New York: Greenwillow, 1977.

Fish, Helen Dean, adapter, illustrated by Dorothy P. Lathrop. *Animals of the Bible*. New York: Frederick A. Stokes, 1937.

Fisher, Leonard Everett. *David and Goliath*. New York: Holiday House, 1993.

―――. *Moses*. New York: Holiday House, 1995.

Freedman, H. and Maurice Simon, eds. and translators. *Midrash Rabbah*. New York: Soncino Press, 1983–1992. 10 volumes.

Freud, Sigmund. *A General Introduction to Psychoanalysis*. Translated by J. Rivera. New Yorks: Perma Books, 1953 (originally published 1916).

―――. *The Interpretation of Dreams*. Translated by James Strachey.

Frye, Northrop. *Fables of Identity: Studies in Poetic Mythology*. New York: Harcourt, Brace, Jovanovitch, 1951.

Gauch, Patricia Lee, illustrated by Jonathan Green. *Noah*. New York: Philomel Book, 1994.

Geisert, Arthur. *The Ark*. New York: Houghton Mifflin, 1988.

Gelman, Rita Golden, illustrated by Frané Lessac. *Queen Esther Saves Her People*. New York: Scholastic, 1998.

Gerson, Mary-Joan, illustrated by Carla Galembe. *Why the Sky is Far Away: A Nigerian Folktale*. Boston: Little, Brown, 1992.

Gerstein, Mordicai. *Jonah and the Two Great Fish*. New York: Simon and Schuster, 1997.

―――. *Queen Esther the Morning Star*. New York: Simon and Schuster, 2000.

Ginzberg, Louis. *Legends of the Jews*. Baltimore, MD: Johns Hopkins University Press, 1998.

Graham, Lorenz, illustrated by Ashley Bryan. *How God Fix Jonah*. 1st rev. ed. Honesdale, PA: Boyds Mills Press, 2000 (originally published 1946).

Green, Roger Lancelyn. *King Arthur and His Knights of the Round Table*. New York: Everyman's Library, 1993.

Grimm, Jacob and Wilhelm, illustrated by Maurice Sendak. *The Juniper Tree and Other Tales from Grimm*, 2 vols. Translated by Lore Segal. New York: Farrar, Straus and Giroux, 1973.

―――. *Tales from Grimm*. Freely translated and illustrated by Wanda Gàg. New York: Coward-McCann, 1936.

―――. *More Tales from Grimm*. Freely translated and illustrated by Wanda Gàg. New York: Coward-McCann, 1947.

Hamilton, Virginia, illustrated by Barry Moser. *In the Beginning: Creation Stories from Around the World*. New York: Harcourt Brace Jovanovich, 1988.

Hayward, Linda, illustrated by Barb Henry. *Baby Moses.* New York: Random House, 1989.

Hiassen, Carl. *Hoot.* New York: Knopf, 2002.

Horn, Geoffrey and Arthur Cavanaugh, illustrated by Arvis Stewart. *Bible Stories for Children.* New York: Simon and Schuster Books for Young Readers, 1980.

Howard, Fern, illustrated by James Needham. *Adam and Eve (Ladybird Bible Story Series).* Leicestershire, England: Ladybird Books, 1990.

Huck, Charlotte, ed. *Children's Literature in the Elementary School, 8th Edition.* Revised by Barbara Keifer. New York: McGraw-Hill, 2004.

Hughes, Thomas. *Tom Brown's Schooldays.* New York: Oxford University Press, 1989 (reprint).

Hunt, Peter. *Children's Literature: An Illustrated History.* New York: Oxford University Press, 1995.

Hutton, Warwick. *Adam and Eve: The Bible Story.* New York: Macmillan, 1987.

———. *Jonah and the Great Fish.* New York: Atheneum, 1983.

———. *Moses in the Bulrushes.* New York: Alladin, 1992.

Hyman, Trina Schart. *Little Red Riding Hood by The Brothers Grimm.* New York: Holiday House, 1983.

Jacobs, Joseph, illustrated by John D. Batten. *English Fairy Tales.* New York: Dover, 1967. (Reprint of 1890 London edition published by David Nutt.)

Janisch, Heinz, illustrated by Lisbeth Zwerger. *Noah's Ark.* New York: North-South Books, 1997.

Jewish Publication Society. *Tanakh.* Philadelphia, PA: Jewish Publication Society, 2000.

Johnson, James Weldon, illustrated by James E. Ransome. *The Creation.* New York: Holiday House, 1994.

Jonas, Ann. *Aardvarks, Disembark!* New York: Greenwillow, 1990.

Kagan, Jerome. *The Nature Of the Child.* New York: Basic Books, 1984.

Kassirer, Sue, illustrated by Danuta Jarecka. *Joseph and His Coat of Many Colors.* New York: Simon and Schuster, 1997.

Keats, Ezra Jack. *Goggles.* New York: Macmillan, 1969.

Kegan, Paul, ed. *William Godwin: His Friends and Contemporaries.* Vol. II. London: Henry S. King & Co., 1876.

Kessler, Brad, illustrated by Phil Huling. *Moses in Egypt: Liberation from Slavery.* New York: Simon and Schuster, 1997.

Kohlberg, Lawrence. *The Meaning and Measurement of Moral Development.* Worcester, MA: Clark University, 1981.

Lang, Andrew. *King Arthur: Tales from the Round Table.* New York: Dover, 2002.

Lanier, Sidney, illustrated by N. C. Wyeth. *Boy's King Arthur*. New York: Scribner, 1924.

Lanning, Rosemary, illustrated by Bernadette Watts. *Jonah and the Whale*. New York: North-South Books, 2001.

Lester, Julius, reteller, illustrated by Jerry Pinkney. *The Tales of Uncle Remus: The Adventures of Brer Rabbit*. New York: Dial, 1987.

Little, Emily, illustrated by Hans Wilhelm. *David and the Giant*. New York: Random House, 1987.

Louie, Ai-Ling, reteller, illustrated by Ed Young. *Yeh-shen: A Cinderella Story from China*. New York: Philomel, 1982.

Mackall, Dandi Daley. *Joseph, King of Dreams*. Nashville, TN: Tommy Nelson, 2000.

Malory, Sir Thomas. *King Arthur and His Knights of the Round Table*. New York: Grosset & Dunlap, 1950.

Manushkin, Fran, illustrated by Uri Shulevitz. *Daughters of Fire: Heroines of the Bible*. New York: Harcourt, 2001.

Martin, Mary, illustrated by Bryn Barnard. *Adam and Eve* (Family Time Bible Stories Series). Alexandria, VA: Time Life Kids, 1995.

May, Herbert G. and Bruce M. Metzger, eds. *New Oxford Annotated Bible with the Apocrypha* (Revised Standard Version 8914a). Oxford: Oxford University Press, 1977.

McDermott, Gerald. *Creation*. New York: Dutton's Children's Books, 2003.

McDonough, Yona Zeldis, with paintings by Malcah Zeldis. *Eve and her Sisters: Women of the Old Testament*. New York: Greenwillow, 1994.

McKissack, Patricia and Fredrick, illustrated by James E. Ransome. *Let My People Go*. New York: Atheneum, 1998.

Miller, J. B. "The Development of Women's Sense of Self," in J. V. Jordan, A. G. Kaplan, J. B. Miller, I. P. Stiver, and J. L. Surrey, eds., *Women's Growth In Connection: Writings for the Stone Center*. New York: Guilford Press, 1991.

Monte, Richard, illustrated by Izhar Cohen. *The Flood Tales*. London: Pavilion Books, 2000.

Myers, Walter Dean, illustrated by Christopher Myer. *A Time to Love: Stories from the Old Testament*. New York: Scholastic, 2003.

Opie, Iona and Peter. *The Classic Fairy Tales*. London: Oxford University Press, 1974.

———, ed., illustrated by Maurice Sendak. *I Saw Esau: The Schoolchild's Pocket Book*. Cambridge, MA: Candlewick; 1992.

Orenstein, Catherine. *Little Red Riding Hood Uncloaked*. New York: Basic Books, 2002.

Paparone, Pam. *Who Built the Ark?* New York: Simon and Schuster, 1994.

Parton, Dolly, illustrated by Judith Sutton. *Coat of Many Colors.* New York: HarperCollins, 1994.

Patterson, Geoffrey. *Jonah and the Whale.* New York: Lothrop, Lee and Shepard Books, 1991.

Paul, C. Kegan, ed. *William Godwin: His Friends and Contemporaries,* vol. 2, chapter VII. London: Henry S. King & Co, 1876.

Perrault, Charles, illustrated by Gustav Doré. *Perrault's Fairy Tales.* New York: Dover, 1969.

———, illustrated by Sarah Moon. *Little Red Riding Hood.* Mankato, MN: Creative Editions, 2002.

Piaget, Jean. *The Moral Judgment of the Child.* Translated by M. Gabin. New York: Free Press, 1965 (originally published in 1932).

———. "Comments on Vygotsky's Critical Remarks Concerning the Language and Thought of the Child, and Judgment and Reasoning In the Child," in L. S. Vygotsky, *Thought and Language.* Cambridge, MA: MIT Press, 1962.

———. *The Origins of Intelligence in Children.* New York: International Universities Press, 1952.

———. *The Constructions of Reality in the Child.* New York: Basic Books, 1954.

Pinkney, Jerry. *Noah's Ark.* New York: SeaStar Books, 2002.

Plaut, W. Gunther, ed. *The Torah: A Modern Commentary.* New York: UAHC Press, 1981.

Potter, Beatrix. *The Tale of Jemima Puddle-Duck.* New York: Frederick Warne, 1936, 1908.

Pyle, Howard. *Story of the Champions of the Round Table.* New York: Dover, 1968.

Rank, Otto. "The Myth of the Birth of the Hero" in *In Quest of the Hero,* with an introduction by Robert A. Segal. Princeton, NJ: Princeton University Press, 1990.

Ray, Jane. *Noah's Ark: Words from the Book of Genesis.* New York: Puffin Books, 1990.

Reed, Gwendolyn, illustrated by Helen Siegl. *Adam and Eve.* New York: Lothrop, Lee and Shepard Books, 1968.

Reid, Barbara. *Two by Two.* New York: Scholastic, 1992.

Rosenbach, A.S.W. *Early American Children's Books.* New York: Dover, 1977 (originally published in 1933 by The Southworth Press in Portland Maine).

Ross, Lillian Hammer, illustrated by Kyra Teis. *Daughters of Eve: Strong Women of the Bible.* New York: Barefoot Books, 2000.

Rounds, Glen. *Casey Jones, the Story of a Brave Engineer*. New York: Children's Press, 1968.

———. *Ol' Paul the Mighty Logger*. New York: Holiday House, 1976.

———. *The Three Little Pigs and the Big Bad Wolf*. New York: Holiday House, 1992.

———. *Washday on Noah's Ark*. New York: Holiday House, 1985.

Rowling, J. K., illustrated by Mary GrandPré. *Harry Potter and the Sorcerer's Stone*. New York: Scholastic, 1998.

Sachar, Louis. *Holes*. New York: Farrar, Strauss and Giroux, 1998.

Santore, Charles. *A Stowaway on Noah's Ark*. New York: Random House, 2000.

Sasso, Sandy Eisenberg, illustrated by Bethanne Andersen. *A Prayer for the Earth: The Story of Naamah, Noah's Wife*. Woodstock, VT: Jewish Lights Publishing, 1996.

Schaie, K. Warner. "Toward a Stage Theory of Adult Cognitive Development," in *Journal of Aging and Human Development*, 1979, p. 129–38.

Segal, Lore and Maurice Sendak. *The Juniper Tree and Other Tales from Grimm*. Selected by Lore Segal and Maurice Sendak; translated by Lore Segal, with four translations by Randall Jarrell; illustrated by Maurice Sendak. New York: Farrar, Straus, and Giroux, 1976. 2 volumes.

Sendak, Maurice. *Pierre: A Cautionary Tale in Five Chapters and a Prologue*. New York: HarperCollins, 1962.

———. *Where the Wild Things Are*. New York: HarperCollins, 1963.

Sherman, Ori, with text by Stephen Mitchell. *The Creation*. New York: Dial Books, 1990.

Spier, Peter. *Noah's Ark*. New York: Doubleday, 1977.

———. *The Book of Jonah*. Grand Rapids, MI: Baker Books, 1985.

Spinelli, Jerry. *Maniac Magee*. Boston: Little, Brown, 1990.

———. *Wringer*. New York: HarperCollins, 1997.

Stanley, Diane. *Joan of Arc*. New York: HarperCollins, 1998.

Stewart, Mary. *Mary Stewart's Merlin Trilogy*. New York: Eos Books, 1980–2003.

Stewig, John. *The Animals*. New York: Holiday House, 2005.

Sting, illustrated by Hugh Whyte. *Rock Steady*. New York: HarperCollins, 2001.

Suess. *The Cat in the Hat*. New York: Random House, 1957.

Van Eyssen, Shirley. *In the Beginning*. New York: Harlin Quist, 1970.

Waddell, Martin, illustrated by Geoffrey Patterson. *Stories from the Bible*. London: Frances Lincoln Limited, 1993.

Walker, Barbara K. *Once there Was and Once There Wasn't*. New York: Follett, 1986.

Weil, Lisl. *Esther.* New York: Atheneum, 1980.

White, T. H. *The Sword in the Stone.* New York: Laurel Leaf, 1978.

Wildsmith, Brian, as told by Philip Turner. *Brian Wildsmith's Illustrated Bible Stories.* New York: Franklin Watts, 1968.

Wildsmith, Brian. *Exodus.* Grand Rapids, MI: Wm. B. Eerdmans, 1998.

———. *Joseph.* Grand Rapids, MI: Wm. B. Eerdmans, 1997.

Williams, Marcia. *Joseph and His Magnificent Coat of Many Colors.* Cambridge, MA: Candlewick Press, 1994.

———. *Jonah and the Whale.* New York: Random House, 1989.

Wolkstein, Diane, illustrated by Juan Wijngaard. *Esther's Story.* New York: Mulberry Books, 1996.

Yolen, Jane. *Sword of the Rightful King: A Novel of King Arthur.* New York: Harcourt, 2003.

———. *Touch Magic: Fantasy, Faerie & Folklore in the Literature of Childhood.* Little Rock, AR: August House, 2000.

Young, Ed. *Genesis.* New York: HarperCollins, 1997.

Zwerger, Lisbeth. *Stories from the Bible.* New York: North-South Books, 2000.

The Holy Bible, New International Version. New York: International Bible Society, 1984.

Index of Biblical Books

Genesis
1:27, 26
1:28, 55
1:29–31, 27–28
2:1–10, 25
2:16–17, 33
2:17, 25
2:22, 25
2:25, 45
3:1, 37
3:1–5, 25
3:4, 37
3:6, 34
3:6–7, 25
3:7, 45
3:12, 49
3:13, 49
6:4, 58
6:8–9, 57
6:9, 66
6:11, 59
6:11–13, 58
6:18, 70
6:19, 75
7:7, 83
8:7–8, 71
8:22, 80
9:19, 77
12–18, 104
25:28, 217n. 10
34, 217
37, 107
37:2, 98, 100

37:3, 93, 94
37:5–8, 91
37:5–11, 98
37:9–11, 91
37:14, 100
37:18–20, 102
37:18–25, 92
38, 217
39:1–18, 105
39:6, 104
39:7–10, 104
40:8, 107
42–43, 110
45:3–15, 111
45:4, 113
45:4–5, 109
45:15, 109
Exodus
1:22—2:23, 118
2:2, 119
2:6, 125
2:6–7, 126
3:9–10, 140
4:6–17, 132
4:10, 131, 135
5–14, 118
11:4–5, 145
13:19, 91
17:1–7, 139
17:4, 138
19–34, 118
20, 138
32:9, 138

32:19, 135, 136, 138
32:30–32, 136
45, 93
Deuteronomy
3:23–27, 118
3:26, 139
Judges
4–5, 217
I Samuel
9:15–17, 158
16, 155
16:1, 157
16:1–3, 158
16:11, 181
16:11–12, 157
16:13, 164
16:19, 181
16:21, 181
16:23, 183
17:14, 181
17:15, 169
17:17–18, 170
17:25, 180
17:28–29, 173
17:31–37, 173
17:33, 163
17:34–36, 174
17:38–40, 177
17:55–56, 181
18:2–5, 179
18:20, 217n. 10
19:12, 217
25, 217

II Samuel
  6:14–20, 155
  8, 155
  11, 155
Esther
  1, 221
  2:3–4, 227
  2:5, 7, 10, 229
  2:7, 236
  2:14, 238
  2:17, 238
  2:20, 220

3:1, 242
4, 258
4:11, 244
4:13, 243
4:13–14, 244
4:15–16, 244
4:16, 244, 258
5:2, 239
7:8, 239
9, 252
9:5, 251
9:25, 252

Jonah
  1:1, 190
  1:2, 189
  1:5, 196
  1:13, 197
  2:1–2, 201
  2:7–8, 206
  3:10, 208
  4, 209
  4:10–11, 210

Index

Aardvarks, Disembark, 82–83
Aaron, 160, 218
Abel, 52. *See also* Cain and Abel
Abraham, 14, 160
Achbar the mouse (fictional character), 71, 76–77
Adam. *See also* Adam and Eve
  portrayals of, 29–30, 41
Adam and Eve, 19, 20, 25, 31–37, 262
  adulthood, transition to, 45–49
  age, interpretation of, 46–47
  growing up and, 37–45
  inconsistencies in accounts, 26
  innocence, loss of, 37–45
  responsibility and consequences, 49–55
Adam and Eve (Martin), 32
Adam and Eve: The Bible Story (Hutton), 38
Adulthood, transition to, 45–49
African Americans, 235
  slavery, 140–42
African, depiction of Noah's family as, 78–79
Ahasuerus (King), 20, 219, 230, 232, 234, 242, 256
ALA Best Book for Young Adults, 166
Ammitai, 191
Anansi, 37
Andäch-tiger Catholischer Schriften Gott-heiligter Bibel-Lust, 15
Animals of the Bible (Fish), 57, 75
Animals, role of in Noah's Ark, 75–77
The Animals (Stewig), 72

Anti-Semitism, 233
Apple. *See* Tree of knowledge of good and evil
The Arbuthnot Anthology of Children's Literature, 16
Ark. *See* Noah's Ark
The Ark (Geisert), 68, 76, 84
Aser (fictional character), 127–28, 149–50
Auld, Mary
  David and Goliath, 159, 168
  Exodus from Egypt, 150–51
  Joseph and His Brothers, 94, 98, 105, 107, 111
  The Story of Jonah, 194–95, 200, 203, 209
Award Books, 57

Baby floating in basket symbol, 119
Baby Moses (Hayward), 121
Bach, Alice, 221–22, 242
Barrie, J. M., 40–41
"Beauty and the Beast" (fairy tale), 230, 236, 243, 249
Beauty, problem of, 236–43
Benjamin, 110
Berlin, Adele, 239
Bethlehem, 158–59
Bettelheim, Bruno, 38
  on fairy tales, 17, 22–23, 120, 146–49, 257–58, 260
  on Moses, 146
  number three, significance of, 244–45
  princess, winning hand of, 182–183
  on sibling rivalry, 92–93

The Uses of Enchantment (Bettelheim), 19, 92–93, 103

Bible in Miniuture [sic]; *or, A Concise History of the Old and New Testaments* (Newbery), 13

Bible Stories for Children (Cavanaugh and Horn), 30

Biblia Hebraica Stuttgartensia, 23

The Book of Jonah (Spier), 192, 201–2, 207, 209–10

The Borrowers, 156–58

Bottigheimer, Ruth, 14

Brer Rabbit, 37

Brett, Jan, 77

Brian Wildsmith's Illustrated Bible Stories (Wildsmith), 41

"Brothers Got Bad Heart for Joseph" (Graham), 101, 133–34, 144

Bryan, Ashley, 167, 202, 261

Bulla, Clyde Robert, 195–96

Bullying behavior, 165–69

Cain and Abel, 52, 53, 92

Caldecott Medal, 57, 65, 75, 166

Cameron, Scott, 171–72

Campbell, Joseph
on fairy tales, 18
"herald" role, 244
hero figures, 19–20, 22, 118, 130–32, 136, 158, 160, 176–77, 186, 191, 206, 251, 259
on Joseph, 93
on Moses, 118–19, 130–32, 136
princess, winning hand of, 180
on risk taking, 245
separation from world, 259–60
serpent, symbolism of, 42
on spiritual growth, 245, 246
and "threshold of transformation," 205, 251
and "unconscious content," 201
youngest son as theme, 160

Casey Jones, the Story of a Brave Engineer, 73

The Cat in the Hat (Dr. Seuss), 215

Cavanaugh, Arthur, 30, 38, 42

Chaikin, Miriam
Children's Bible Stories from Genesis to Daniel, 31–32, 51–52, 63, 67–68, 74–75, 102, 111, 124–25, 195, 197–98, 210
Exodus, 132, 135–37, 150

Character, importance of, 66–70

Chess, Victoria, 200–201

Children's Bible Stories from Genesis to Daniel (Chaikin)
Adam and Eve, 51–52
creation, 31–32
Jonah, portrayal of, 195, 197–98, 210
Joseph, portrayal of, 102, 111
Moses, portrayal of, 124–25
Noah, portrayal of, 63, 67–68, 74–75

Children's Literature in the Elementary School (Huck), 16

The Chocolate War (Cormier), 166

"Cinderella" (fairy tale), 199, 229, 236, 243

City of Gold and Other Stories of the Old Testament (Dickinson), 28–29, 39, 53

The Classic Fairy Tales (Opie and Opie), 253

Coat of Many Colors (Patton), 94–95

Cohen, Barbara, 159–60, 179

Cohen, Izhar, 69

Coles, Elisha, 14

Comestor, Peter, 12

"The Coming of Sorrow" (Turner), 41

Consequences, 49–55

Cook, Elizabeth, 16

Cormier, Robert, 166

Cousins, Lucy, 62–63

Creation, 24–55. *See also* Adam and Eve

The Creation (Mitchell), 28

Curious Hieroglyphic Bible . . . for the Amusement of Children (Thomas), 15

Daughters of Eve: Strong Women of the Bible (Ross), 224, 232–33, 241, 248

Daughters of Fire: Heroines of the Bible (Manushkin), 46–47, 223, 226, 240–42, 245–46

David, 22, 132, 155–87, 217, 220. *See also* David and Goliath
  as hero, 177–79
  lion and bear, 174–76, 179
  as obedient son, 169–74
  overview of story, 155–57
  princess, winning hand of, 180–83
  as psalmist, 183–87
  trials of, 174–77
  as young boy, 163–69
  as youngest son, 157–63

David: A Biography (Cohen), 159–60, 179

David and Goliath, 20, 157, 164–70, 173–83, 185–86

David and Goliath (Auld), 159, 168

David and Goliath (De Regniers), 171–73, 178–79, 182, 183

David and Goliath (Fisher), 169–71, 178–79

David and the Giant (Little), 165, 167, 178, 182, 183

David's Songs: His Psalms and Their Story (Eisler), 184

Death, comprehension of, 48–49

Deborah, 217

dePaola, Tomie, 21, 224, 227–28, 233, 243, 250

"Deep River" (spiritual), 141

Delilah, 218

De Regniers, Beatrice Schenk, 171–73, 178–79, 182, 183

DiCamillo, Kate, 166, 254

Dickens, Charles, 165

Dickinson, John, 68

Dickinson, Peter, 28, 39, 53

Dina, 217

Douglas, Kirk, 96–97, 103, 108

"The Dove Who Served Noah" (Fish), 75

"The Dragon and His Grandmother" (fairy tale), 176

Dr. Seuss, 215

Dumbkin (fictional character), 163

Dumbledore (fictional character), 121

Duncehead (fictional character), 162–63

"The Earth Gnome" (fairy tale), 176

Eisler, Colin, 184

Eliab, 158

Emberley, Barbara, 57, 75–76

Emberley, Ed, 57, 76

Environment
  interaction with, 58–59
  Noah's Ark, environmental themes, 80–83

Erbaulich Erzählungen, 15

Erikson, Erik, 19
  on authority, 212–13
  eight stages of development, 49
  on emotional development, 45
  identity, establishment of, 131
  on Joseph, 98–99, 113
  on Moses, 146
  stages of personality development, 87–88
  on tattling, 98–99

Esau, 160

Estes, Eleanor, 166

Esther, 19, 20, 22, 217–60
  beauty, problem of, 236–43
  identity, 229–35
  obedience of, 220–29
  overview of story, 217–20
  risk taking, 243–51
  violence, 251–60

Esther's Story (Wolkstein), 224–27, 231, 234–35, 239–41, 243, 247–48, 256

Esther (Weil), 224, 233–34, 236, 239, 248

Eve. *See also* Adam and Eve
  creation of, 30
  and serpent, 34–35, 37–45

Eve and Her Sisters: Women of the Old Testament (McDonough), 242

Eve (Manushkin), 46–47
Exodus (Chaikin and Mikolaycak), 132, 135–37, 150
Exodus from Egypt (Auld), 150–51
Exodus (Wildsmith), 21, 128, 139–40, 149
Exum, J. Cheryl, 221–22, 242

Fairy tales. *See also specific fairy tale*
    beauty portrayed in, 236–38
    brothers, relationships, 161–62
    children, killing of, 145–49
    knowledge about the future, 199–200
    success stories, 120
    violence in, 252–253
Fall of Man, 26
Farber, Norma, 200–201
Favoritism. *See* Parental favoritism
First-born, killing of, 119, 145–53
Fisher, Leonard Everett
    David and Goliath, 169–71, 178–79
    Moses, 125–27, 132–33, 137–39, 150
Fish, Helen Dean, 57, 75
The Flood Tales (Monte), 69, 73, 80–81, 83–84, 86
Foreman, Michael, 28
Forgiveness, 109–15
"Free at Last" (spiritual), 143
Freedom, slavery and, 140–15
Freeway (film), 237–38
Freud, Sigmund, 42, 45, 148
"The Frog Prince" (fairy tale), 42, 230, 238, 249
Fruit. *See* Tree of knowledge of good and evil

Gamiel (fictional character), 127–28, 149–50
Garden of Eden, 28–29, 31–32. *See also* Tree of knowledge of good and evil
Gauch, Patricia Lee, 78–79
Geisert, Arthur, 68, 76, 84
Gelman, Rita Golden, 223, 225–26, 232, 240, 247, 250–51, 255
Gender roles, Noah's Ark, 83–89

Gerson, Mary-Joan, 50
Gerstein, Mordicai
    Jonah and the Two Great Fish, 193, 198–99, 203–4, 208, 211–12
    Queen Esther the Morning Star, 222–23, 225, 227, 231, 234, 240–43, 246–47, 255
Giant figures, 148, 156. *See also* David and Goliath
Gilbert, Yvonne, 32, 67–68
Giuenivere, 180
Glover, Danny, 143
God
    description, 29
    loving care, 35–36
    as parent, 29–37
    as protagonist, 206–8
    punishment by, 50–53. *See also* Noah's Ark
    representations of, 15
    rules of, 34
"Go Down, Moses" (spiritual), 141, 143
Godwin, William, 12, 261
Goggles (Keats), 166
Golden calf, 118
Goliath. *See* David and Goliath
Good character, importance of, 66–70
Graham, Lorenz, 101, 123–24, 133–34, 144, 167–68, 193, 202, 248–49
Green, Jonathan, 78–79
Grimm brothers, 17
Grimm's fairy tales. *See specific fairy tale*
Growing up, inevitability, 40–41

Hadassah, 224, 226, 229–32, 241
Haman, 20, 219–20, 223, 227, 232, 234, 235, 239–40, 246, 248, 251–57
Hamilton, Virginia, 27
"Hansel and Gretel" (fairy tale), 17, 36–38, 42–44, 125, 145, 147, 252, 253
Harry Potter series, 120–21, 166
Hayward, Linda, 121
Henry, Barb, 121
Hercules, 148, 176, 180

Hero figures, 19–20, 22, 118, 130–32, 136, 148, 158, 160, 176–79, 186, 191, 206, 251, 259
Hiasson, Carl, 166
Hieroglyphic Bibles, 14–15
Historia Scholastica (Comestor), 12
Hodgson, T., 15
Holes (Sachar), 166
Holy Bible abridged . . . for the use of children (Newbery), 13
Hoot (Hiasson), 166
Horn, Geoffrey, 30, 38, 42
House of Potiphar, 104–6
How God Fix Jonah (Graham), 261
    David, portrayal of, 167–68
    Esther, portrayal of, 248–49
    Jonah, portrayal of, 193, 202
    Joseph, portrayal of, 101
    Moses, portrayal of, 123–24, 133–34, 144
Huck, Charlotte, 16
Hughes, Thomas, 165
Humanity, 27–28
Hunting, Phil, 143
Hutton, Warwick
    Adam and Eve: The Bible Story, 38
    Jonah and the Great Fish, 199–200, 202
    Moses in the Bulrushes, 122–23

Icones Biblicae, 15
Identity
    establishment of, 131
    Esther, 229–35
Innocence, loss of, 37–45
In the Beginning (Hamilton), 27
In the Beginning (Van Eyssen), 29, 52
Isaac, 14, 160
I Saw Esau: The Schoolchild's Pocket Book (Opie and Sendak), 167
Ishtar, 231

"Jack and the Beanstalk" (fairy tale), 148, 163–64, 180, 253
Jacob, 91, 92, 112, 113, 160, 217
    favoritism, 95–97

Janisch, Heinz, 64–65
Jarecka, Danuta, 110
Jealousy, 39
Jeffries, Price (fictional character), 141–42
Jemima Puddleduck, 37
Jephthah, daughter of, 218
Jesse, 156, 158, 172–73
Jesus, 148
Jonah, 20, 189–215
    God as protagonist, 206–8
    and huge fish, 201–6
    overview of story, 189–190
    and sailors, 196–200
Jonah and the Great Fish (Bulla), 195–96
Jonah and the Great Fish (Hutton), 199–200, 202
Jonah and the Two Great Fish (Gerstein), 193, 198–99, 203–4, 208, 211–12
"Jonah and the Whale" (Chaikin), 195, 197–98
Jonah and the Whale (Lanning), 192–93, 202, 207, 209
Jonah and the Whale (Patterson), 192, 198, 202, 206–7
Jonah and the Whale (Williams), 191–92
Jonas, Ann, 82–83
Joseph, 18, 20, 22, 91–115, 171, 191, 262
    accusation against, 104–6
    coat of many colors, 91–92
    culpability, 98–101
    and forgiveness, 109–15
    parental favoritism theme, 93–98
    the pit, 91–92, 102–4
    plot to kill, 91–92
    and Potiphar's wife, 104–6
    responsibility for gift, 107–9
Joseph and His Brothers (Auld), 94, 98, 105, 107, 111
Joseph and His Coat of Many Colors (Kassirer), 105, 107–8, 110
Joseph and his Magnificent Coat of Many Colors (Williams), 94, 95–96, 99–100, 105, 111

Joseph, King of Dreams (Mackall), 21, 102–3, 106, 109

Joseph (Wildsmith), 21, 94, 103–6, 108, 111–12

Joshua, 218

Judah, 91, 217

Kassirer, Sue, 105, 107–8, 110

Keats, Ezra Jack, 166

Keloglan and the Magic Hairs, 157–58

Kessler, Brad, 122, 128–29, 133, 143–44, 149

"King Arthur," 120, 132, 180, 199, 229

King James Version of the Bible, 57, 62, 67, 135–36, 144–45

Kohlberg, Lawrence, 130, 249

Lamb, Charles, 12, 261

Lanning, Rosemary, 192–93, 202, 207, 209

Lathrop, Dorothy P., 57, 75

Leah, 217

Lessac, Frané, 223, 250–51, 255

Let My People Go: Bible Stories Told by a Freeman of Color (McKissack and McKissack)

David, portrayal of, 173–74

Esther, portrayal of, 226, 235, 242, 254–55

Jonah, portrayal of, 193–94, 207–8, 210–11

Joseph, portrayal of, 96, 103

Moses, portrayal of, 141–42

"The Liberty Song" (Dickinson), 68

Limits, setting, 33–37

Literature for the Child (Cullinan and Galda), 16

Little, Emily, 165, 167, 178, 182, 183

"Little Red Riding Hood" (fairy tale), 37, 145, 190, 201, 237–38

Lot, wife of, 218

Luther, Martin, 12

Mackall, Dandi Daley, 21, 102–3, 106, 109

Maniac Magee (Spinelli), 166

Manushkin, Fran, 46–47, 223, 226, 240–42, 245–46

Martin, Mary, 32, 34, 50–51

Max (fictional character), 214–15

Mayo, Diana, 94, 150–51, 168, 194

McDonough, Yona Zeldis, 242

McKissack, Patricia and Frederick, 96, 103, 141–42, 173–74, 193–94, 207–8, 210–11, 226, 235, 242, 254–55

Merlin (fictional character), 121

Michal, 217

Mikolaycak, 135–37

Miriam, 218

Miriam's Well: Stories about Women in the Bible (Bach and Exum), 221–22, 242

Mitchell, Stephen, 28

Monte, Richard, 69, 73, 80–81, 83–84, 86

Moral judgment, 129–30

Moral realism, 113

Mordecai (king), 218–20, 222–29, 231–34, 239, 241, 244, 246–49, 255–59

Moses, 18, 20, 22, 91, 117–53, 214, 218, 220, 230, 262

baby Moses, 119–25

and first-born, killing of, 119, 145–53

as human being, 135–40

as leader of Hebrews, 125–31

overview of story, 117–19

Pharaoh, negotiations with, 118

reluctance in leader role, 131–35

slavery and freedom, 140–45

Ten Commandments, 118

Moses (Fisher), 125–27, 132–33, 137–39, 150

Moses in Egypt (Kessler), 122, 128–29, 133, 143–44, 149

Moses in the Bulrushes (Hutton), 122–23

Mutual respect, 113

Myers, Christopher, 112–13

Myers, Michael Dean, 112

Myers, Walter Dean, 112–13, 127, 149–50

The Myth of the Birth of the Hero (Rank), 148

Nabal, 217
Nakedness/nudity themes, 47–48
Nemean Lion, 176
Newbery Award, 166, 254
Newbery, John, 13
New Jewish Publication Society, 23
Nineveh (city), 20, 189, 192–96, 202–15
Noah, 19, 20, 22, 57–89, 186, 189, 191, 220.
    See also Noah's Ark
  character of, 61, 63
  as father of many nations, 77–80
  wife of, 218
"Noah and the Flood" (Chaikin), 63,
    67–68, 74–75
Noah (Gauch), 78–79
Noah's Ark, 57–89
  animals, role of, 75–77
  character, importance of, 66–70
  environmental themes, 80–83
  gender roles, 83–89
  God, role of, 70–75
  wrongdoing of people, flood caused
    by, 59–66
Noah's Ark (Cousins), 62–63
Noah's Ark (Janisch), 64–65
Noah's Ark (Pinkney), 57, 65–66, 73–74
Noah's Ark (Spier), 57, 60, 61, 86
Noah's Ark: Words from the Book of Gene-
    sis (Ray), 62, 71, 78, 84
Nolens Volens; or, You shall make Latin
    whether you Will or No (Coles), 14
Number three, significance of, 244–45

Obedience, 169–74, 186, 220–29
Oedipus, 148
"The Old Man Made Young Again," 17
Oliver Twist (Dickens), 165
Ol' Paul the Mighty Logger, 73
The 100 Dresses (Estes), 166
One Wide River to Cross (Emberley), 57,
    75–76, 79
On Noah's Ark (Brett), 77
Opie, Iona, 167, 253
Opie, Peter, 253

The Ordinary and the Fabulous (Cook),
    16
Orenstein, Catherine, 237–38
Original sin, 26

Paparone, Pam, 79–80
Parental favoritism, 93–98
Parton, Dolly, 95
Passional (Luther), 12
Passover, 151
Patterson, Geoffrey, 46, 192, 198, 202,
    206–7
Persia, 231–33, 241
Peter Pan (Barrie), 40–41
Pharaoh, 234. See also Moses
  first-born, killing of, 119, 145–53
  Moses, negotiations with, 118
Piaget, Jean, 19
  on environment, interaction with,
    58–59
  on Joseph, 98–99, 113
  learning, young children, 75
  moral judgment, 129–30
  moral realism, 113
  mutual respect, 113
  stages of development, 191
  on tattling, 98–99
Pierre (Sendak), 190
Pinkney, Jerry, 57, 65–66, 73–74, 184, 261
"Pinocchio," 190, 201
The Pit. See Joseph
Plagues, 149–50
Pocket Bible for Little Masters and Misses
    (Newbery), 13
Police (rock band), 81
Potiphar's wife, 104–6
Potter, Beatrix, 37
A Prayer for the Earth: The Story of Naa-
    mah, Noah's Wife (Sasso), 21, 85–86
Princess, winning hand of, 180–83
Psalmist, David as, 183–187
Punishment, 50–53
  flood. See Noah's Ark
Purim, 218–19, 255–56

"The Queen Bee" (fairy tale), 161, 162
Queen Esther (dePaola), 224, 227–28, 233, 249
Queen Esther Saves Her People (Gelman), 223, 225–26, 232, 240, 247, 249–51, 255
Queen Esther the Morning Star (Gerstein), 222–23, 225, 227, 231, 234, 240–43, 246–47, 255

Rachel, 91, 96, 217
Rahab, 218
Rank, Otto, 119, 148, 259
Ransome, James, 226
"Rapunzel" (fairy tale), 37, 125, 199, 229, 238
Ray, Jane, 62, 71, 78, 84
Rebecca, 217
"Red Ettin" (folktale), 180
Reed, Gwendolyn, 29, 44, 48
Reid, Barbara, 62
Responsibility and consequences, 49–55
Reuben, 91, 101, 112, 113
Revius, Jacobus, 60
Rhea, 120
Risk taking, 243–51
Rites of passage, 20
Rock Steady (Sting), 81–82, 87
Ross, Lillian Hammer, 224, 232–33, 241, 248
Rounds, Glen, 72–73, 84–85
Rowling, J. K., 120–21, 166
Rules, breaking, 33–37
"Rumpelstilskin" (fairy tale), 125
Ruth, 217–18

Sachar, Louis, 166
Sailors, Jonah and, 196–200
Samson, 218
Samuel, 172
Santore, Charles, 71–72, 86
Sarah, 217
Sargon, 119

Sasso, Sandy Eisenberg, 21, 85–86
Saul (King), 156, 160, 163, 170–74, 177–79, 181–82
Sendak, Maurice, 36, 167, 190, 214–15
Serpent, Garden of Eden, 34–35, 37–45, 103. See also Tree of knowledge of good and evil
"Seven at One Blow" (fairy tale), 176
"The Seven Ravens," 17
Sexuality
  awakening of, 37–45
  beauty and, 238–39
Shame, 47–48
A Ship in a Storm on the Way to Tarshish (Farber), 200–201
Sibling rivalry, 92–93, 114
Slavery, 129–30, 140–45
"Sleeping Beauty" (fairy tale), 38, 145, 229, 236–38, 252, 253
Snake. See Serpent, Garden of Eden
"Snow White" (fairy tale), 145, 229, 237, 238, 243, 252
Spier, Peter
  The Book of Jonah, 192, 201–2, 207, 209–10
  Noah's Ark, 57, 60, 61, 86
Spinelli, Jerry, 166
Spirituals, African American, 140–41
Steuart, Andrew, 13
Stewart, Arvis, 30
Stewig, John W., 72
Sting, 81–82, 87
Stories from the Bible (Waddell), 28, 46
Stories from the Bible (Zwerger), 46, 67, 144–45, 168–69
"The Story of Animals Saved in the Ark" (Fish), 75
The Story of Jonah (Auld), 194–95, 200, 203, 209
A Stowaway on Noah's Ark (Santore), 71–72, 86
Sutton, Judith, 95
"Swing Low Sweet Chariot" (spiritual), 141

The Tale of Despereaux (DiCamillo), 166, 254

Tamar, 217

Tarshish, 200–201, 204–5

Tattling, 98–99

Teis, Kyra, 224

Ten Commandments, 118

Thebes, King of, 180

Thomas, Isaiah, 15

Thousand and One Nights, 17

"The Three Brothers" (fairy tale), 161

"The Three Feathers" (fairy tale), 161, 162, 244

"The Three Languages" (fairy tale), 244

"The Three Little Pigs," 37

Three, significance of, 244–45

Thumb Bibles, 13

A Time to Love: Stories from the Old Testament (Myers and Myers), 112–13, 127, 149–50

Tom Brown's Schooldays (Hughes), 165

Tomie dePaola's Book of Bible Stories (de-Paola), 21, 243

Translations of biblical text, 23

Tree of knowledge of good and evil, 34–37, 41, 48, 51, 53, 262

Trinitarian triangle, 15

Turner, Philip, 41, 42

Two by Two (Reid), 62

The Uses of Enchantment (Bettelheim), 19, 92–93, 103

Van Eyssen, Shirley, 29, 43–44, 52

Vashti, 224, 225, 228, 236, 238–39, 240

Vashti (Queen), 219, 220–22

Violence, 217
  Story of Esther, 251–60

Voldemort (fictional character), 120–21

Waddell, Martin, 28, 35, 46

Washday on Noah's Ark (Rounds), 72–73, 84–85

Watts, Bernadette, 192

Weil, Lisl, 224, 233–34, 236, 239, 248

Where the Wild Things Are (Sendak), 36, 214–15

Who Built the Ark (Paparone), 79–80

Whuppie, Molly (fictional character), 161

Whyte, Hugh, 81

Why the Sky is Far Away: A Nigerian Folktale (Gerson), 50

Wijngaard, Juan, 224–25

Wildsmith, Brian
  Brian Wildsmith's Illustrated Bible Stories, 41
  Exodus, 21, 128, 139–40, 149
  Joseph, 94, 103–6, 108, 111–12

Wilhelm, Hans, 165, 178

Williams, Marcia
  Jonah and the Whale, 191–92
  Joseph and his Magnificent Coat of Many Colors, 94, 95–96, 99–100, 105, 111

Wives, 83–89, 104–6, 218

A Wizard of Earthsea, 156

Wolkstein, Diane, 224–27, 231, 234–35, 239–41, 243, 247–48, 256

Women in Bible, generally, 217–28

Wringer (Spinelli), 166

Wrongdoing of people, flood caused by, 59–66

Yael, 217

Yeh-Shen: A Cinderella Story from China, 158

Yolen, Jane, 156–57

Young Heroes of the Bible: A Book for Family Sharing (Douglas), 96–97, 103, 108

"The Youths Visible Bible," 14

Zeresh, 228

Zeus, 120

Zipporah, 118, 217

Zwerger, Lisbeth, 46, 64–65, 67, 144–45, 168–69